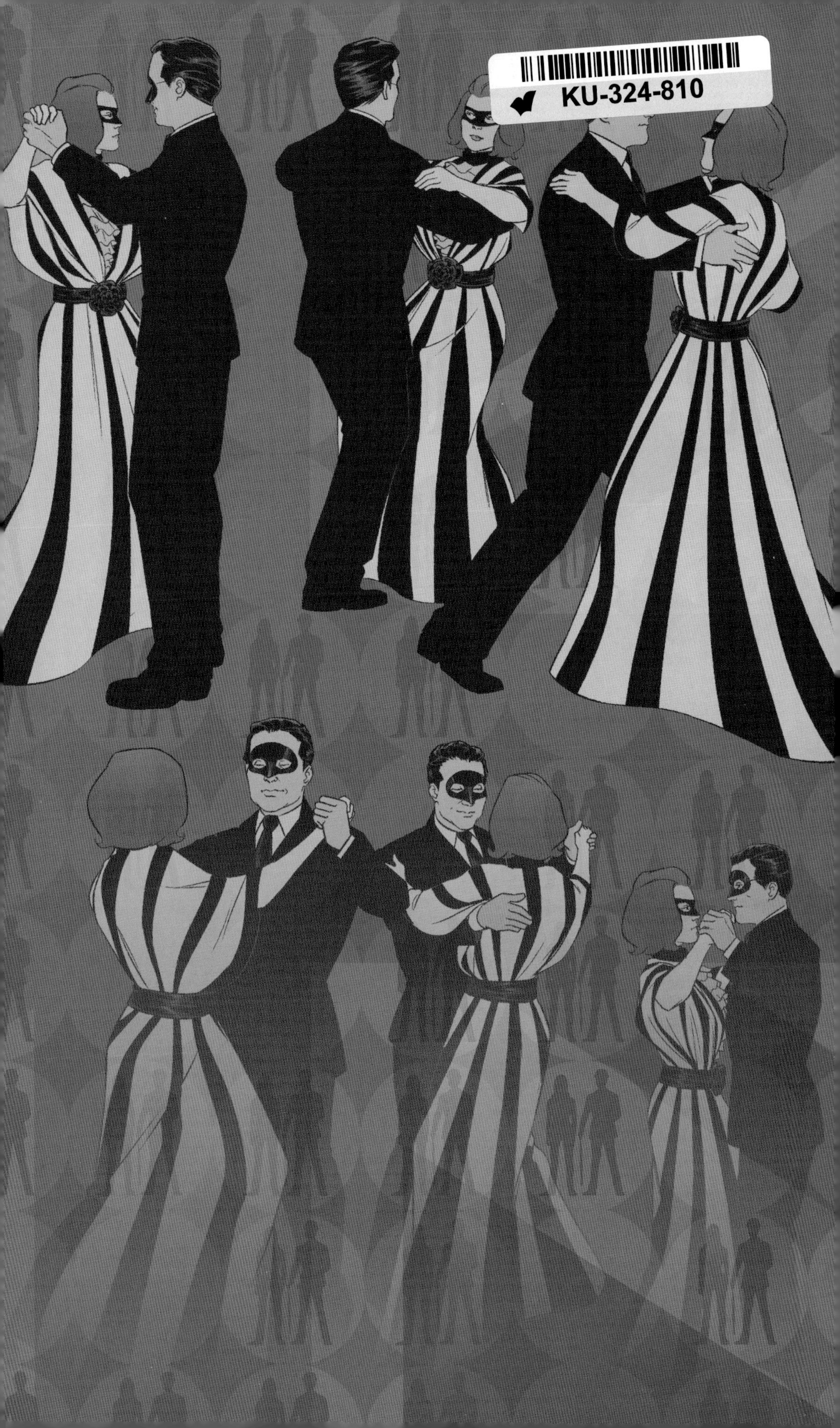

Written by
CALEB MONROE
Art by
YASMIN LIANG

Colors by
RON RILEY

Letters by
ED DUKESHIRE

Cover by
JOSEPH MICHAEL LINSNER

Assistant Editor
CHRIS ROSA

Editor
MATT GAGNON

Trade Design
KASSANDRA HELLER
& PHIL SMITH

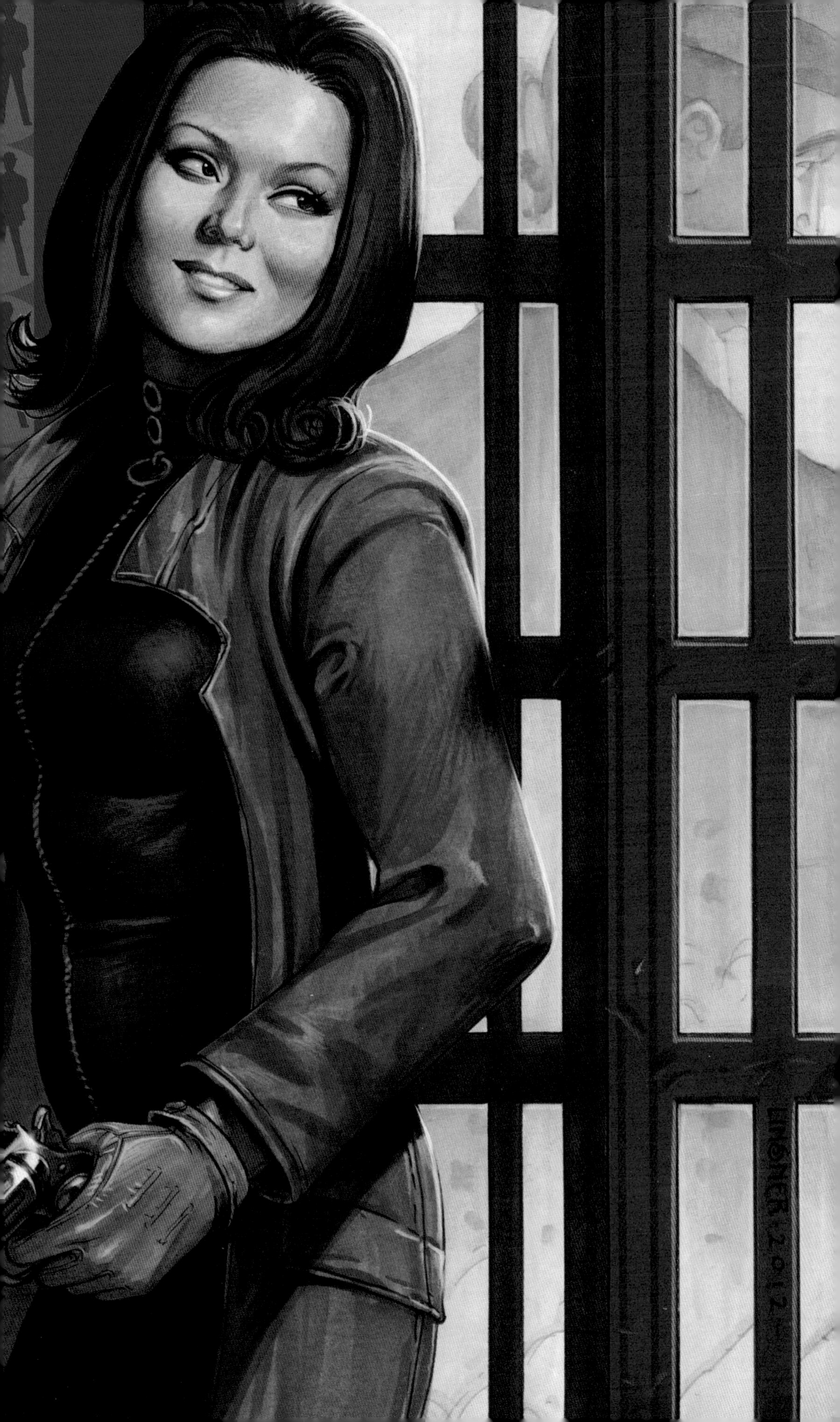

CHAPTER FOUR

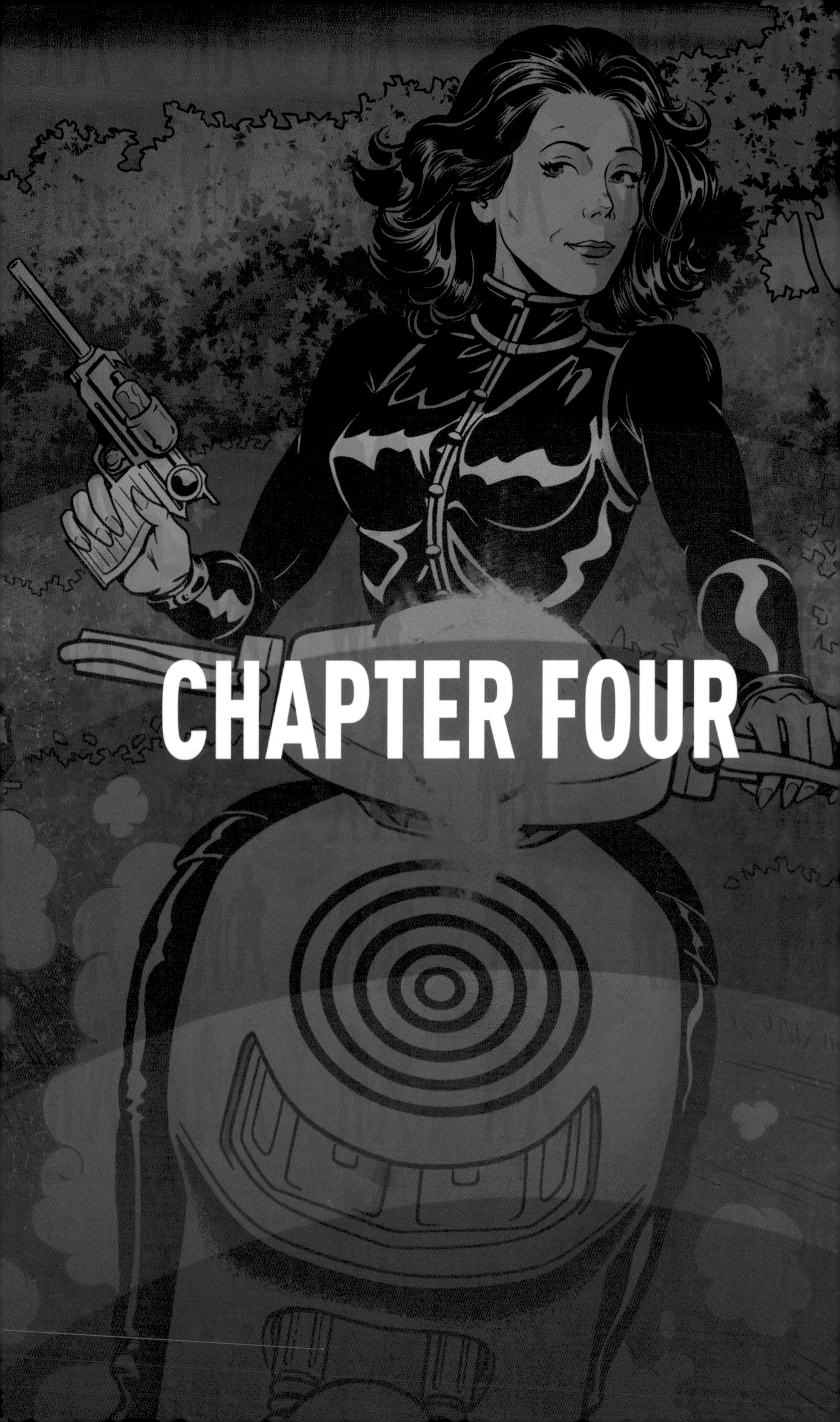

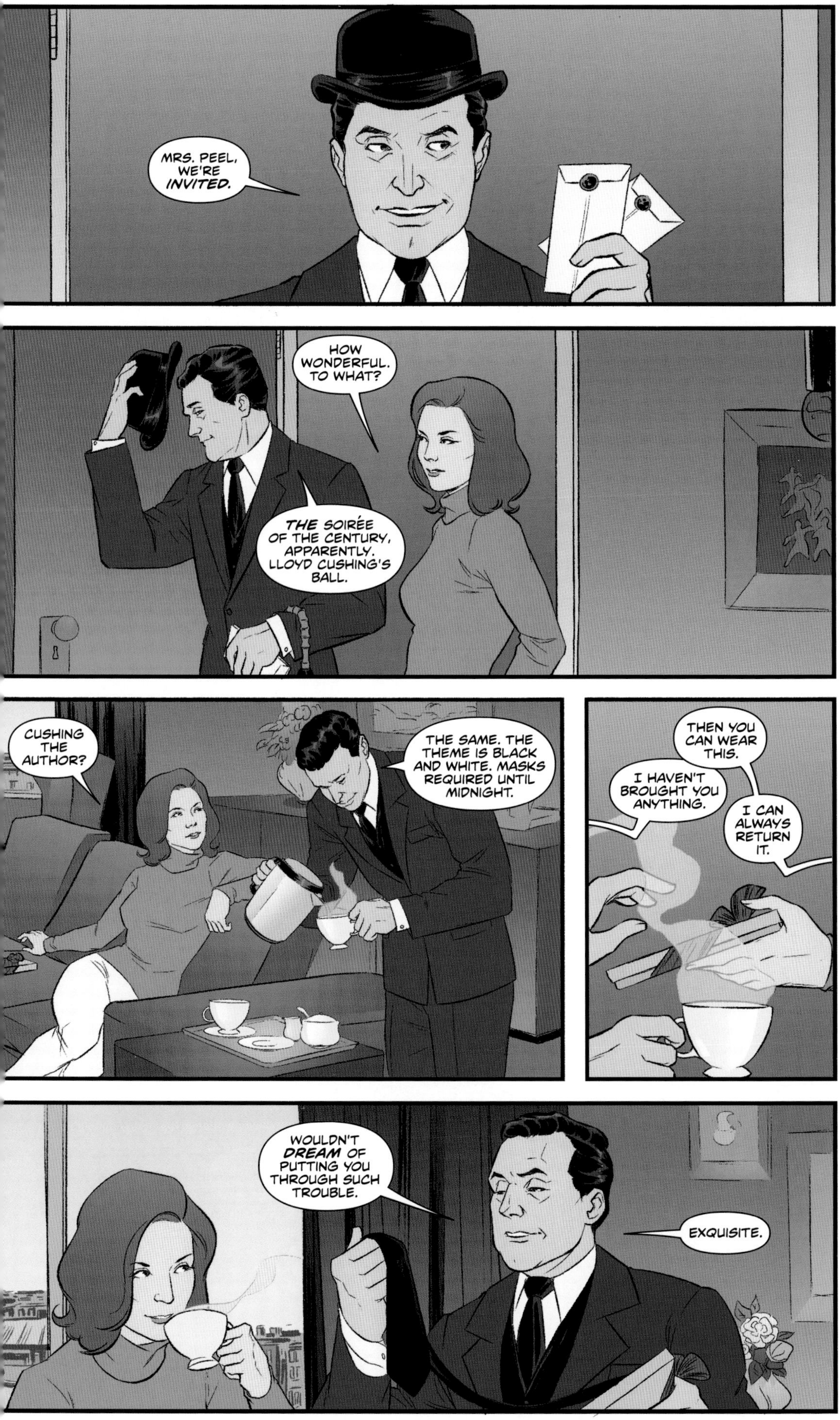
MRS. PEEL, WE'RE *INVITED.*
HOW WONDERFUL. TO WHAT?
THE SOIRÉE OF THE CENTURY, APPARENTLY. LLOYD CUSHING'S BALL.
CUSHING THE AUTHOR?
THE SAME. THE THEME IS BLACK AND WHITE. MASKS REQUIRED UNTIL MIDNIGHT.
I HAVEN'T BROUGHT YOU ANYTHING.
THEN YOU CAN WEAR THIS.
I CAN ALWAYS RETURN IT.
WOULDN'T *DREAM* OF PUTTING YOU THROUGH SUCH TROUBLE.
EXQUISITE.

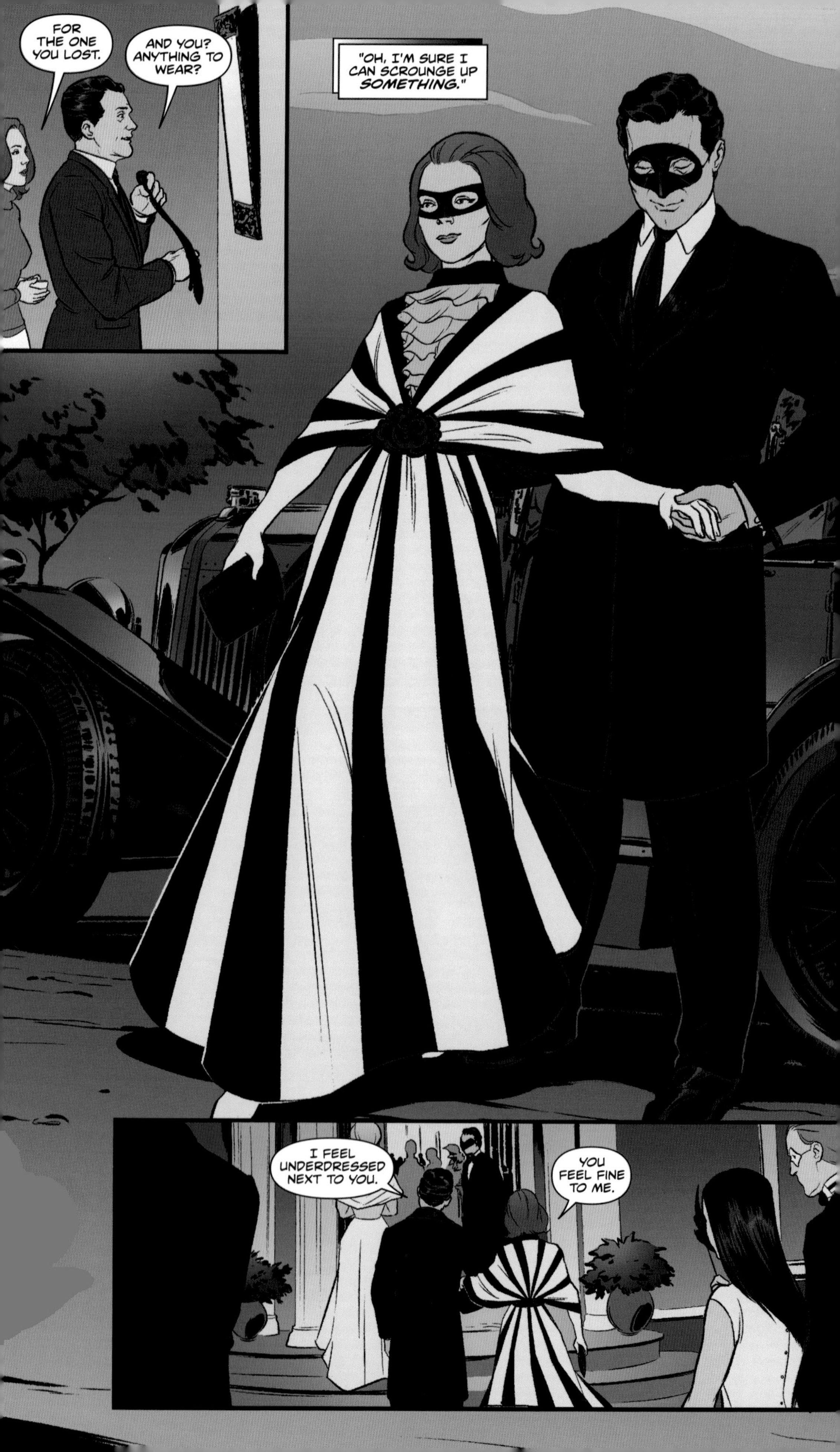
FOR THE ONE YOU LOST.
AND YOU? ANYTHING TO WEAR?
"OH, I'M SURE I CAN SCROUNGE UP SOMETHING."
I FEEL UNDERDRESSED NEXT TO YOU.
YOU FEEL FINE TO ME.

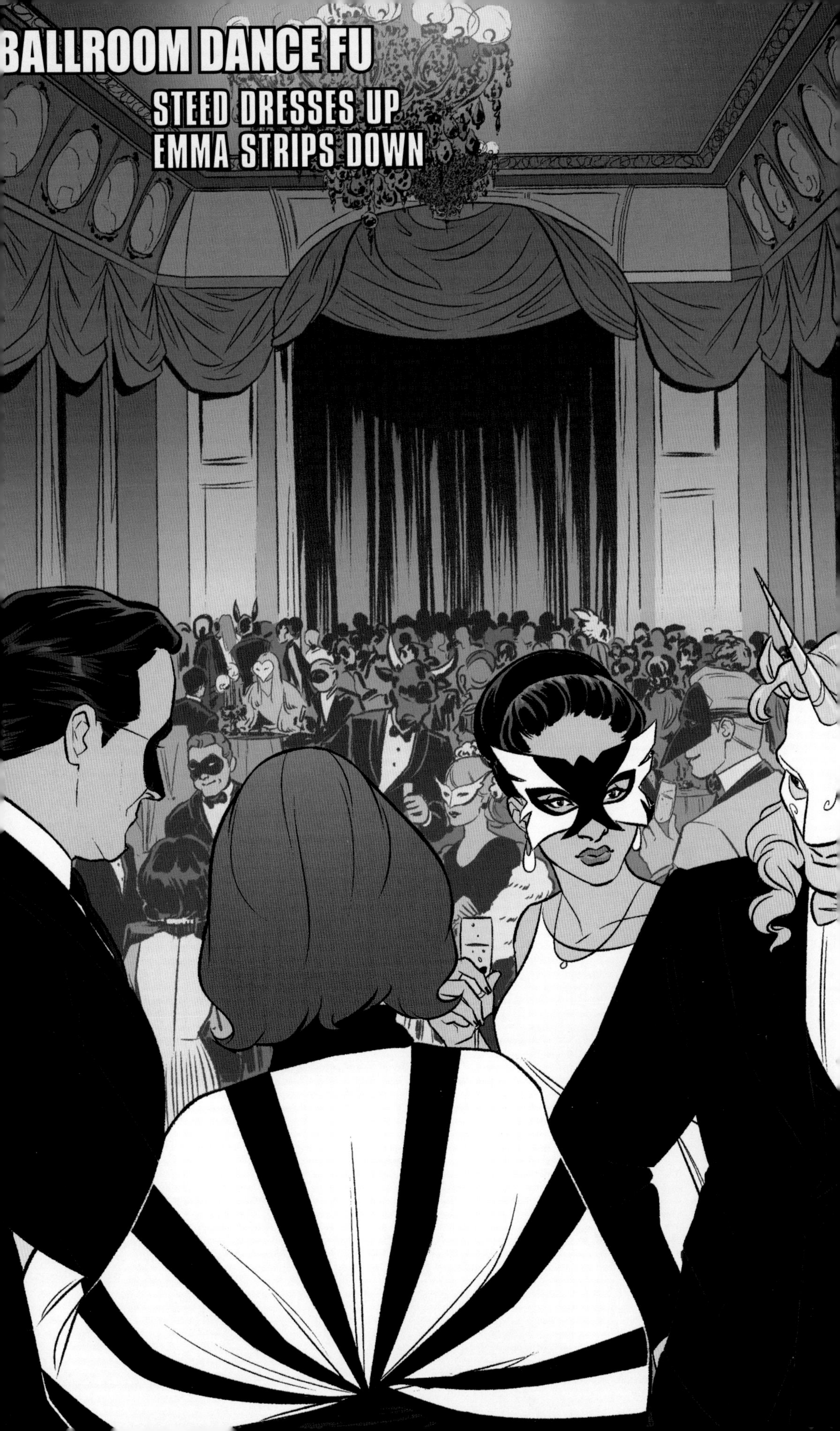

BALLROOM DANCE FU
STEED DRESSES UP
EMMA STRIPS DOWN

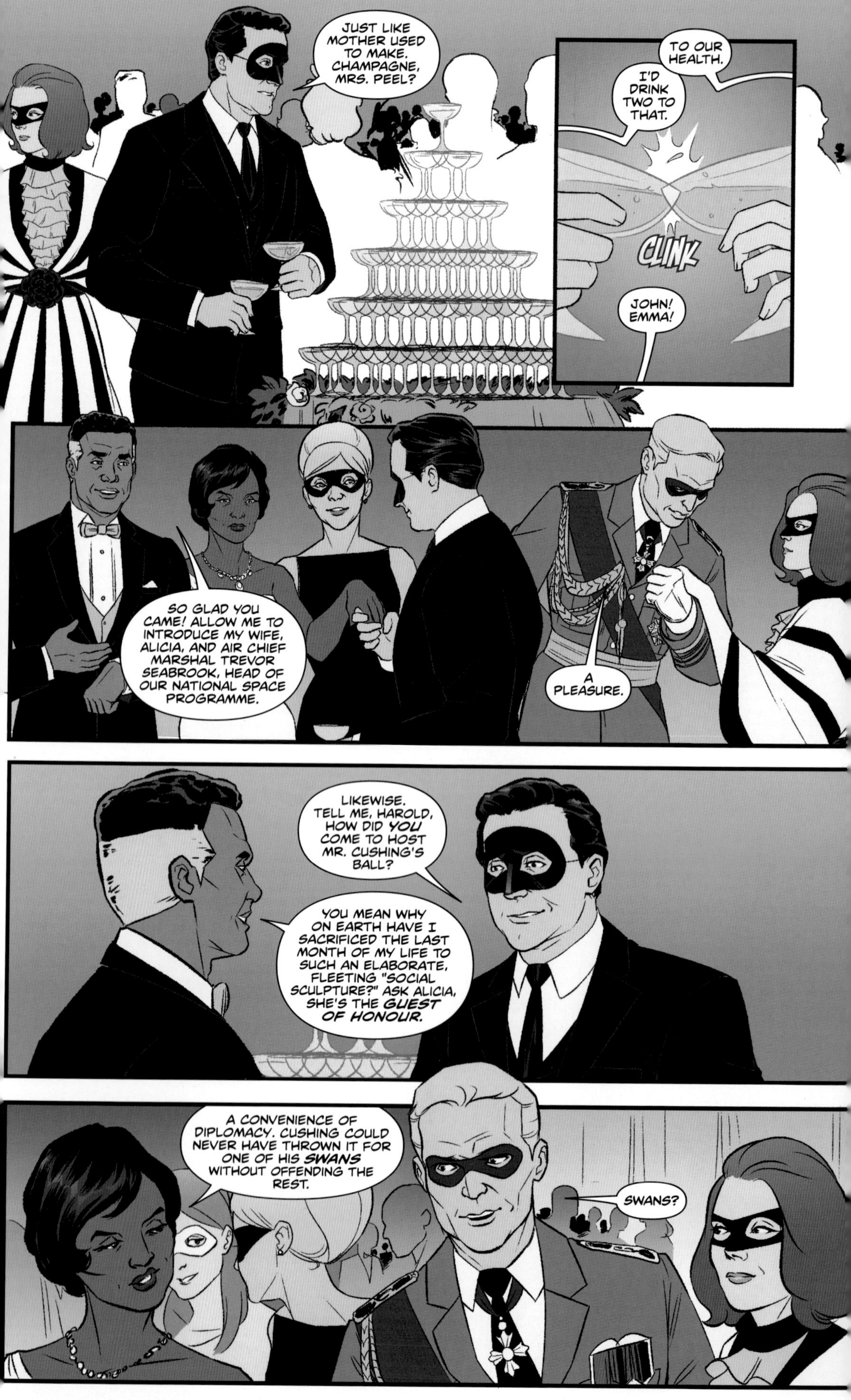
JUST LIKE MOTHER USED TO MAKE. CHAMPAGNE, MRS. PEEL?
TO OUR HEALTH.
I'D DRINK TWO TO THAT.
CLINK
JOHN! EMMA!
SO GLAD YOU CAME! ALLOW ME TO INTRODUCE MY WIFE, ALICIA, AND AIR CHIEF MARSHAL TREVOR SEABROOK, HEAD OF OUR NATIONAL SPACE PROGRAMME.
A PLEASURE.
LIKEWISE. TELL ME, HAROLD, HOW DID YOU COME TO HOST MR. CUSHING'S BALL?
YOU MEAN WHY ON EARTH HAVE I SACRIFICED THE LAST MONTH OF MY LIFE TO SUCH AN ELABORATE, FLEETING "SOCIAL SCULPTURE?" ASK ALICIA, SHE'S THE GUEST OF HONOUR.
A CONVENIENCE OF DIPLOMACY. CUSHING COULD NEVER HAVE THROWN IT FOR ONE OF HIS SWANS WITHOUT OFFENDING THE REST.
SWANS?

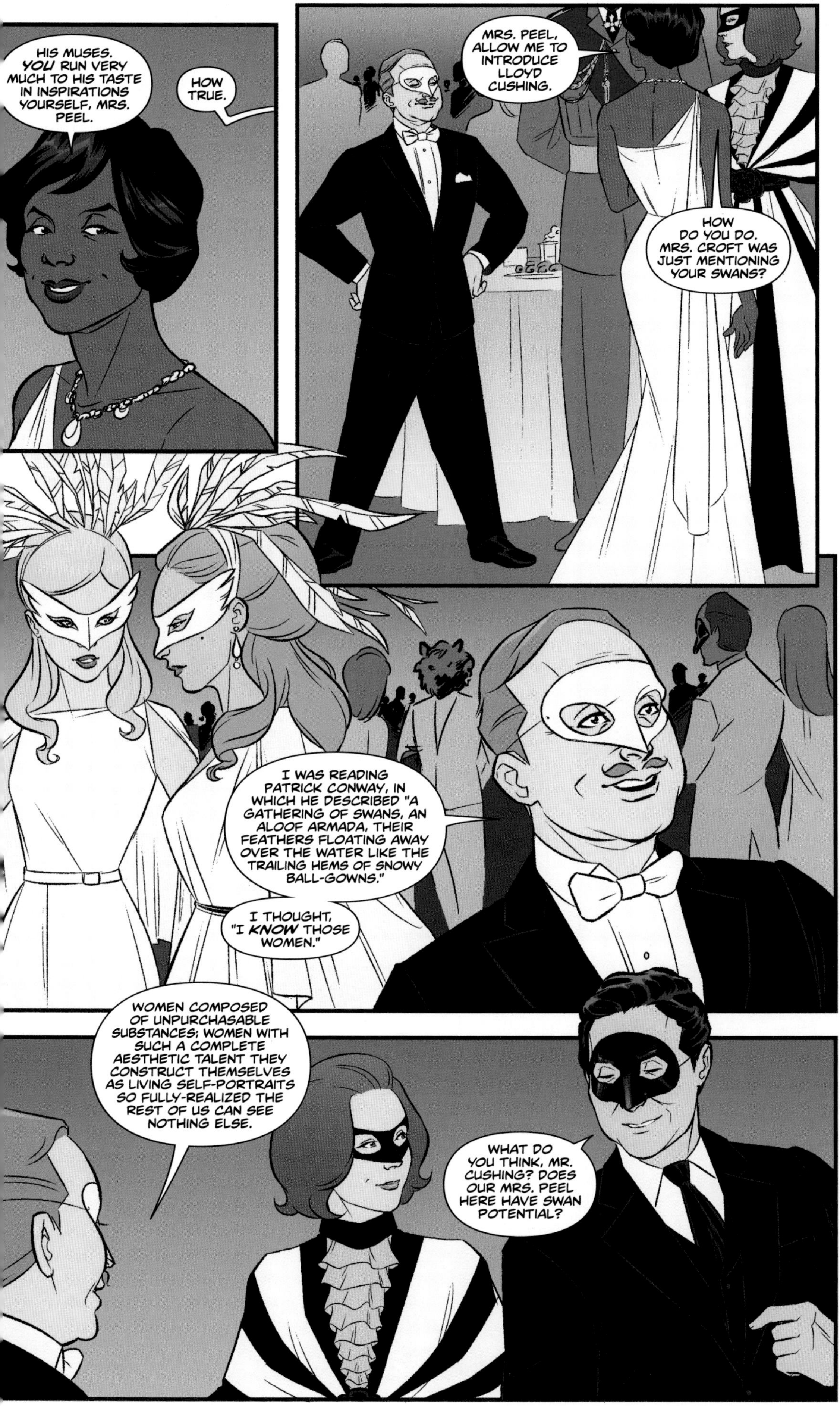
HIS MUSES. YOU RUN VERY MUCH TO HIS TASTE IN INSPIRATIONS YOURSELF, MRS. PEEL.
HOW TRUE.
MRS. PEEL, ALLOW ME TO INTRODUCE LLOYD CUSHING.
HOW DO YOU DO. MRS. CROFT WAS JUST MENTIONING YOUR SWANS?
I WAS READING PATRICK CONWAY, IN WHICH HE DESCRIBED "A GATHERING OF SWANS, AN ALOOF ARMADA, THEIR FEATHERS FLOATING AWAY OVER THE WATER LIKE THE TRAILING HEMS OF SNOWY BALL-GOWNS."
I THOUGHT, "I KNOW THOSE WOMEN."
WOMEN COMPOSED OF UNPURCHASABLE SUBSTANCES; WOMEN WITH SUCH A COMPLETE AESTHETIC TALENT THEY CONSTRUCT THEMSELVES AS LIVING SELF-PORTRAITS SO FULLY-REALIZED THE REST OF US CAN SEE NOTHING ELSE.
WHAT DO YOU THINK, MR. CUSHING? DOES OUR MRS. PEEL HERE HAVE SWAN POTENTIAL?

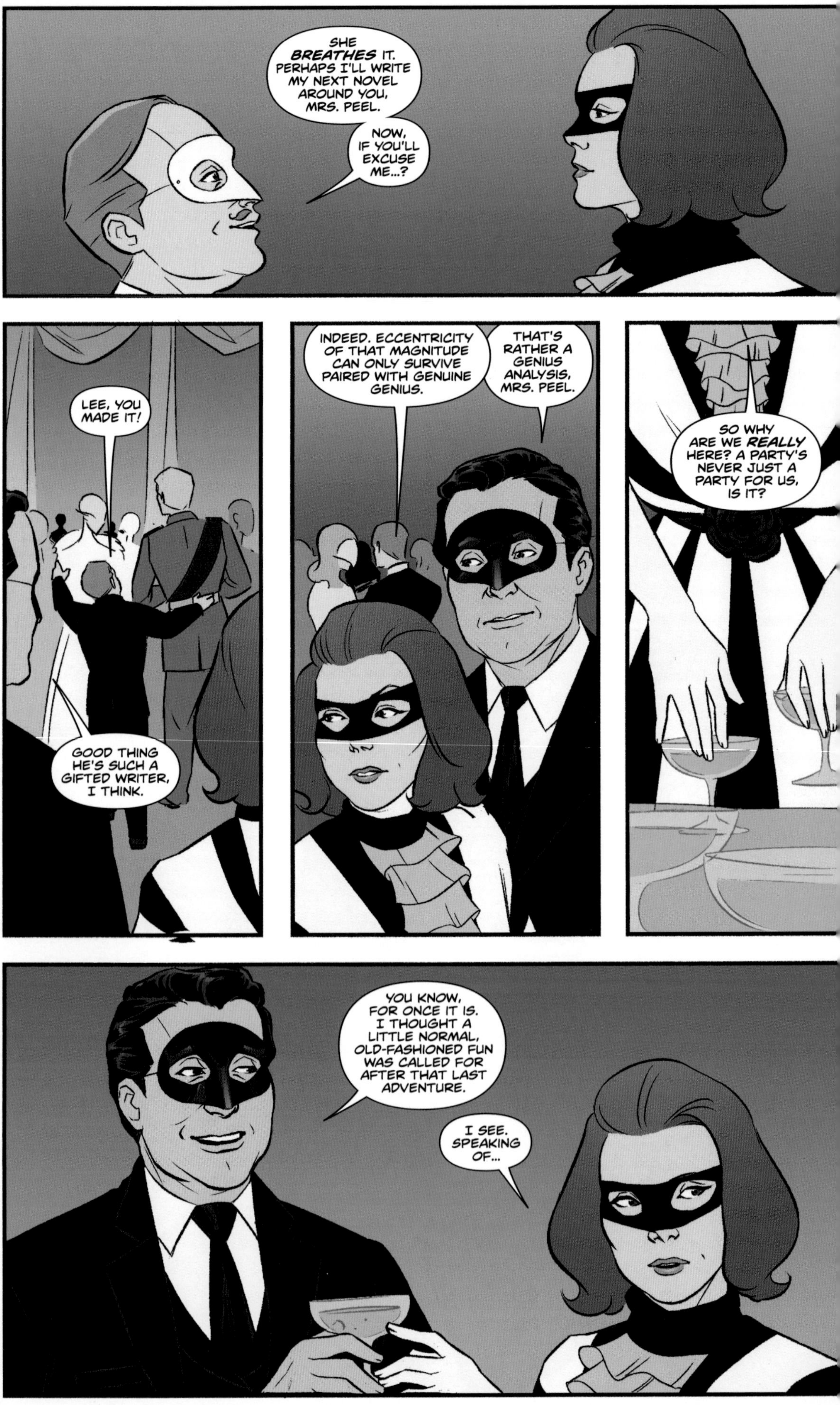
SHE *BREATHES* IT. PERHAPS I'LL WRITE MY NEXT NOVEL AROUND YOU, MRS. PEEL.
NOW, IF YOU'LL EXCUSE ME...?
LEE, YOU MADE IT!
GOOD THING HE'S SUCH A GIFTED WRITER, I THINK.
INDEED. ECCENTRICITY OF THAT MAGNITUDE CAN ONLY SURVIVE PAIRED WITH GENUINE GENIUS.
THAT'S RATHER A GENIUS ANALYSIS, MRS. PEEL.
SO WHY ARE WE *REALLY* HERE? A PARTY'S NEVER JUST A PARTY FOR US, IS IT?
YOU KNOW, FOR ONCE IT IS. I THOUGHT A LITTLE NORMAL, OLD-FASHIONED FUN WAS CALLED FOR AFTER THAT LAST ADVENTURE.
I SEE. SPEAKING OF...

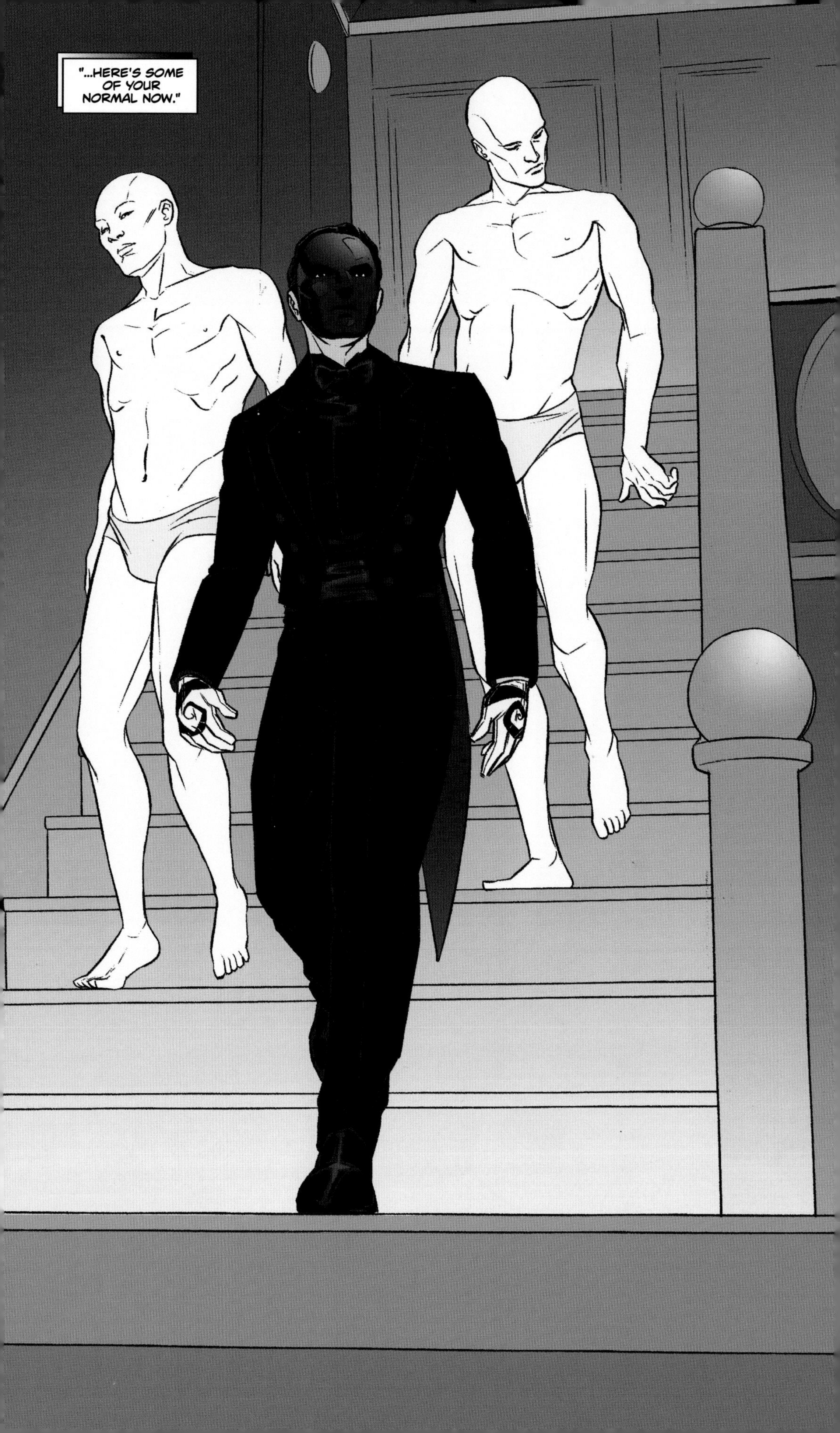
"...HERE'S SOME OF YOUR NORMAL NOW."

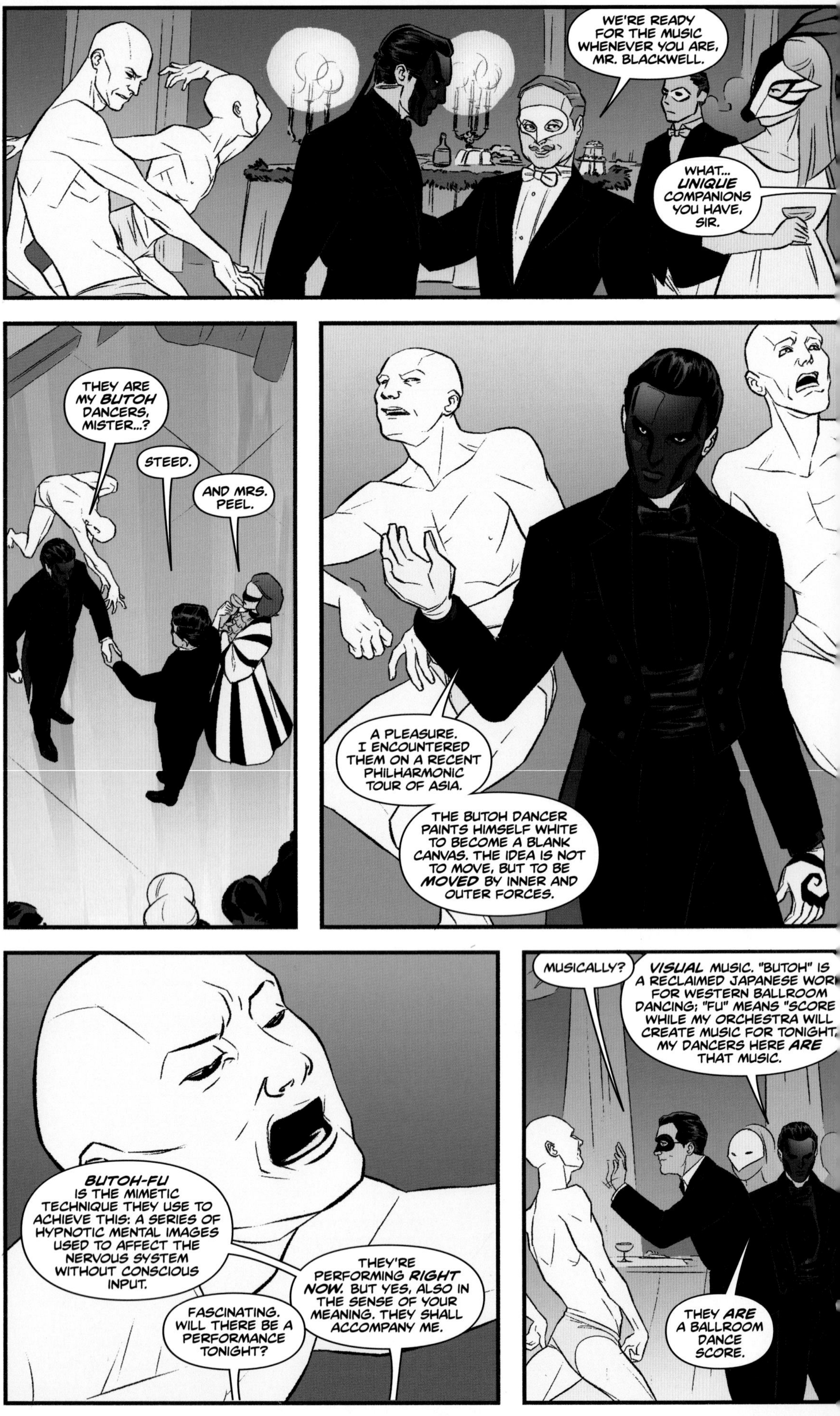
WE'RE READY FOR THE MUSIC WHENEVER YOU ARE, MR. BLACKWELL.
WHAT... UNIQUE COMPANIONS YOU HAVE, SIR.
THEY ARE MY BUTOH DANCERS, MISTER...?
STEED.
AND MRS. PEEL.
A PLEASURE. I ENCOUNTERED THEM ON A RECENT PHILHARMONIC TOUR OF ASIA.
THE BUTOH DANCER PAINTS HIMSELF WHITE TO BECOME A BLANK CANVAS. THE IDEA IS NOT TO MOVE, BUT TO BE MOVED BY INNER AND OUTER FORCES.
BUTOH-FU IS THE MIMETIC TECHNIQUE THEY USE TO ACHIEVE THIS: A SERIES OF HYPNOTIC MENTAL IMAGES USED TO AFFECT THE NERVOUS SYSTEM WITHOUT CONSCIOUS INPUT.
FASCINATING. WILL THERE BE A PERFORMANCE TONIGHT?
THEY'RE PERFORMING RIGHT NOW. BUT YES, ALSO IN THE SENSE OF YOUR MEANING. THEY SHALL ACCOMPANY ME.
MUSICALLY?
VISUAL MUSIC. "BUTOH" IS A RECLAIMED JAPANESE WOR FOR WESTERN BALLROOM DANCING; "FU" MEANS "SCORE WHILE MY ORCHESTRA WILL CREATE MUSIC FOR TONIGHT, MY DANCERS HERE ARE THAT MUSIC.
THEY ARE A BALLROOM DANCE SCORE.

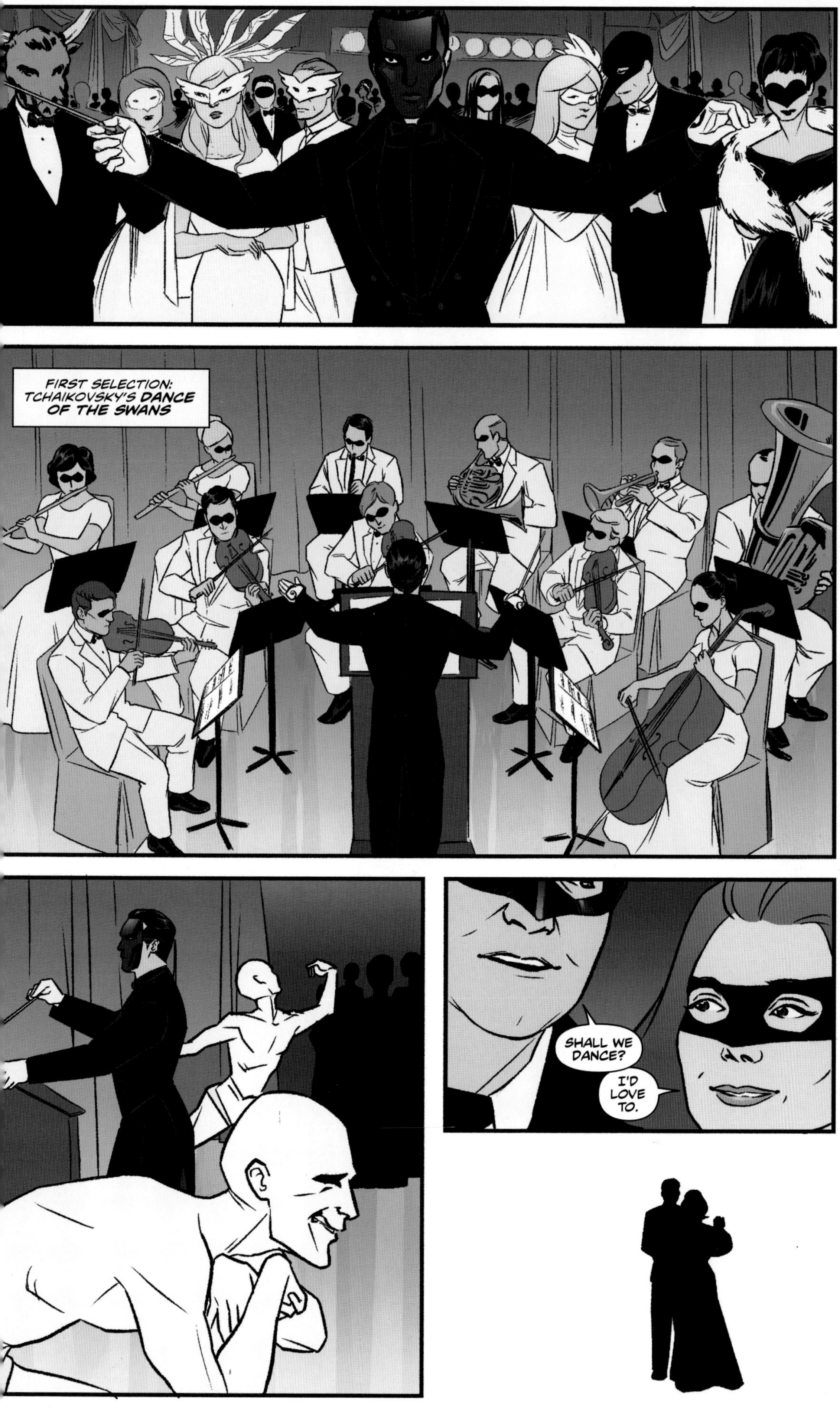
FIRST SELECTION: TCHAIKOVSKY'S DANCE OF THE SWANS
SHALL WE DANCE?
I'D LOVE TO.

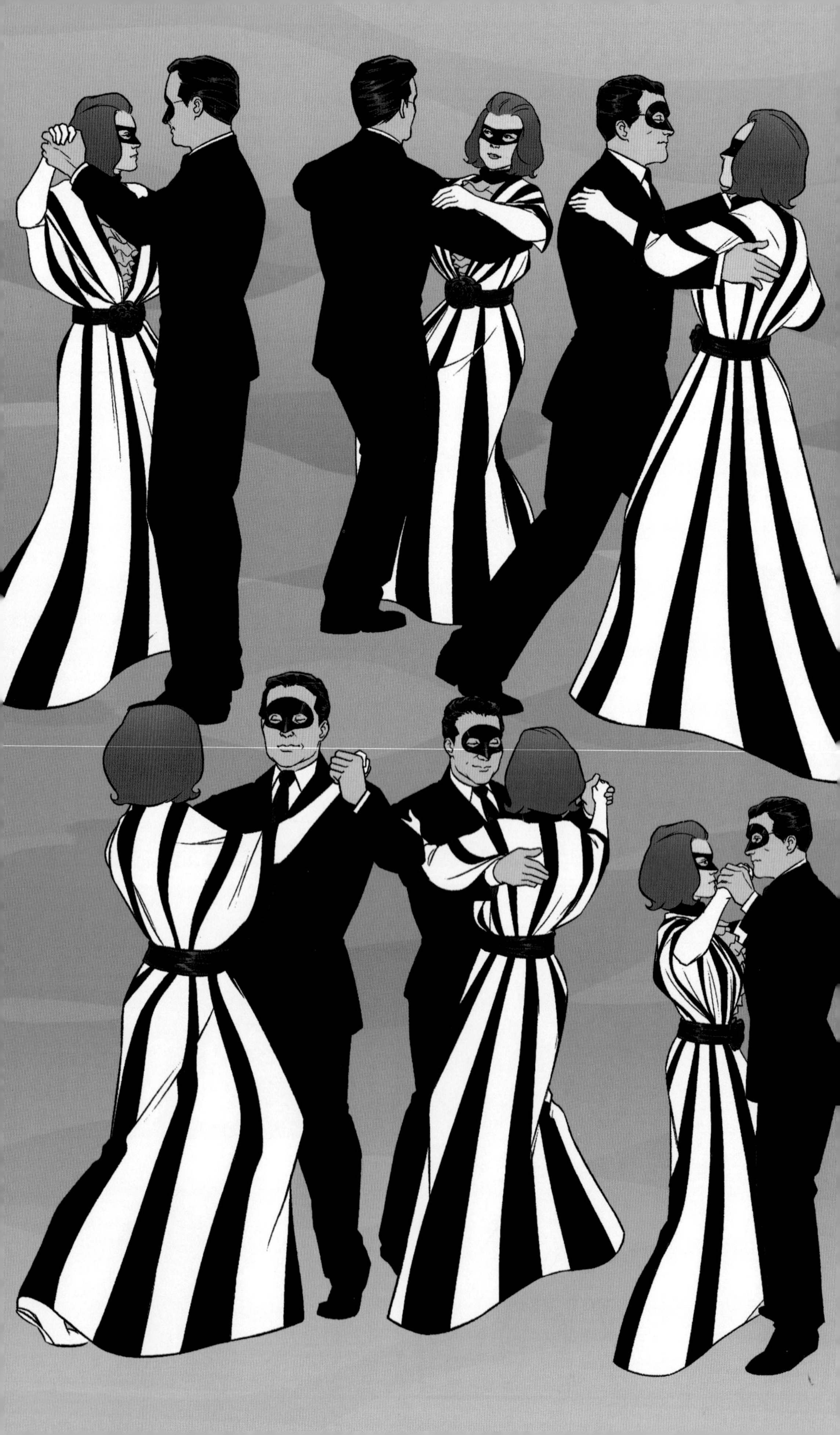

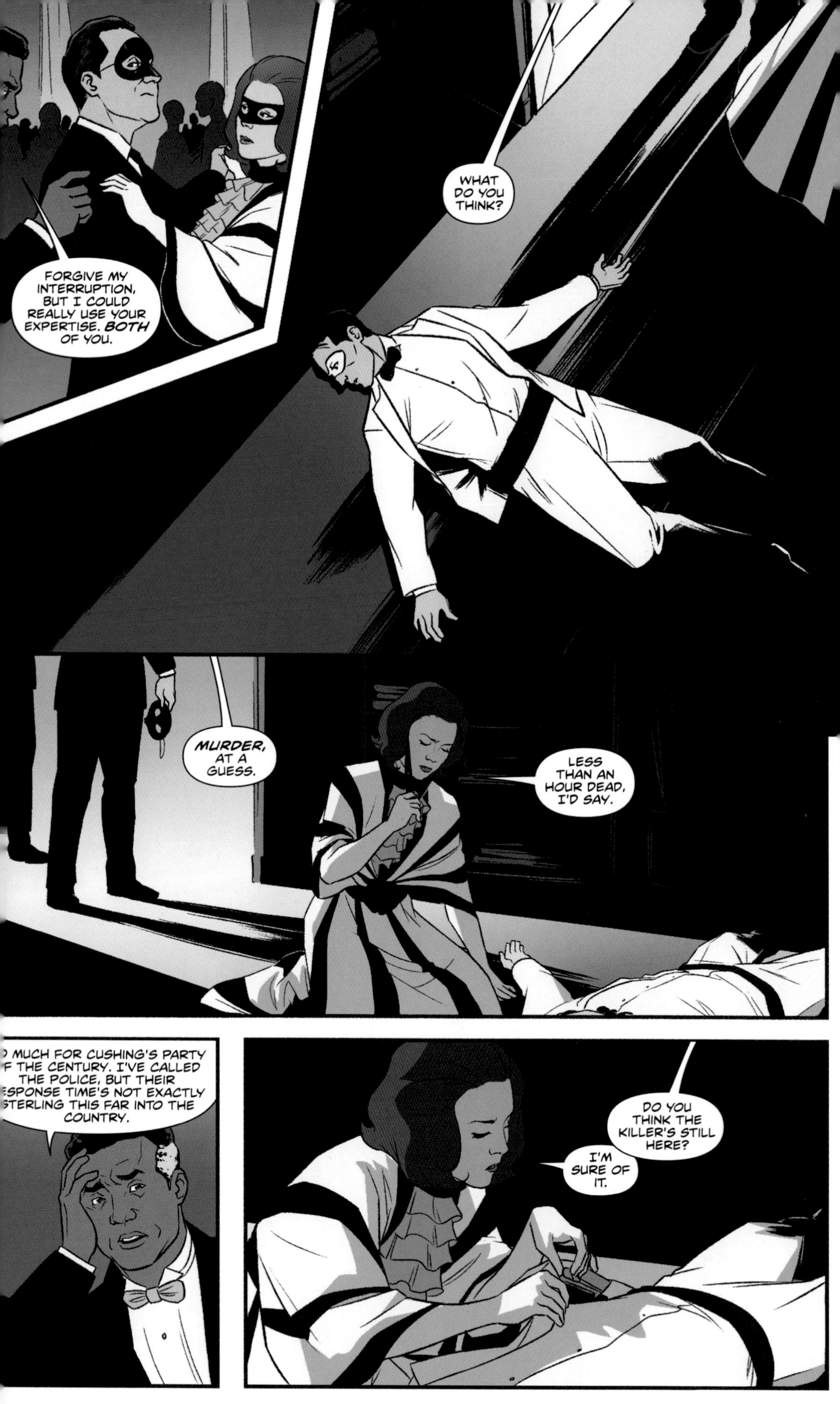

FORGIVE MY INTERRUPTION, BUT I COULD REALLY USE YOUR EXPERTISE. *BOTH* OF YOU.
WHAT DO YOU THINK?
MURDER, AT A GUESS.
LESS THAN AN HOUR DEAD, I'D SAY.
MUCH FOR CUSHING'S PARTY OF THE CENTURY. I'VE CALLED THE POLICE, BUT THEIR RESPONSE TIME'S NOT EXACTLY STERLING THIS FAR INTO THE COUNTRY.
DO YOU THINK THE KILLER'S STILL HERE?
I'M SURE OF IT.

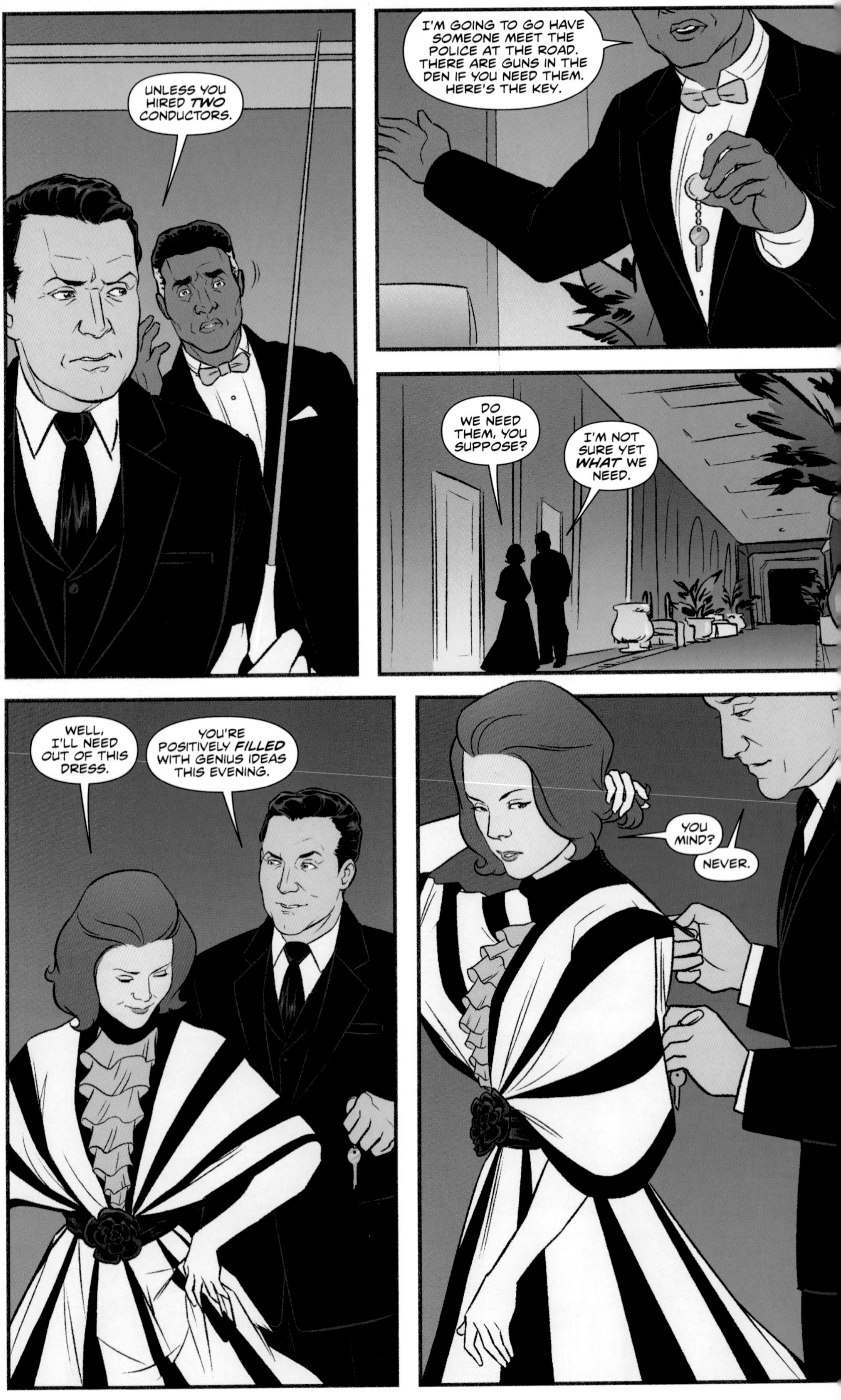
UNLESS YOU HIRED *TWO* CONDUCTORS.
I'M GOING TO GO HAVE SOMEONE MEET THE POLICE AT THE ROAD. THERE ARE GUNS IN THE DEN IF YOU NEED THEM. HERE'S THE KEY.
DO WE NEED THEM, YOU SUPPOSE?
I'M NOT SURE YET *WHAT* WE NEED.
WELL, I'LL NEED OUT OF THIS DRESS.
YOU'RE POSITIVELY *FILLED* WITH GENIUS IDEAS THIS EVENING.
YOU MIND?
NEVER.

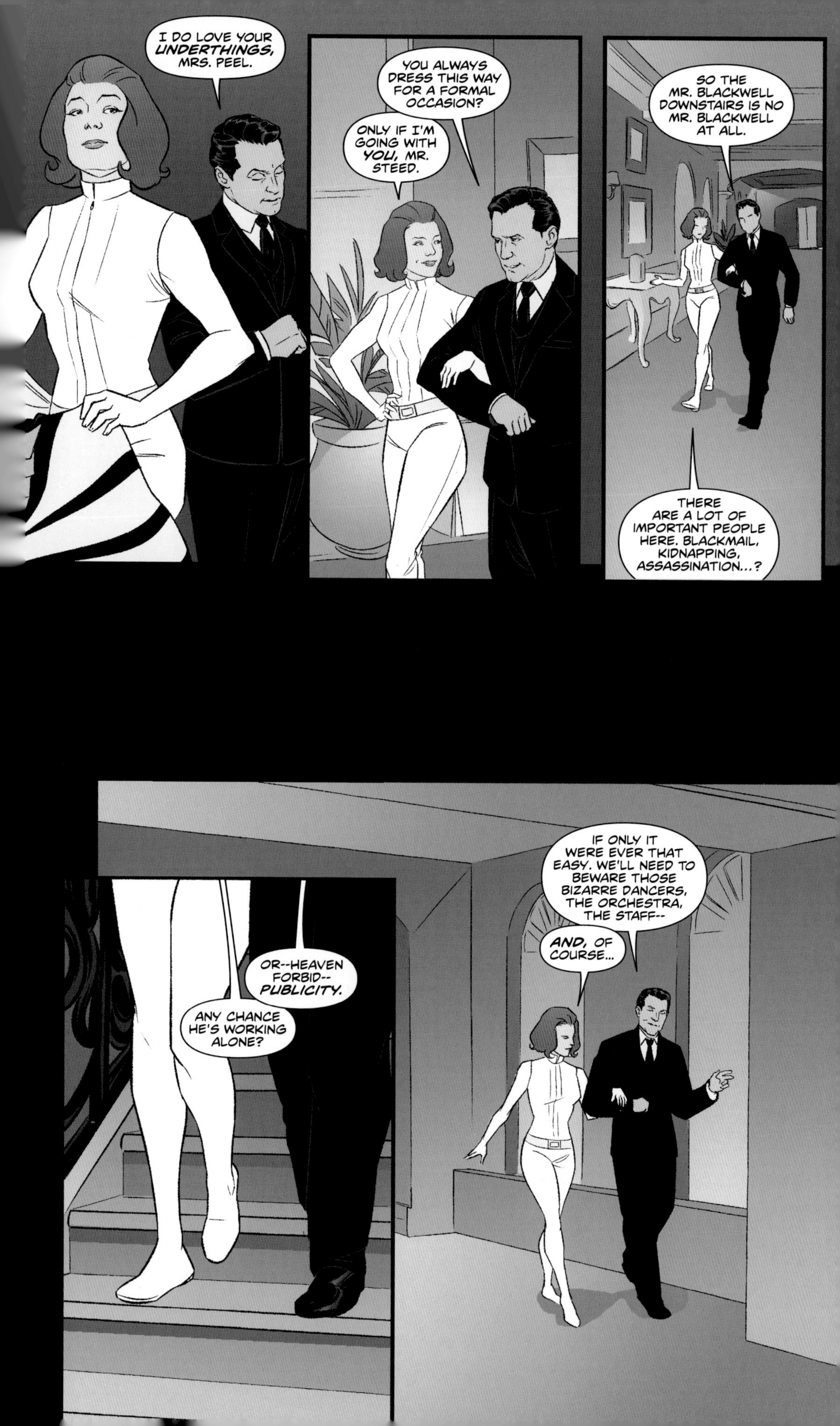
I DO LOVE YOUR *UNDERTHINGS,* MRS. PEEL.
YOU ALWAYS DRESS THIS WAY FOR A FORMAL OCCASION?
ONLY IF I'M GOING WITH *YOU,* MR. STEED.
SO THE MR. BLACKWELL DOWNSTAIRS IS NO MR. BLACKWELL AT ALL.
THERE ARE A LOT OF IMPORTANT PEOPLE HERE. BLACKMAIL, KIDNAPPING, ASSASSINATION...?
ANY CHANCE HE'S WORKING ALONE?
OR--HEAVEN FORBID--*PUBLICITY.*
IF ONLY IT WERE EVER THAT EASY. WE'LL NEED TO BEWARE THOSE BIZARRE DANCERS, THE ORCHESTRA, THE STAFF--
AND, OF COURSE...

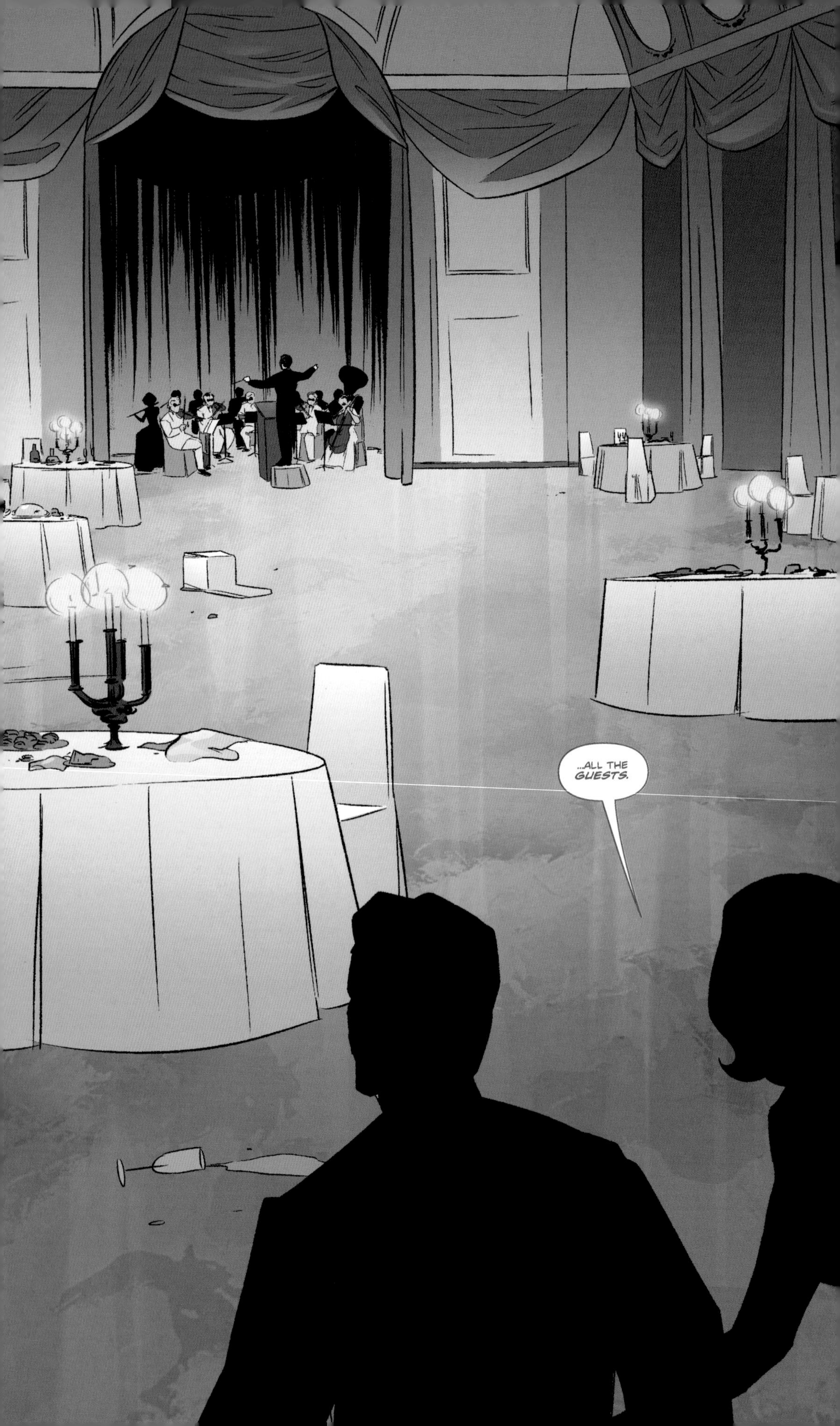
...ALL THE GUESTS.

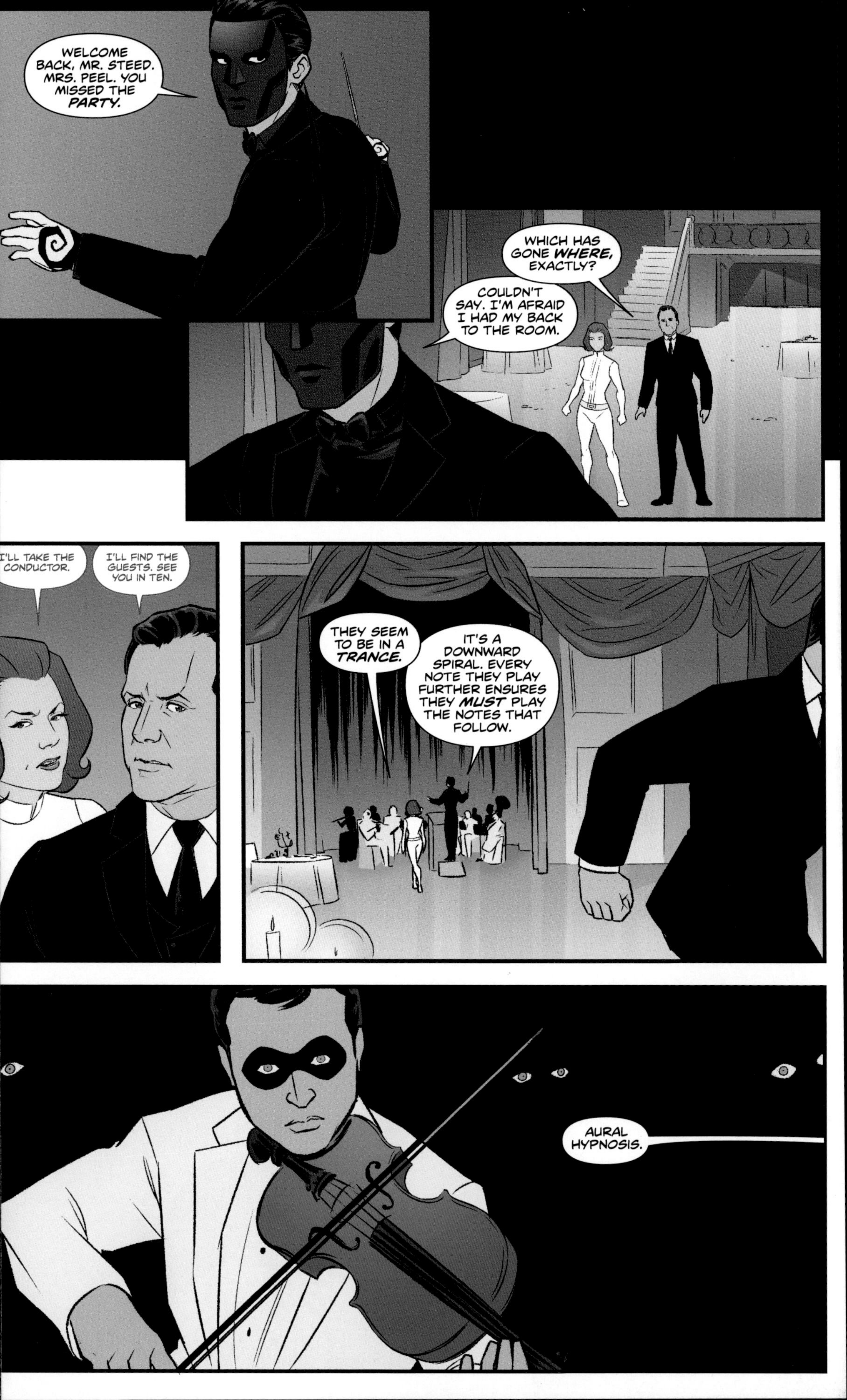
WELCOME BACK, MR. STEED. MRS. PEEL. YOU MISSED THE PARTY.
WHICH HAS GONE WHERE, EXACTLY?
COULDN'T SAY. I'M AFRAID I HAD MY BACK TO THE ROOM.
I'LL TAKE THE CONDUCTOR.
I'LL FIND THE GUESTS. SEE YOU IN TEN.
THEY SEEM TO BE IN A TRANCE.
IT'S A DOWNWARD SPIRAL. EVERY NOTE THEY PLAY FURTHER ENSURES THEY MUST PLAY THE NOTES THAT FOLLOW.
AURAL HYPNOSIS.

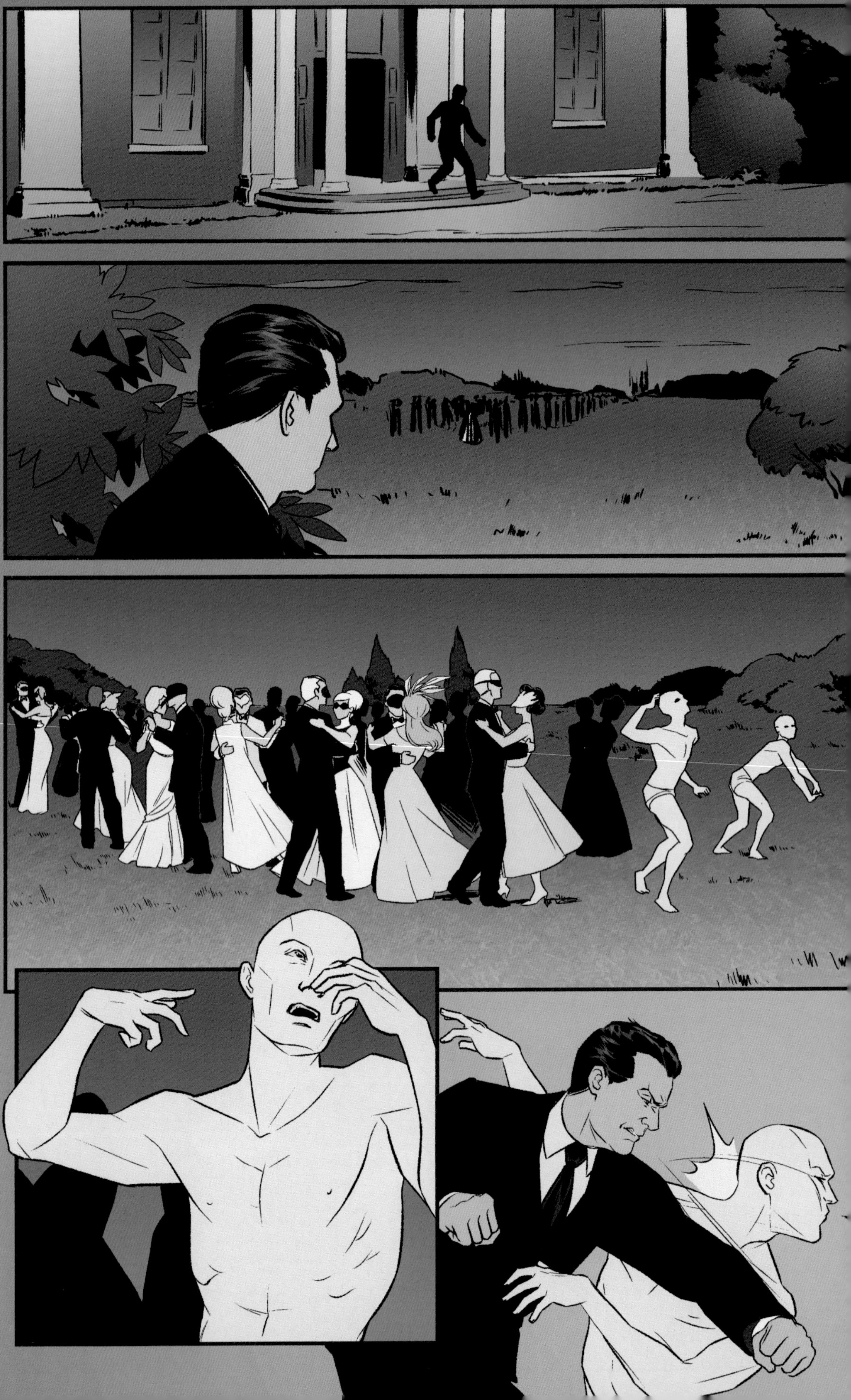

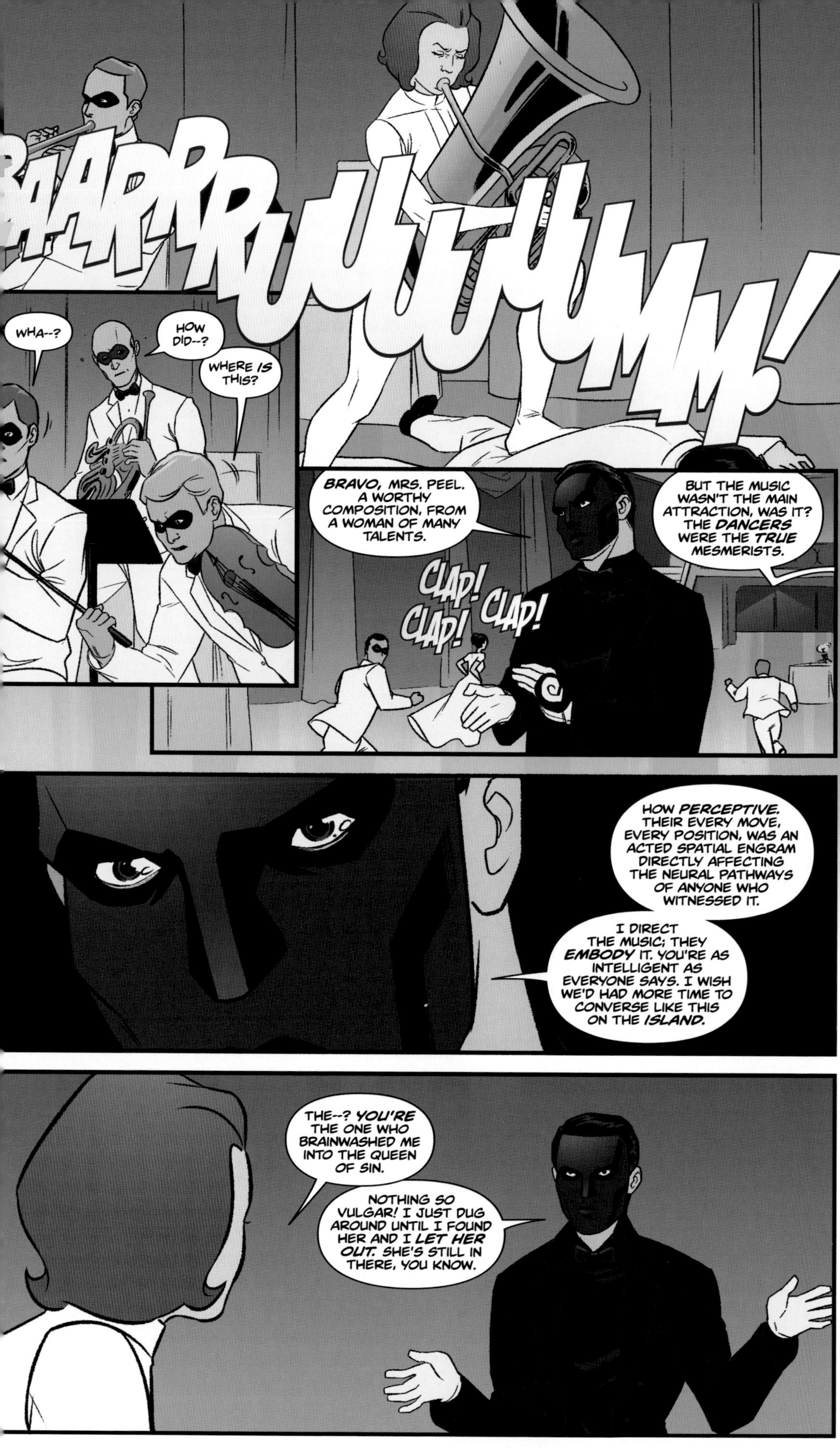
BAARRRUUUUUMMM!
WHA--?
HOW DID--?
WHERE IS THIS?
BRAVO, MRS. PEEL. A WORTHY COMPOSITION, FROM A WOMAN OF MANY TALENTS.
CLAP! CLAP! CLAP!
BUT THE MUSIC WASN'T THE MAIN ATTRACTION, WAS IT? THE DANCERS WERE THE TRUE MESMERISTS.
HOW PERCEPTIVE. THEIR EVERY MOVE, EVERY POSITION, WAS AN ACTED SPATIAL ENGRAM DIRECTLY AFFECTING THE NEURAL PATHWAYS OF ANYONE WHO WITNESSED IT.
I DIRECT THE MUSIC; THEY EMBODY IT. YOU'RE AS INTELLIGENT AS EVERYONE SAYS. I WISH WE'D HAD MORE TIME TO CONVERSE LIKE THIS ON THE ISLAND.
THE--? YOU'RE THE ONE WHO BRAINWASHED ME INTO THE QUEEN OF SIN.
NOTHING SO VULGAR! I JUST DUG AROUND UNTIL I FOUND HER AND I LET HER OUT. SHE'S STILL IN THERE, YOU KNOW.

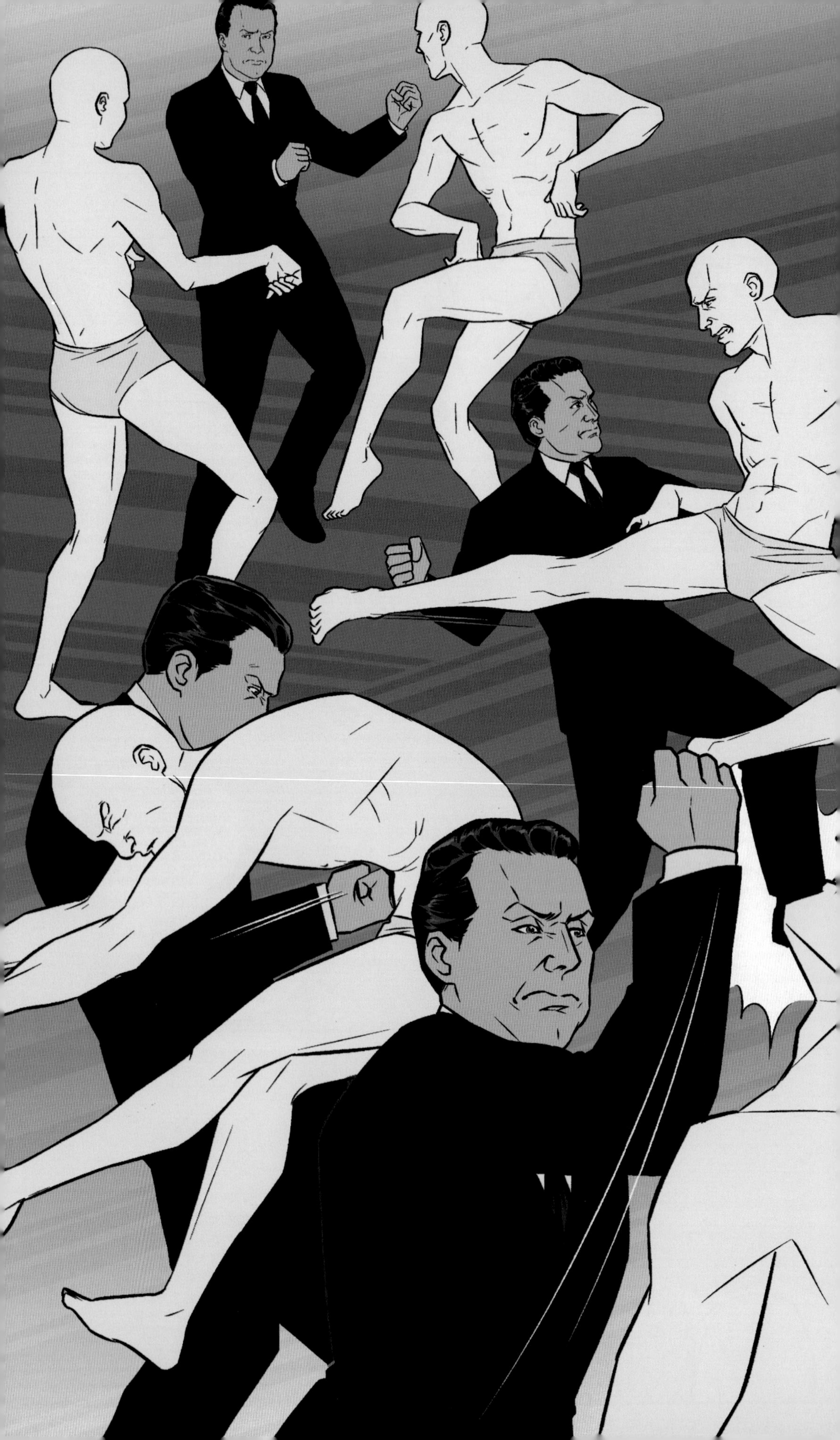

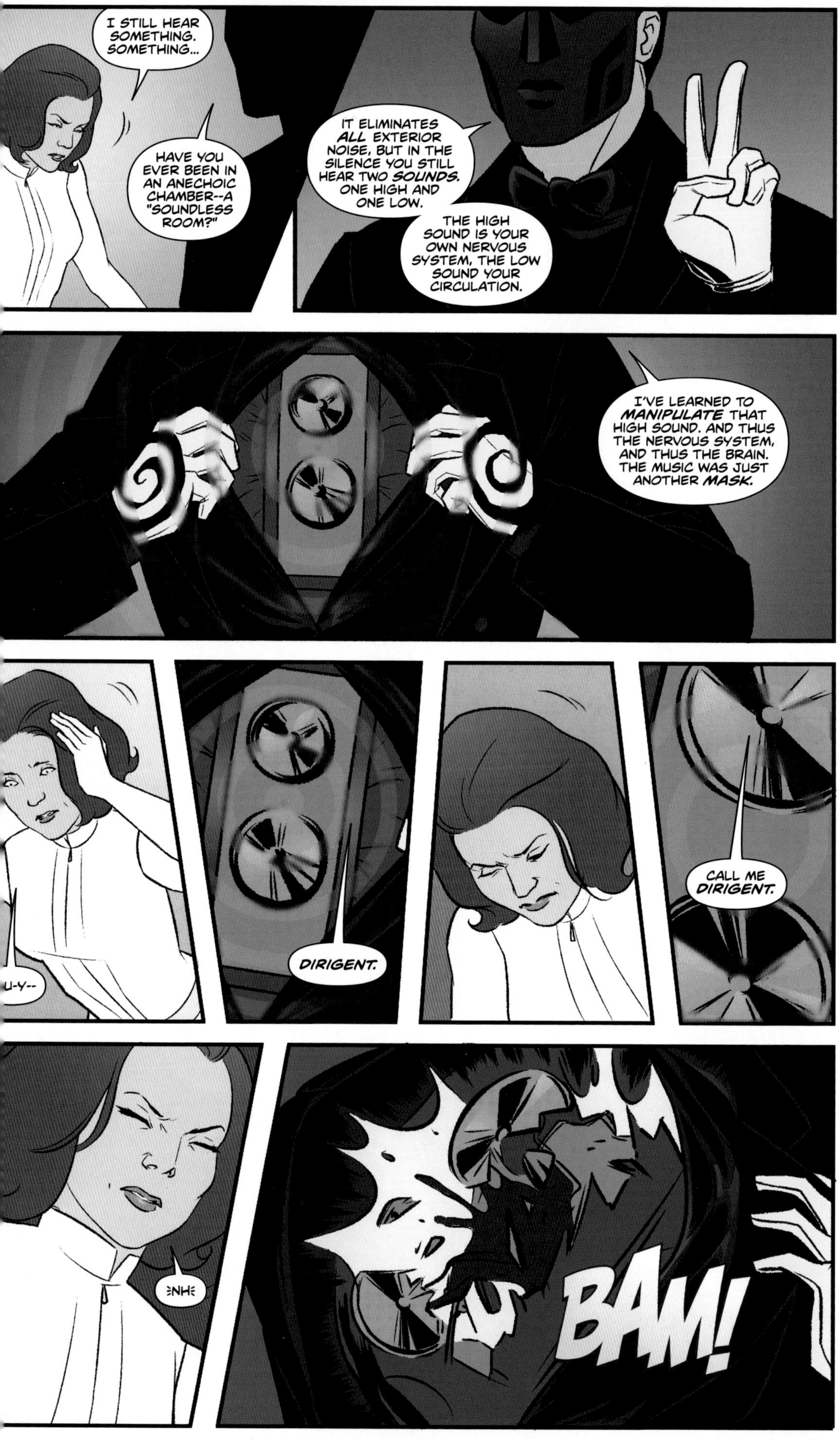
I STILL HEAR SOMETHING. SOMETHING...
HAVE YOU EVER BEEN IN AN ANECHOIC CHAMBER--A "SOUNDLESS ROOM?"
IT ELIMINATES ALL EXTERIOR NOISE, BUT IN THE SILENCE YOU STILL HEAR TWO SOUNDS. ONE HIGH AND ONE LOW.
THE HIGH SOUND IS YOUR OWN NERVOUS SYSTEM, THE LOW SOUND YOUR CIRCULATION.
I'VE LEARNED TO MANIPULATE THAT HIGH SOUND. AND THUS THE NERVOUS SYSTEM, AND THUS THE BRAIN. THE MUSIC WAS JUST ANOTHER MASK.
U-Y--
DIRIGENT.
CALL ME DIRIGENT.
NH
BAM!

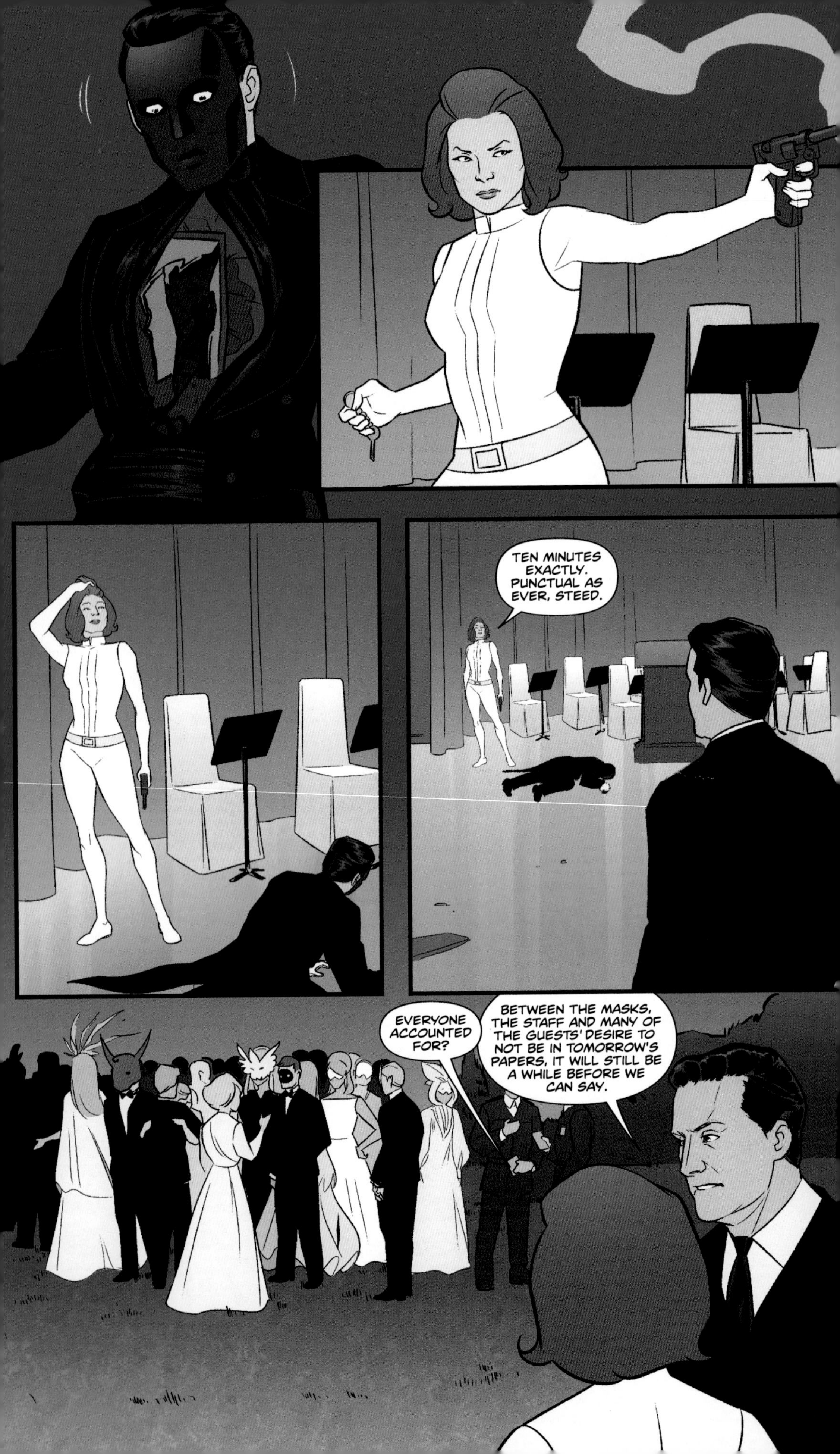
TEN MINUTES EXACTLY. PUNCTUAL AS EVER, STEED.
EVERYONE ACCOUNTED FOR?
BETWEEN THE MASKS, THE STAFF AND MANY OF THE GUESTS' DESIRE TO NOT BE IN TOMORROW'S PAPERS, IT WILL STILL BE A WHILE BEFORE WE CAN SAY.

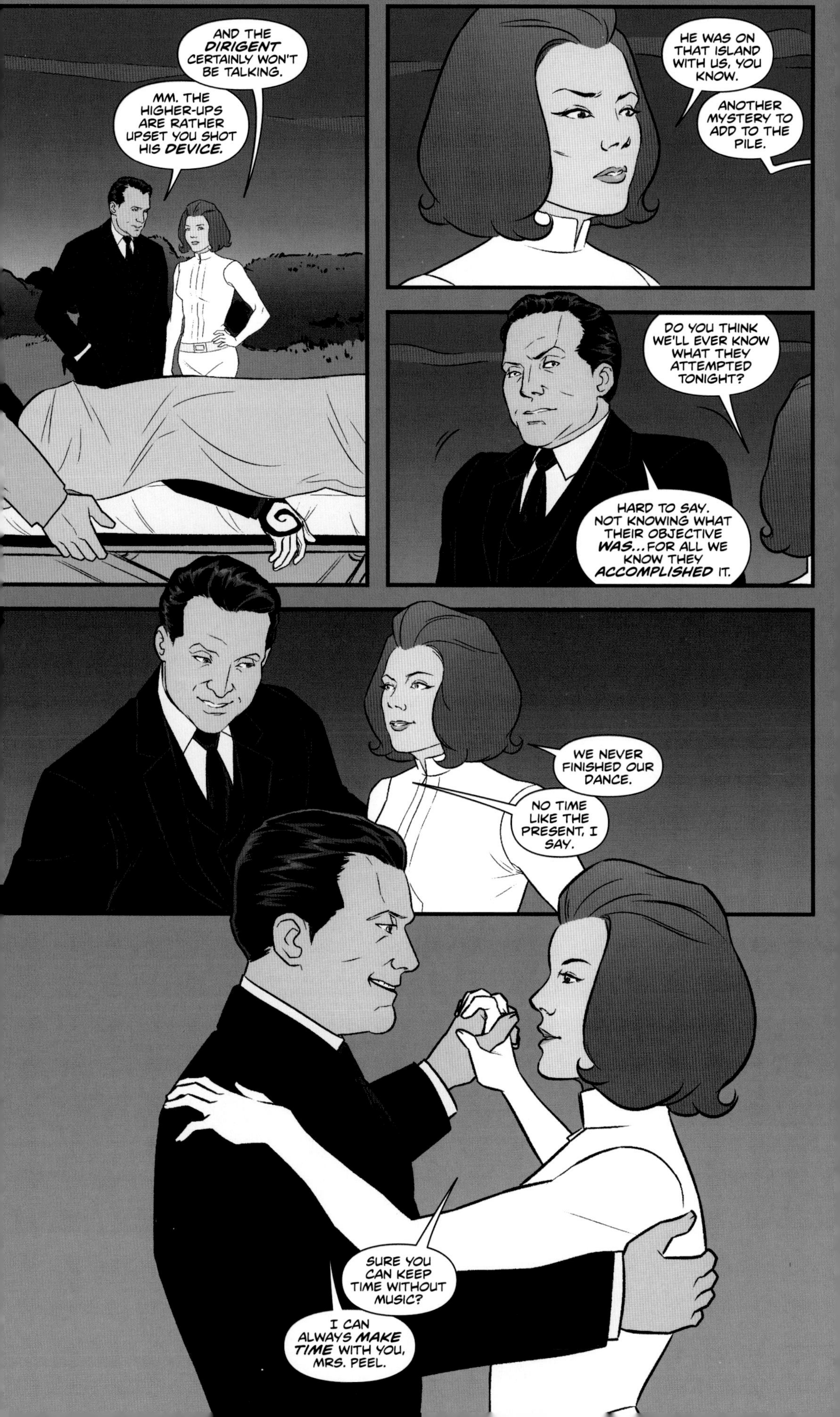

MM. THE HIGHER-UPS ARE RATHER UPSET YOU SHOT HIS *DEVICE.*
AND THE *DIRIGENT* CERTAINLY WON'T BE TALKING.
HE WAS ON THAT ISLAND WITH US, YOU KNOW.
ANOTHER MYSTERY TO ADD TO THE PILE.
DO YOU THINK WE'LL EVER KNOW WHAT THEY ATTEMPTED TONIGHT?
HARD TO SAY. NOT KNOWING WHAT THEIR OBJECTIVE *WAS...* FOR ALL WE KNOW THEY *ACCOMPLISHED* IT.
WE NEVER FINISHED OUR DANCE.
NO TIME LIKE THE PRESENT, I SAY.
SURE YOU CAN KEEP TIME WITHOUT MUSIC?
I CAN ALWAYS *MAKE TIME* WITH YOU, MRS. PEEL.

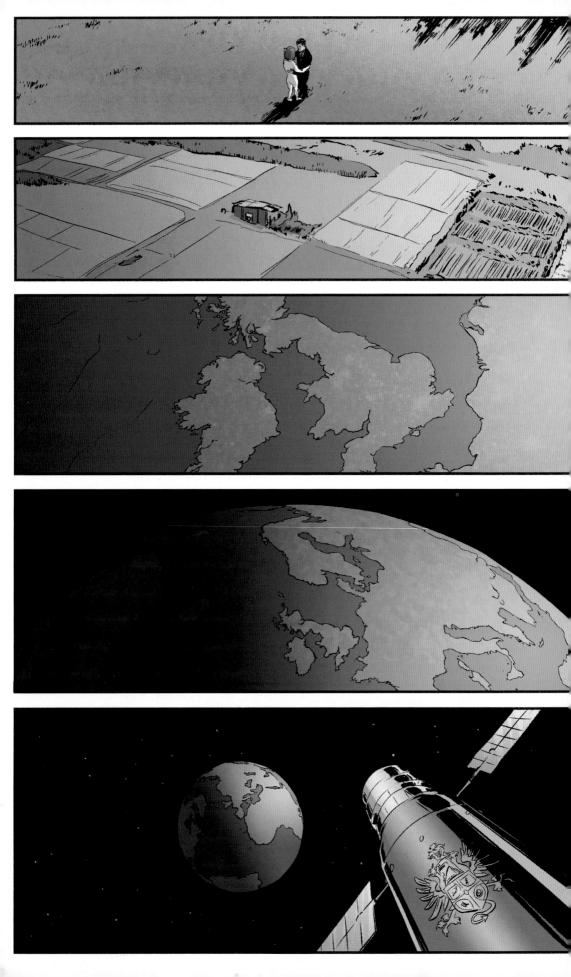

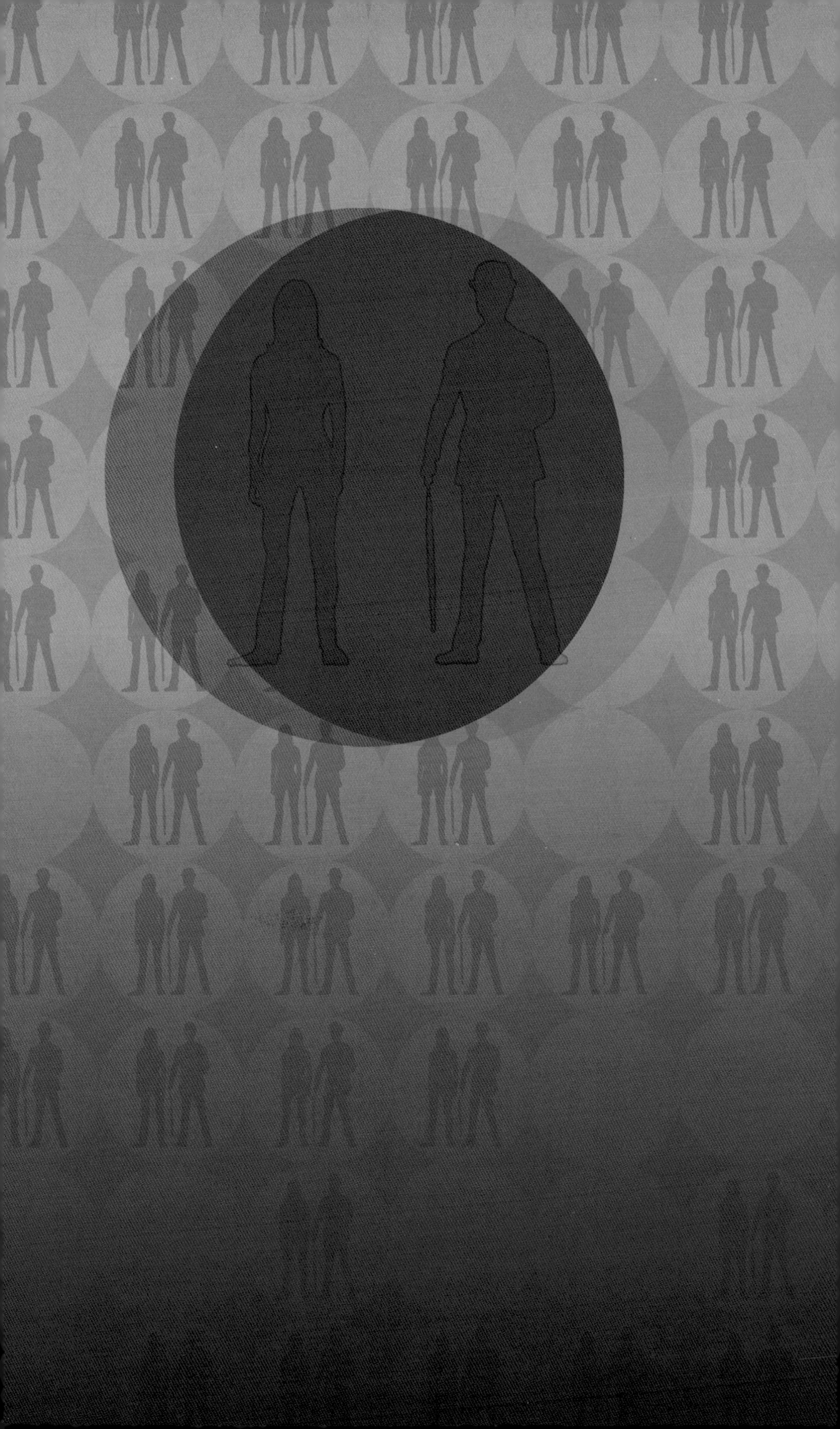

CHAPTER FIVE

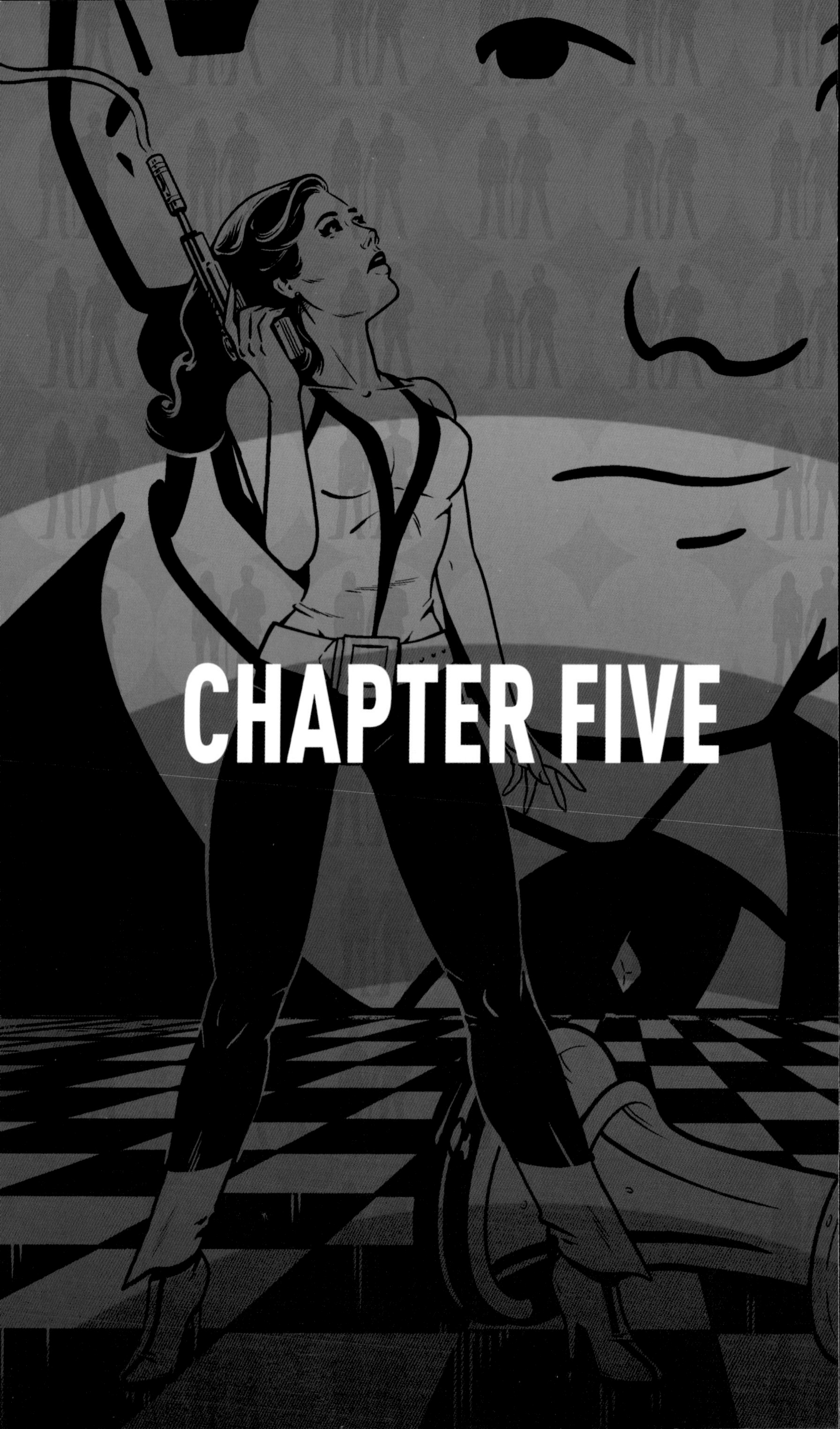

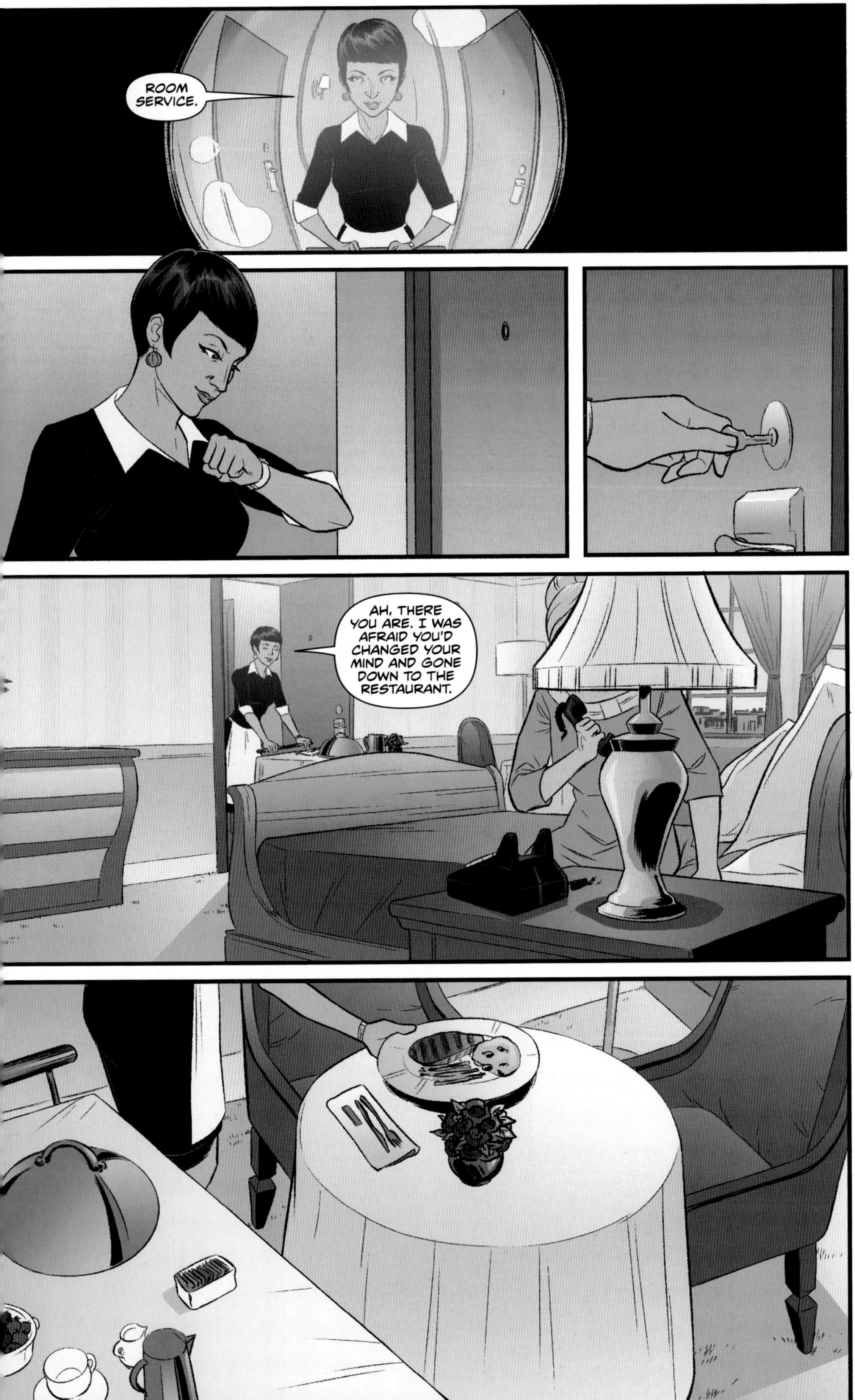
ROOM SERVICE.
AH, THERE YOU ARE. I WAS AFRAID YOU'D CHANGED YOUR MIND AND GONE DOWN TO THE RESTAURANT.

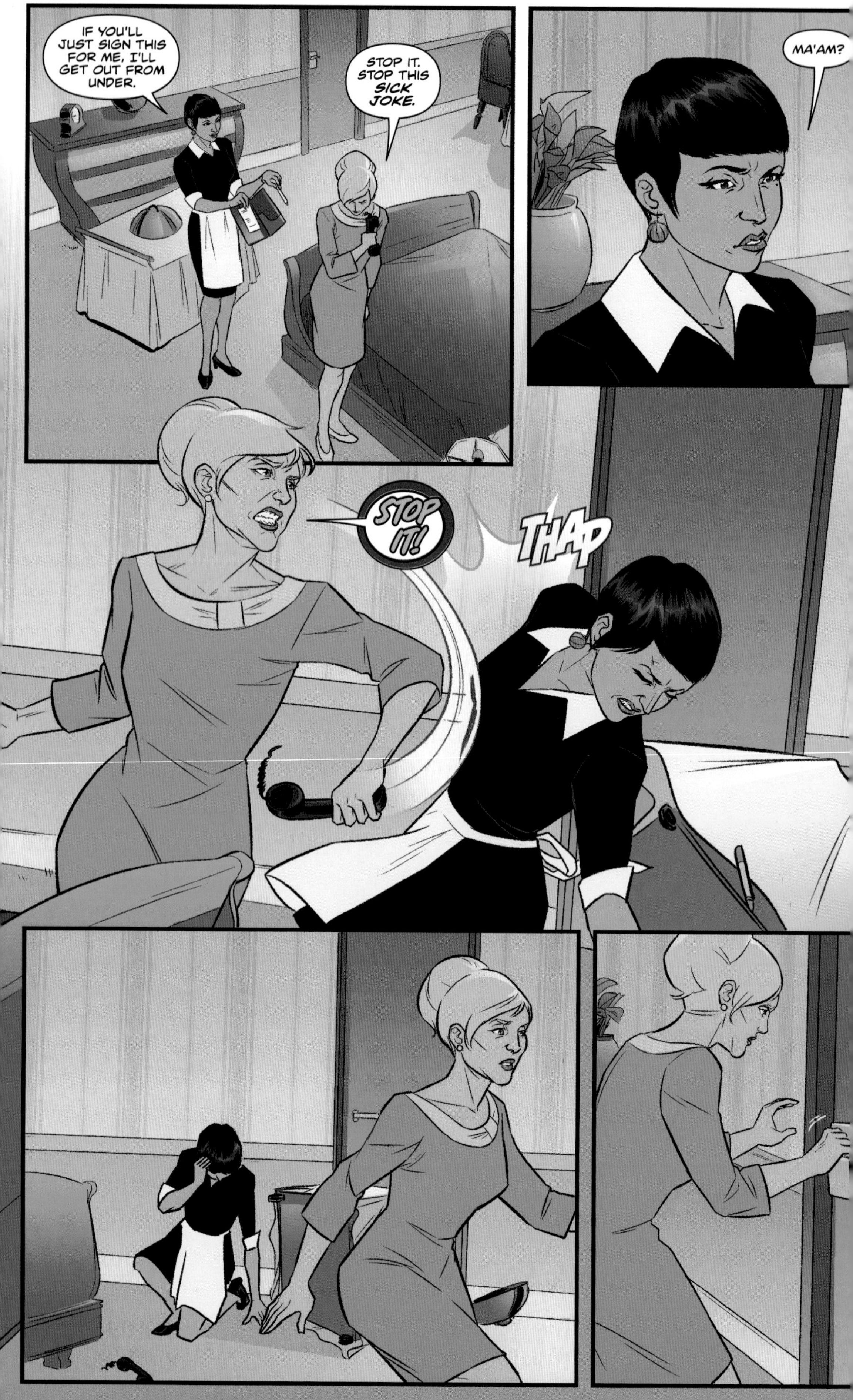
IF YOU'LL JUST SIGN THIS FOR ME, I'LL GET OUT FROM UNDER.
STOP IT. STOP THIS SICK JOKE.
MA'AM?
STOP IT!
THAP

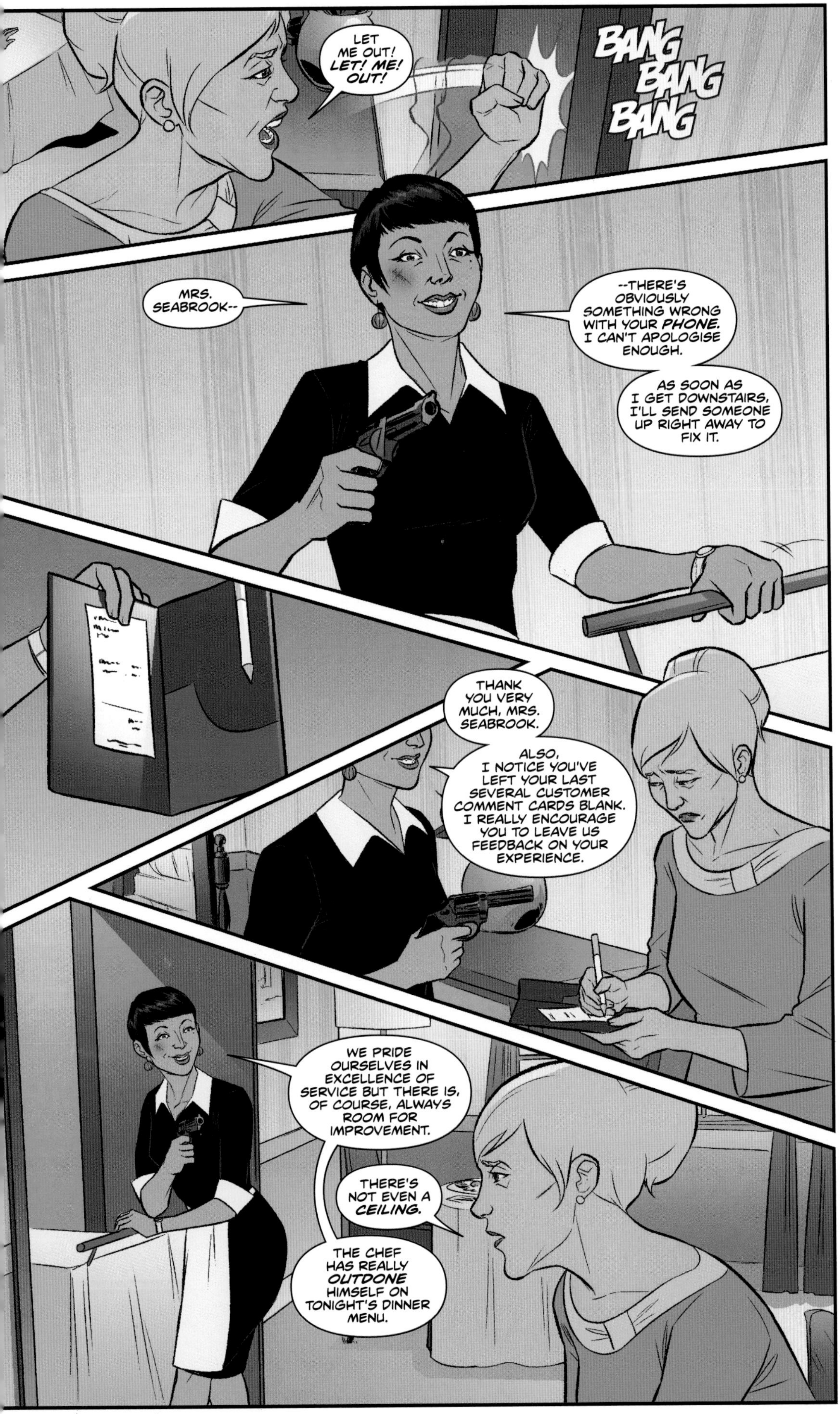

LET ME OUT! LET! ME! OUT!
BANG BANG BANG
MRS. SEABROOK--
--THERE'S OBVIOUSLY SOMETHING WRONG WITH YOUR PHONE. I CAN'T APOLOGISE ENOUGH.
AS SOON AS I GET DOWNSTAIRS, I'LL SEND SOMEONE UP RIGHT AWAY TO FIX IT.
THANK YOU VERY MUCH, MRS. SEABROOK.
ALSO, I NOTICE YOU'VE LEFT YOUR LAST SEVERAL CUSTOMER COMMENT CARDS BLANK. I REALLY ENCOURAGE YOU TO LEAVE US FEEDBACK ON YOUR EXPERIENCE.
WE PRIDE OURSELVES IN EXCELLENCE OF SERVICE BUT THERE IS, OF COURSE, ALWAYS ROOM FOR IMPROVEMENT.
THERE'S NOT EVEN A CEILING.
THE CHEF HAS REALLY OUTDONE HIMSELF ON TONIGHT'S DINNER MENU.

THE SECRET HISTORY OF SPACE

STEED DRIES OFF
EMMA DRIFTS OFF

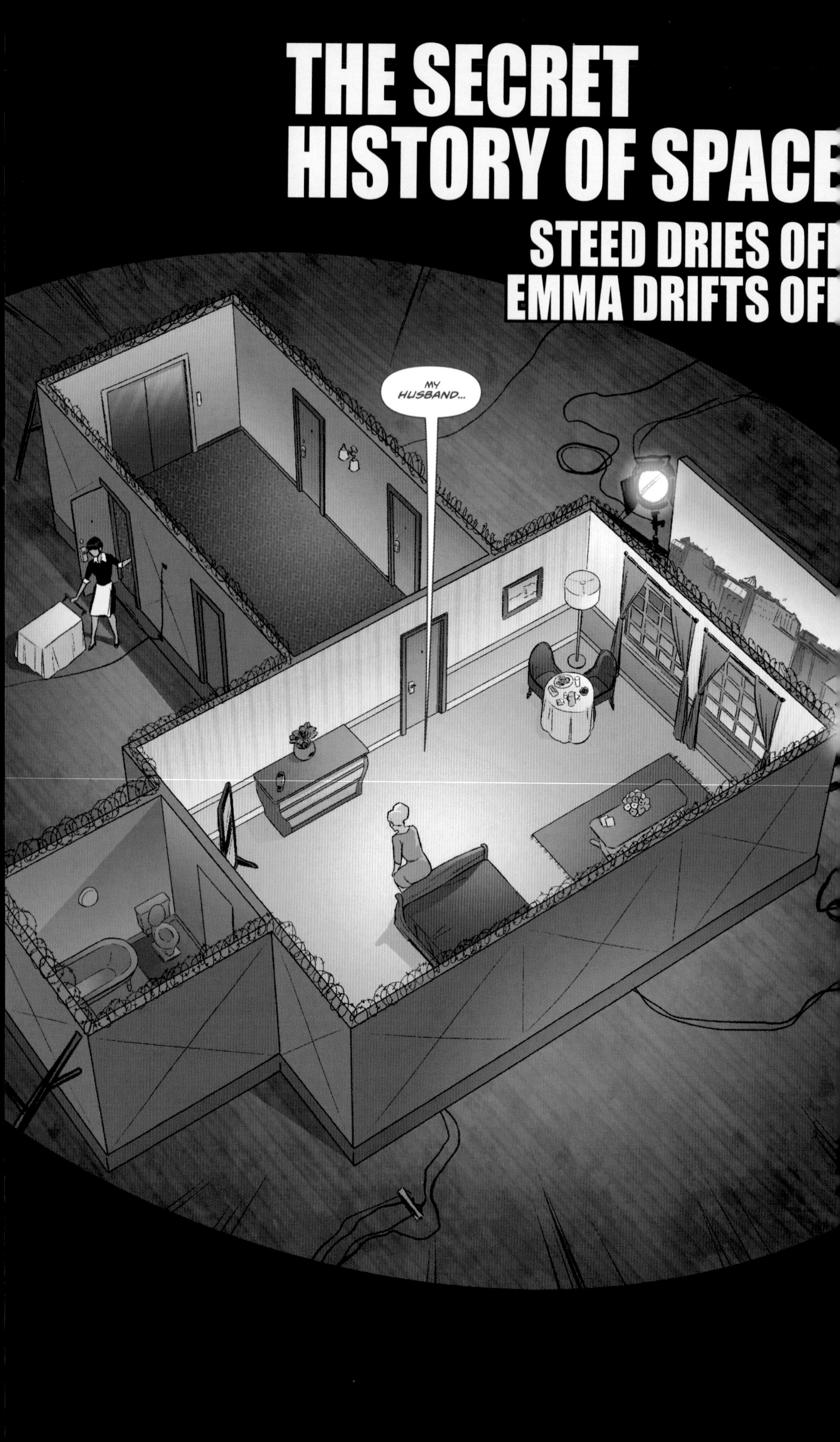

MY HUSBAND...

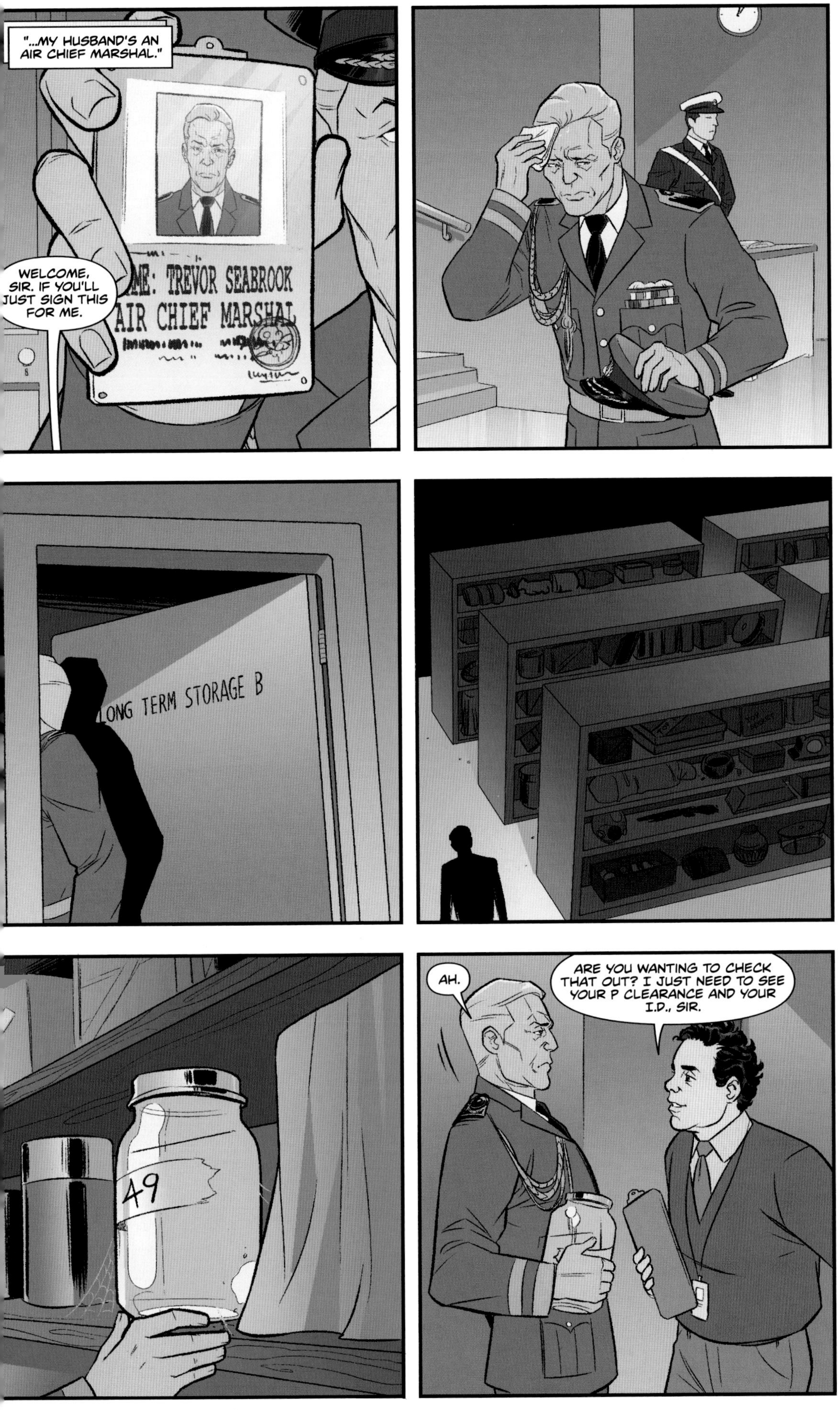
"...MY HUSBAND'S AN AIR CHIEF MARSHAL."
WELCOME, SIR. IF YOU'LL JUST SIGN THIS FOR ME.
AIR CHIEF MARSHAL
LONG TERM STORAGE B
49
AH.
ARE YOU WANTING TO CHECK THAT OUT? I JUST NEED TO SEE YOUR P CLEARANCE AND YOUR I.D., SIR.

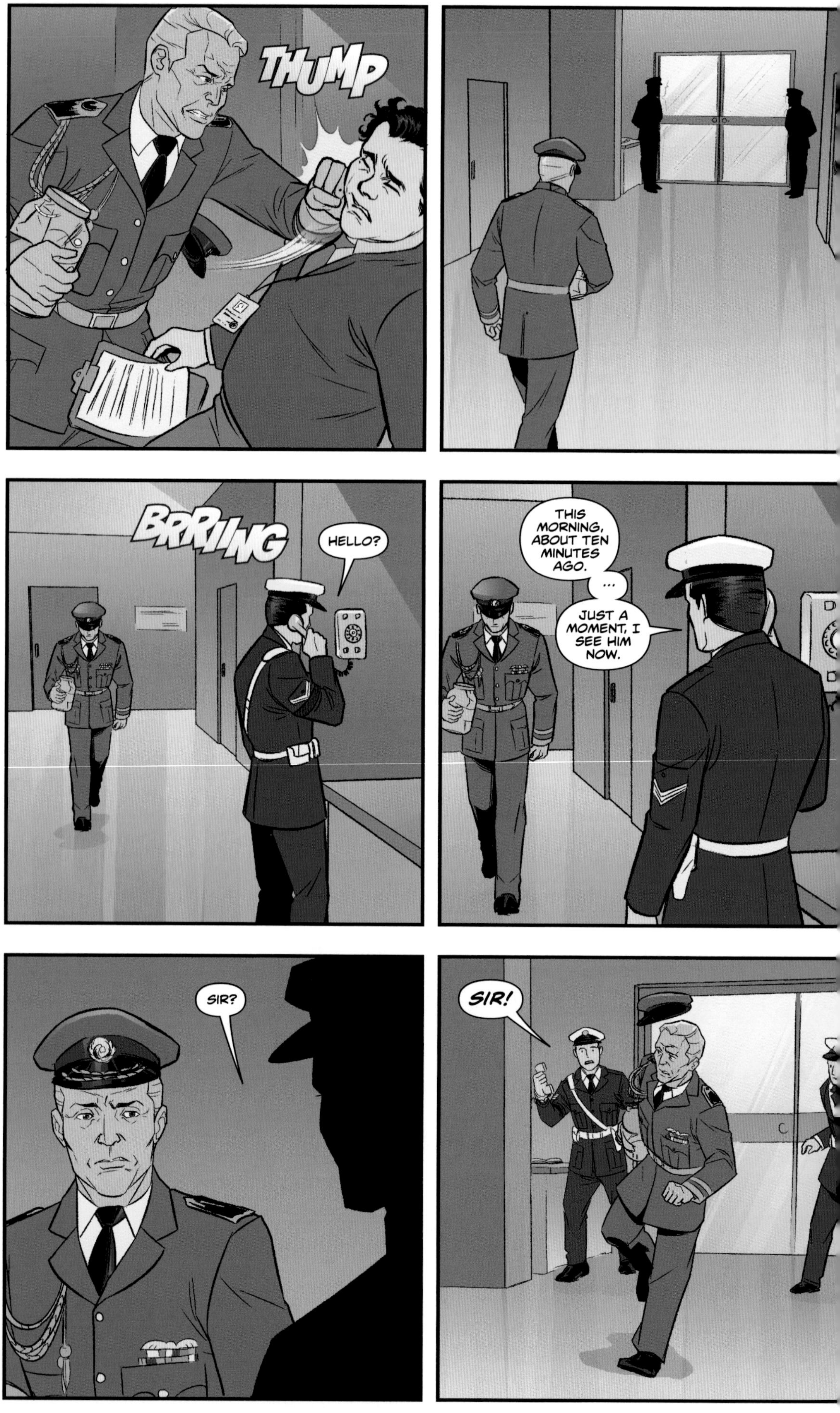
THUMP
BRRIING
HELLO?
THIS MORNING, ABOUT TEN MINUTES AGO.
...
JUST A MOMENT, I SEE HIM NOW.
SIR?
SIR!

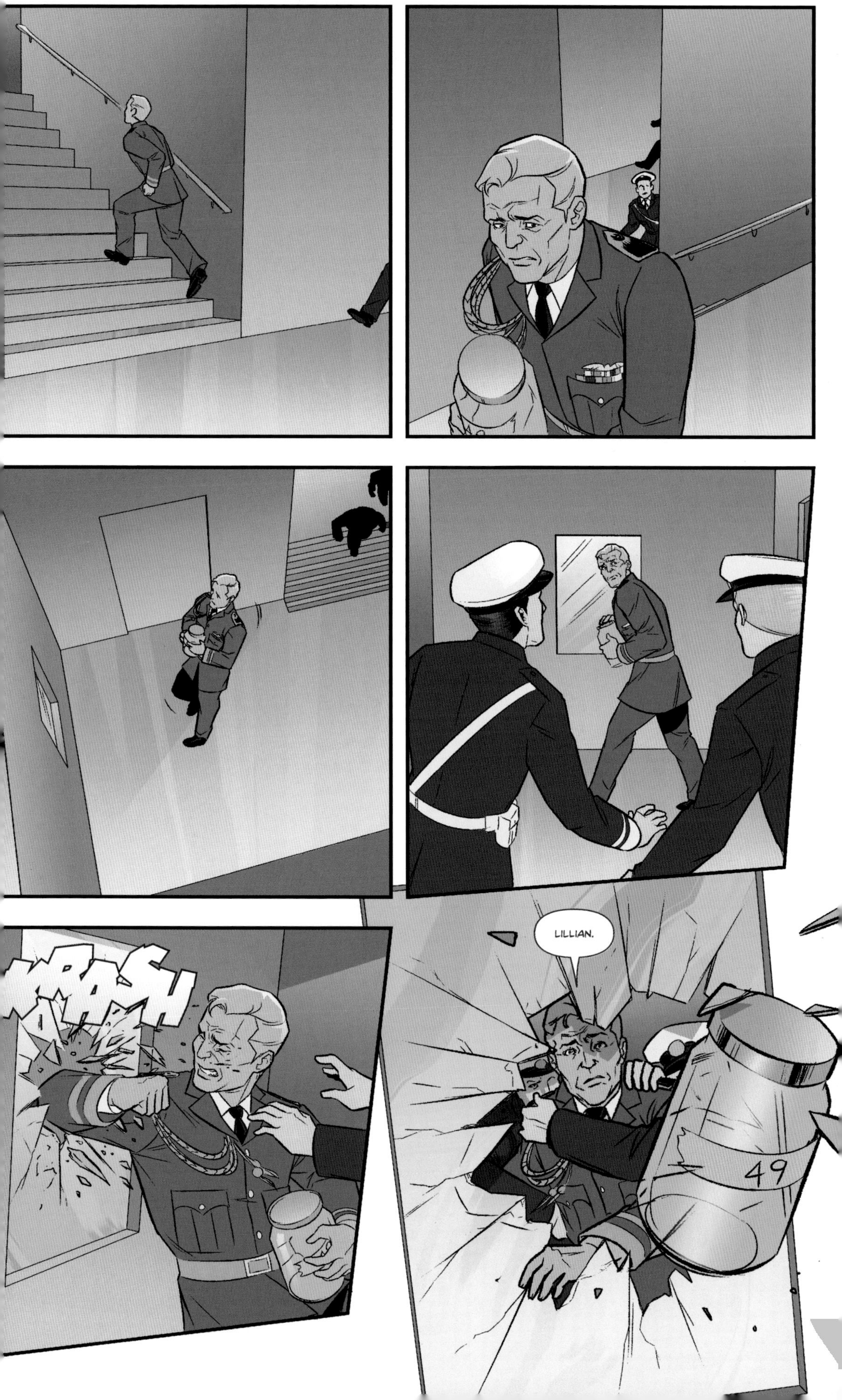
KRASH
LILLIAN.
49

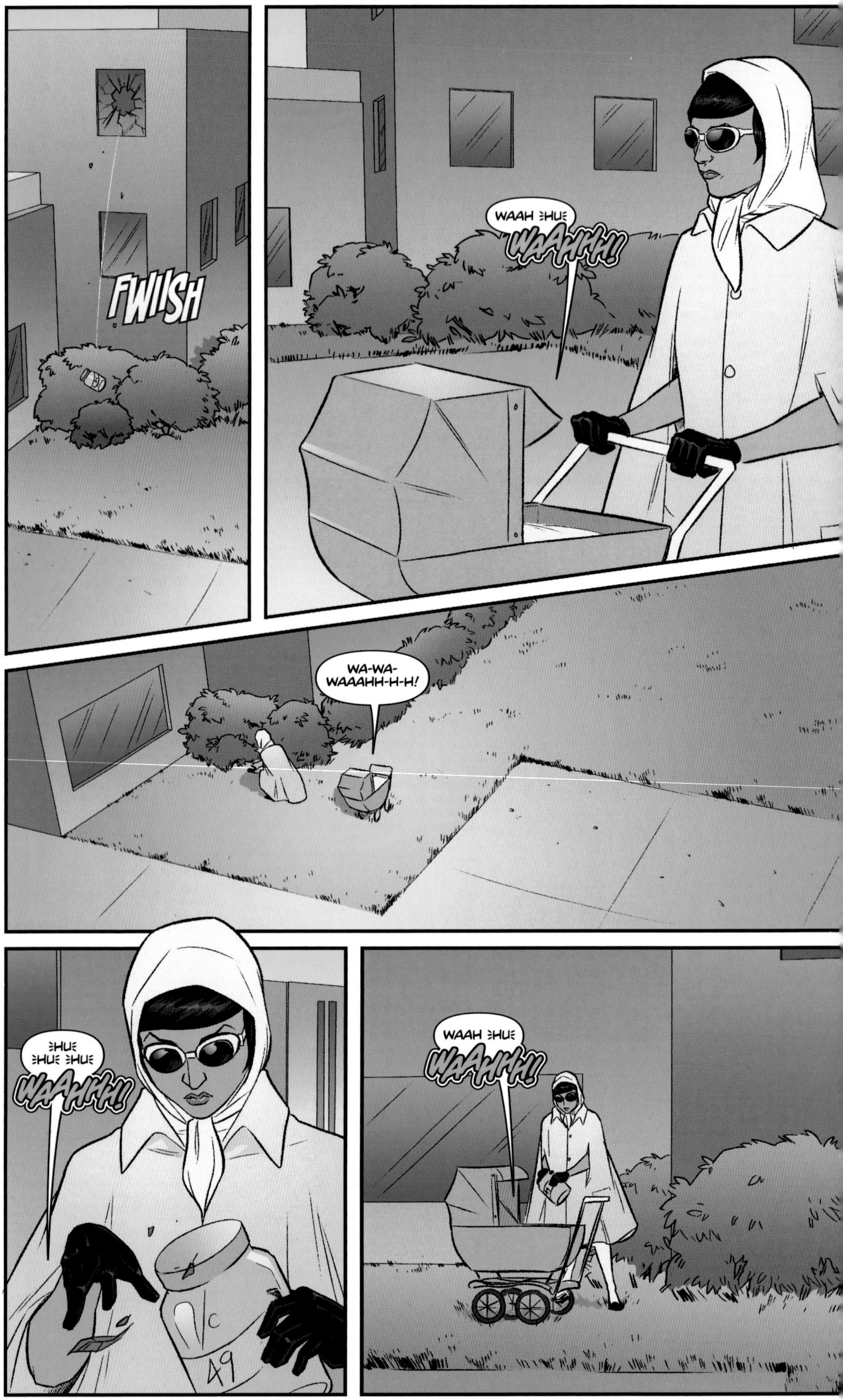
FWIISH
WAAH HU WAAHHH!
WA-WA-WAAAHH-H-H!
HU HU HU WAAHHH!
WAAH HU WAAHHH!

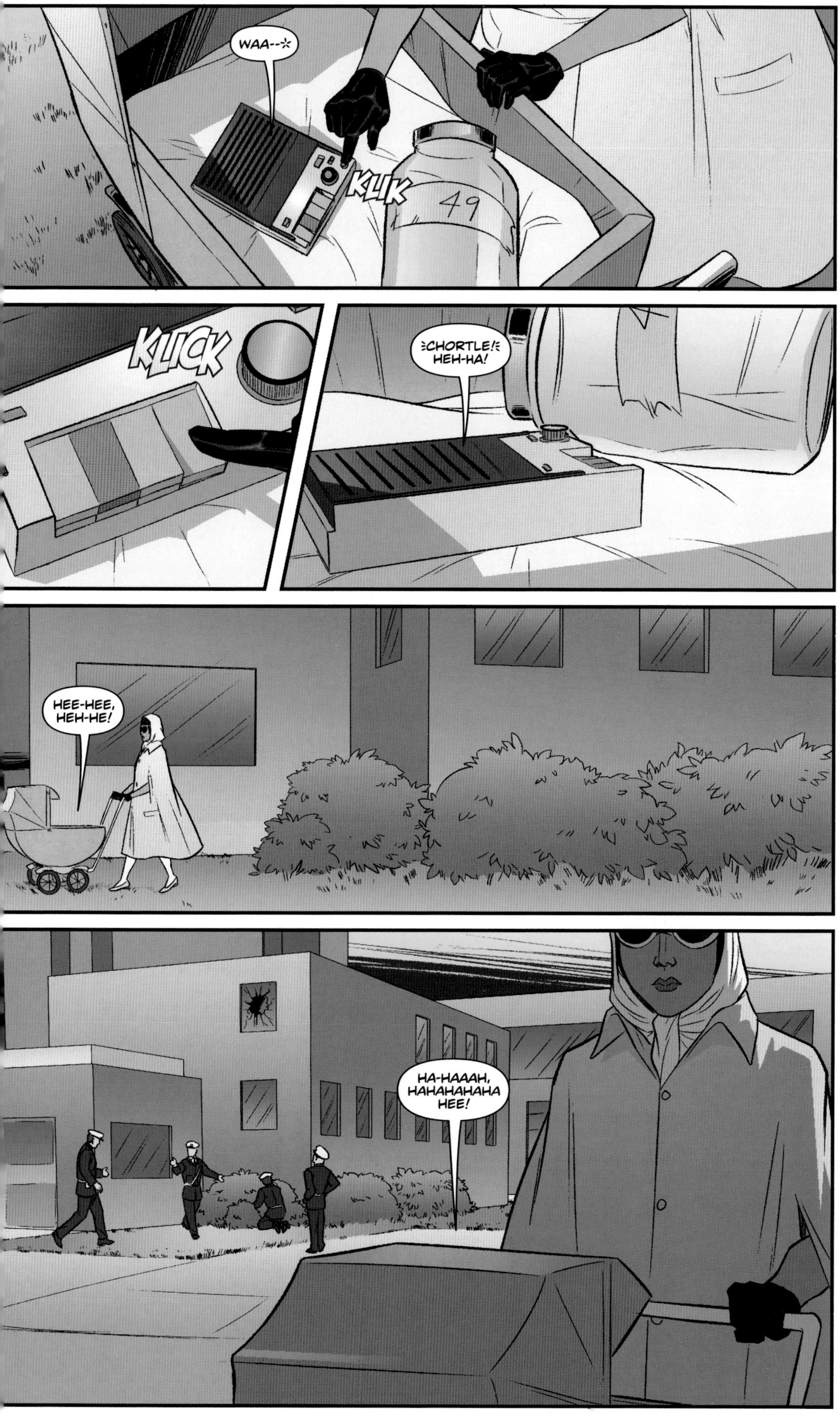
WAA--
KLIK
49
KLICK
CHORTLE! HEH-HA!
HEE-HEE, HEH-HE!
HA-HAAAH, HAHAHAHAHA HEE!

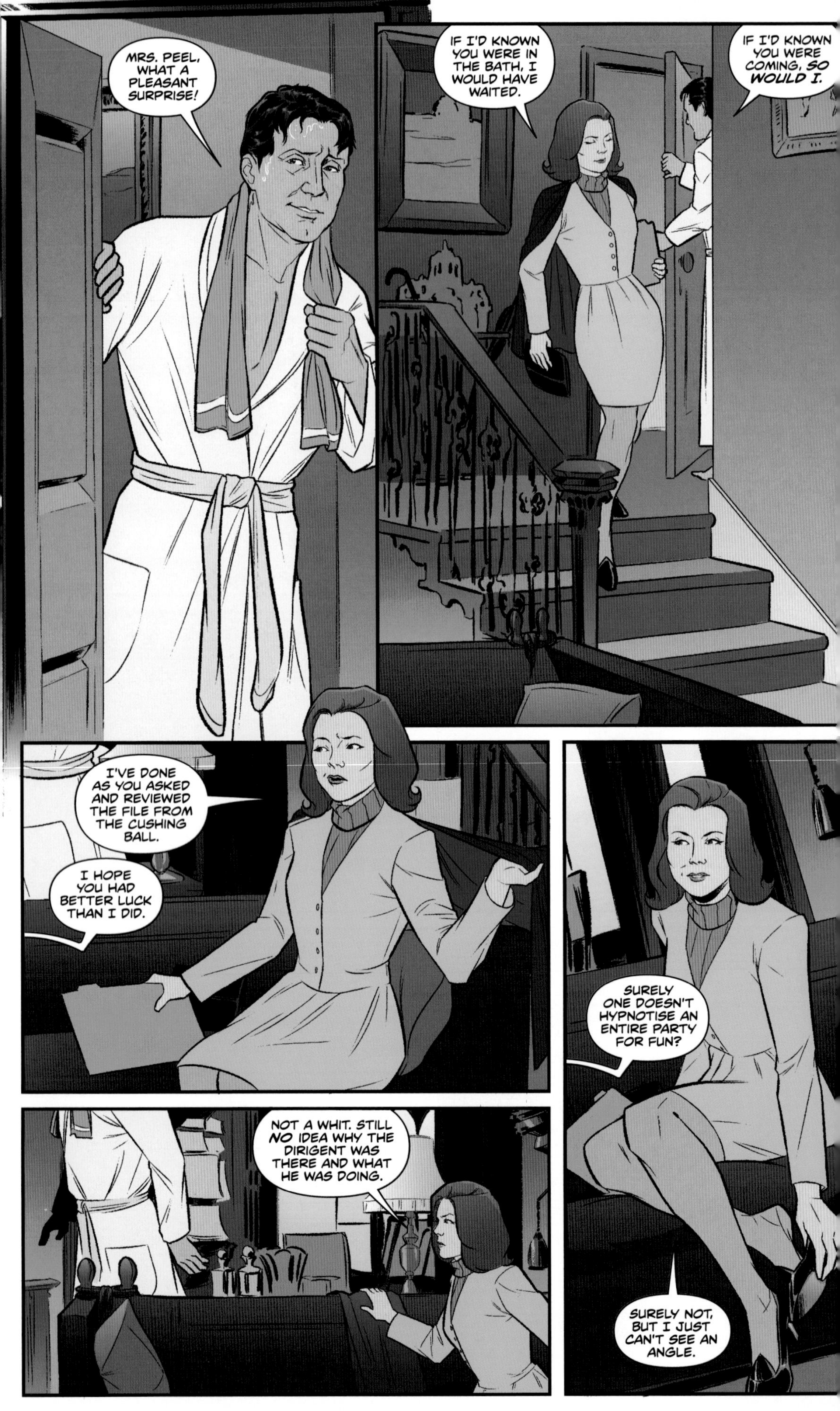
MRS. PEEL, WHAT A PLEASANT SURPRISE!
IF I'D KNOWN YOU WERE IN THE BATH, I WOULD HAVE WAITED.
IF I'D KNOWN YOU WERE COMING, SO WOULD I.
I'VE DONE AS YOU ASKED AND REVIEWED THE FILE FROM THE CUSHING BALL.
I HOPE YOU HAD BETTER LUCK THAN I DID.
NOT A WHIT. STILL NO IDEA WHY THE DIRIGENT WAS THERE AND WHAT HE WAS DOING.
SURELY ONE DOESN'T HYPNOTISE AN ENTIRE PARTY FOR FUN?
SURELY NOT, BUT I JUST CAN'T SEE AN ANGLE.

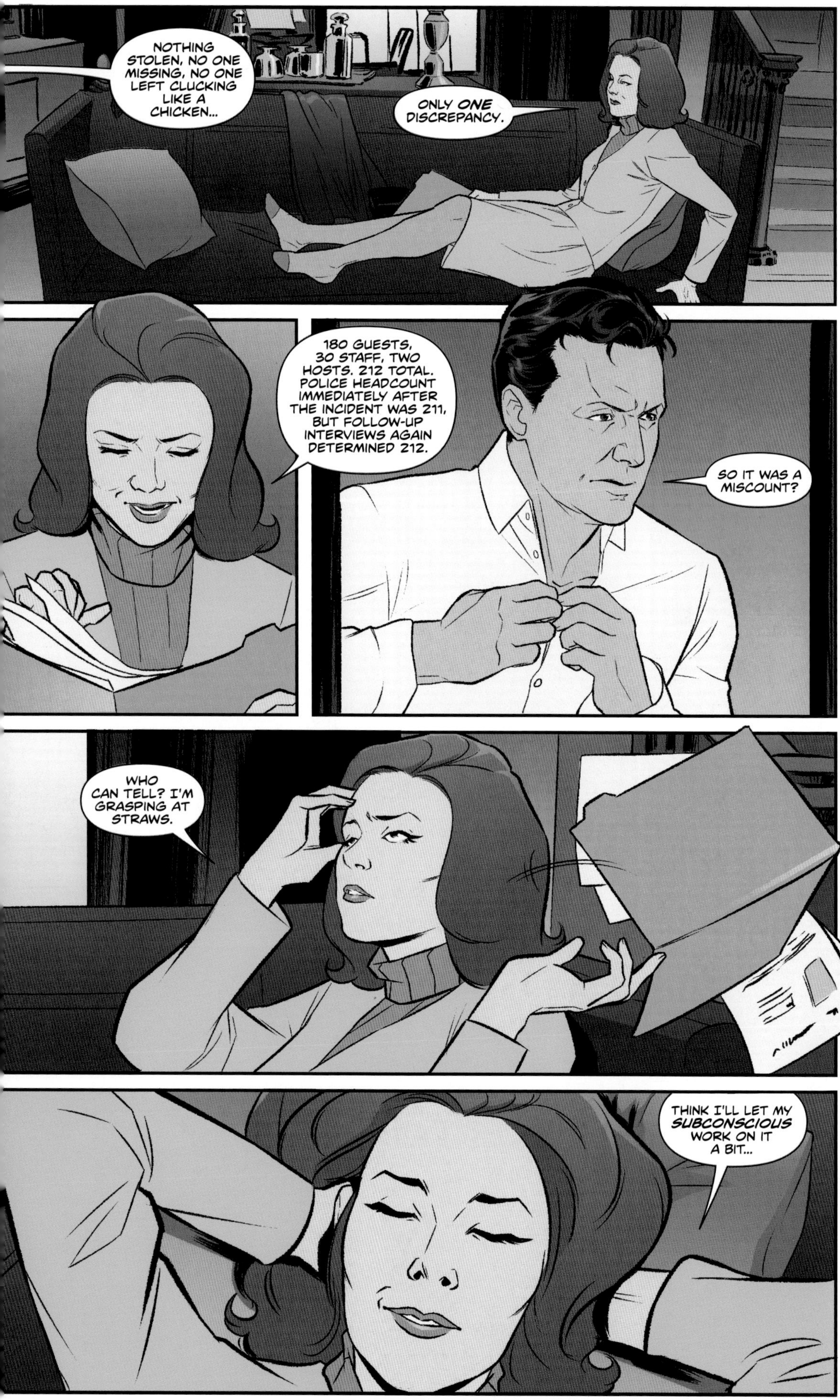
NOTHING STOLEN, NO ONE MISSING, NO ONE LEFT CLUCKING LIKE A CHICKEN...
ONLY *ONE* DISCREPANCY.
180 GUESTS, 30 STAFF, TWO HOSTS. 212 TOTAL. POLICE HEADCOUNT IMMEDIATELY AFTER THE INCIDENT WAS 211, BUT FOLLOW-UP INTERVIEWS AGAIN DETERMINED 212.
SO IT WAS A MISCOUNT?
WHO CAN TELL? I'M GRASPING AT STRAWS.
THINK I'LL LET MY *SUBCONSCIOUS* WORK ON IT A BIT...

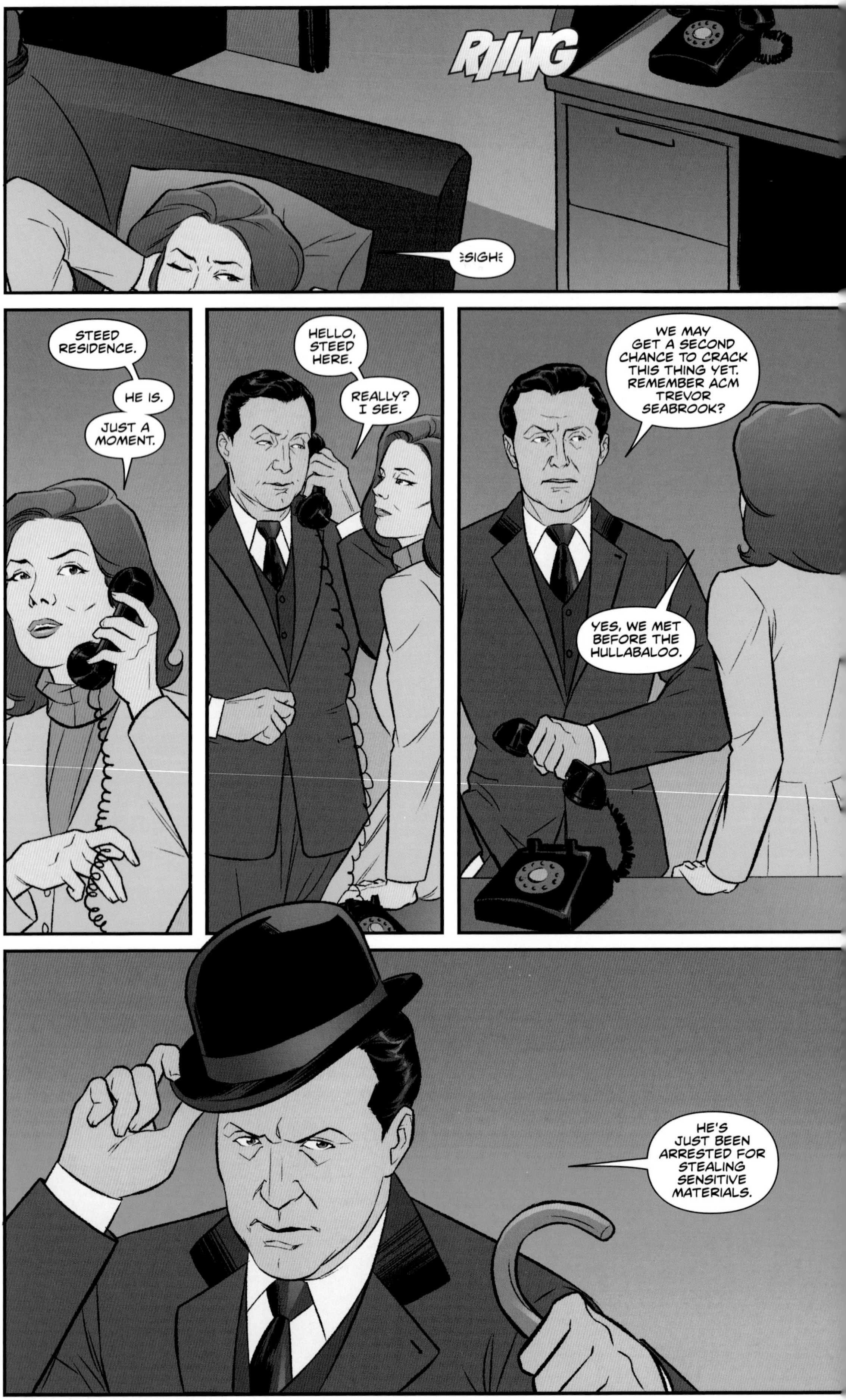
RING
SIGH
STEED RESIDENCE.
HE IS.
JUST A MOMENT.
HELLO, STEED HERE.
REALLY? I SEE.
WE MAY GET A SECOND CHANCE TO CRACK THIS THING YET. REMEMBER ACM TREVOR SEABROOK?
YES, WE MET BEFORE THE HULLABALOO.
HE'S JUST BEEN ARRESTED FOR STEALING SENSITIVE MATERIALS.

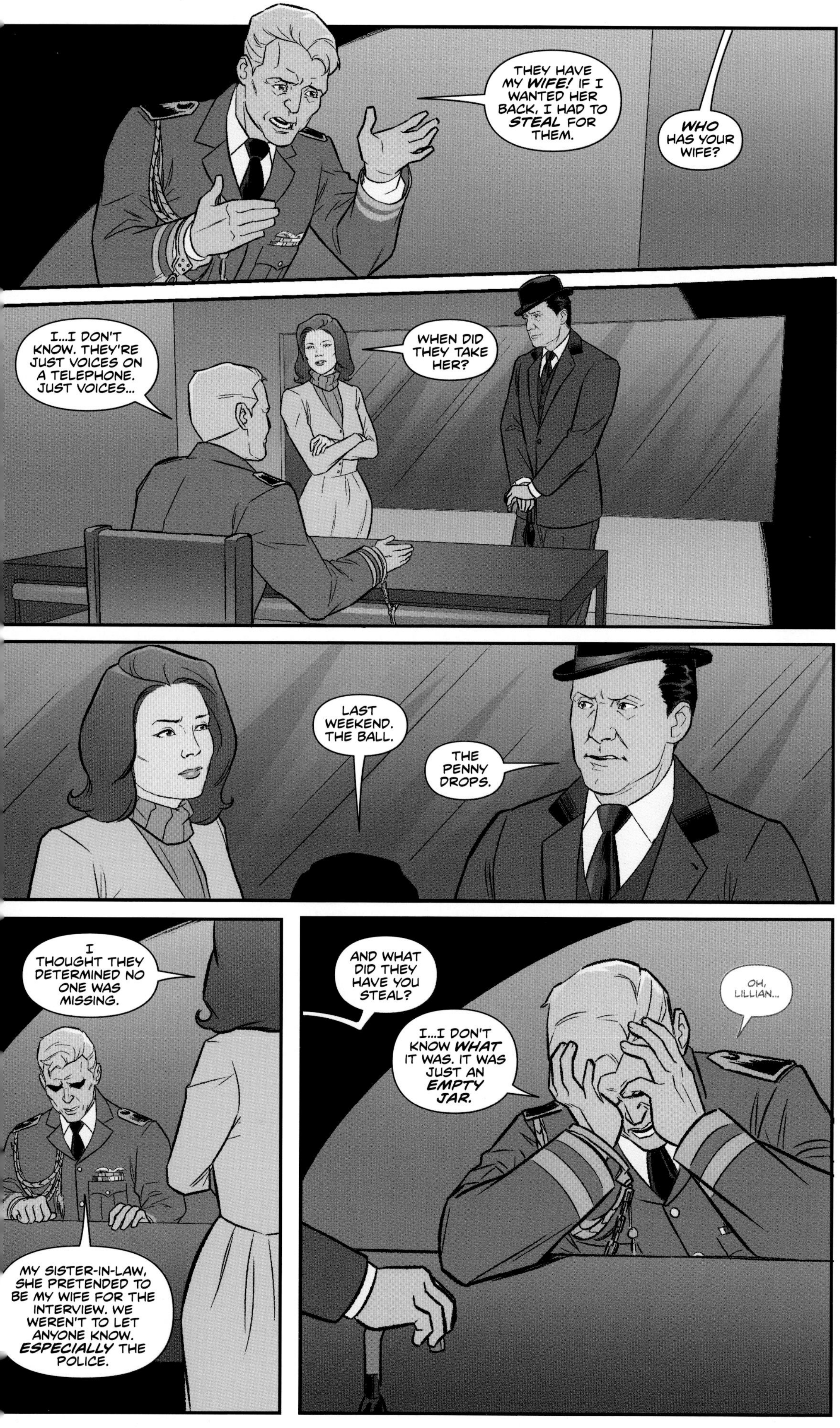
THEY HAVE MY *WIFE!* IF I WANTED HER BACK, I HAD TO *STEAL* FOR THEM.
WHO HAS YOUR WIFE?
I...I DON'T KNOW. THEY'RE JUST VOICES ON A TELEPHONE. JUST VOICES...
WHEN DID THEY TAKE HER?
LAST WEEKEND. THE BALL.
THE PENNY DROPS.
I THOUGHT THEY DETERMINED NO ONE WAS MISSING.
MY SISTER-IN-LAW, SHE PRETENDED TO BE MY WIFE FOR THE INTERVIEW. WE WEREN'T TO LET ANYONE KNOW. *ESPECIALLY* THE POLICE.
AND WHAT DID THEY HAVE YOU STEAL?
I...I DON'T KNOW *WHAT* IT WAS. IT WAS JUST AN *EMPTY JAR.*
OH, LILLIAN...

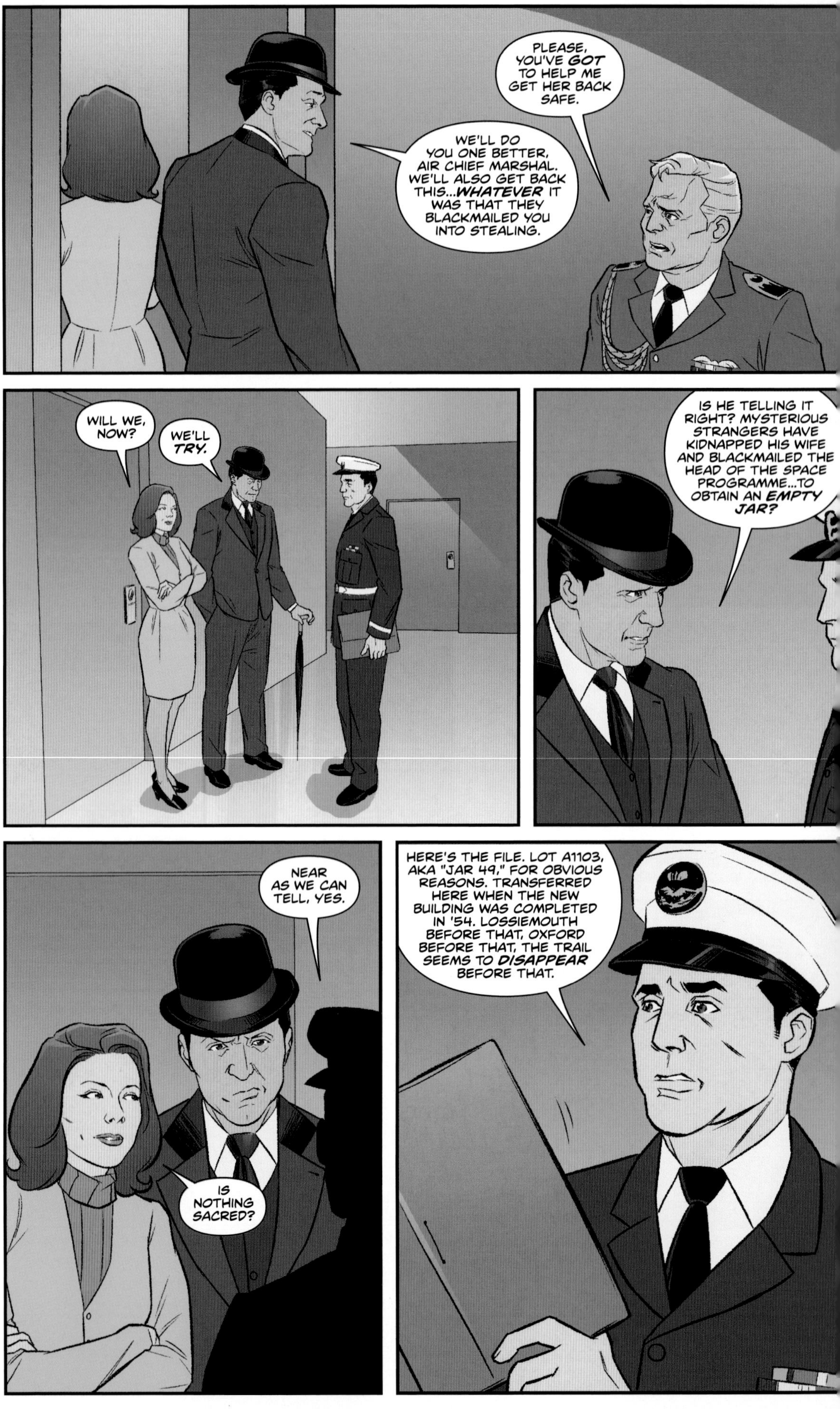
PLEASE, YOU'VE GOT TO HELP ME GET HER BACK SAFE.
WE'LL DO YOU ONE BETTER, AIR CHIEF MARSHAL. WE'LL ALSO GET BACK THIS...WHATEVER IT WAS THAT THEY BLACKMAILED YOU INTO STEALING.
WILL WE, NOW?
WE'LL TRY.
IS HE TELLING IT RIGHT? MYSTERIOUS STRANGERS HAVE KIDNAPPED HIS WIFE AND BLACKMAILED THE HEAD OF THE SPACE PROGRAMME...TO OBTAIN AN EMPTY JAR?
NEAR AS WE CAN TELL, YES.
IS NOTHING SACRED?
HERE'S THE FILE. LOT A1103, AKA "JAR 49," FOR OBVIOUS REASONS. TRANSFERRED HERE WHEN THE NEW BUILDING WAS COMPLETED IN '54. LOSSIEMOUTH BEFORE THAT, OXFORD BEFORE THAT, THE TRAIL SEEMS TO DISAPPEAR BEFORE THAT.

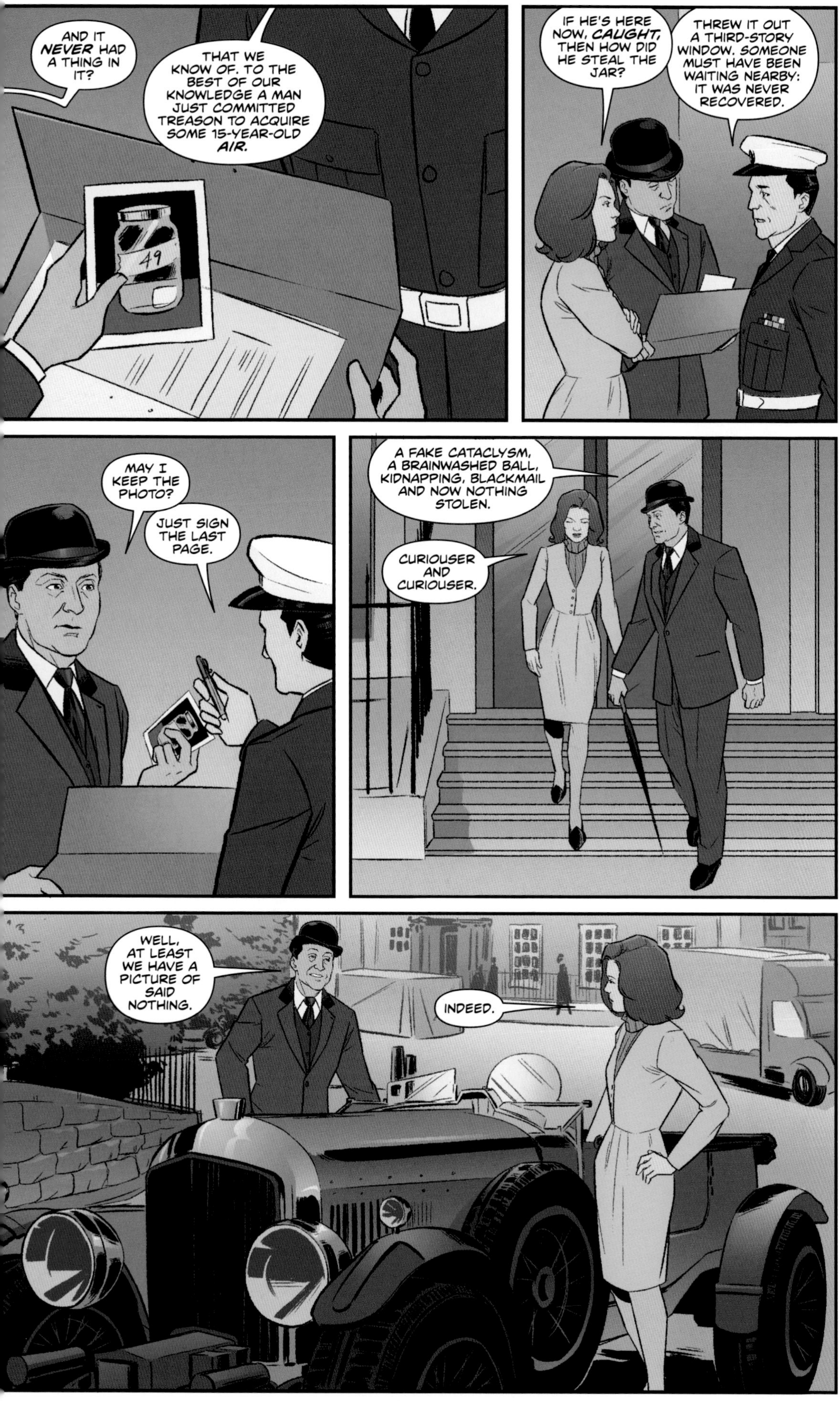
AND IT NEVER HAD A THING IN IT?
THAT WE KNOW OF. TO THE BEST OF OUR KNOWLEDGE A MAN JUST COMMITTED TREASON TO ACQUIRE SOME 15-YEAR-OLD AIR.
49
IF HE'S HERE NOW, CAUGHT, THEN HOW DID HE STEAL THE JAR?
THREW IT OUT A THIRD-STORY WINDOW. SOMEONE MUST HAVE BEEN WAITING NEARBY: IT WAS NEVER RECOVERED.
MAY I KEEP THE PHOTO?
JUST SIGN THE LAST PAGE.
A FAKE CATACLYSM, A BRAINWASHED BALL, KIDNAPPING, BLACKMAIL AND NOW NOTHING STOLEN.
CURIOUSER AND CURIOUSER.
WELL, AT LEAST WE HAVE A PICTURE OF SAID NOTHING.
INDEED.

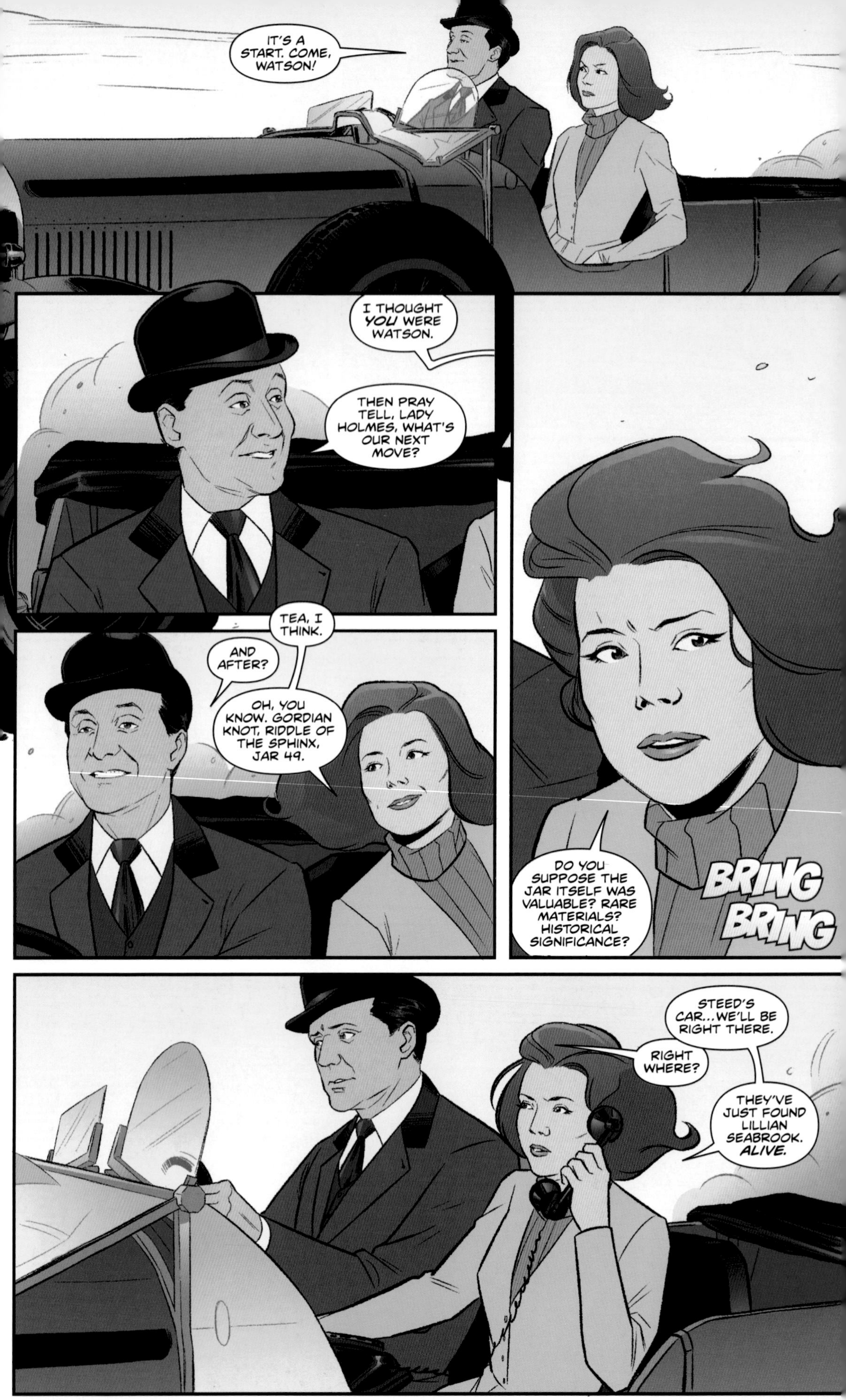
IT'S A START. COME, WATSON!
I THOUGHT *YOU* WERE WATSON.
THEN PRAY TELL, LADY HOLMES, WHAT'S OUR NEXT MOVE?
TEA, I THINK.
AND AFTER?
OH, YOU KNOW. GORDIAN KNOT, RIDDLE OF THE SPHINX, JAR 49.
DO YOU SUPPOSE THE JAR ITSELF WAS VALUABLE? RARE MATERIALS? HISTORICAL SIGNIFICANCE?
BRING BRING
STEED'S CAR...WE'LL BE RIGHT THERE.
RIGHT WHERE?
THEY'VE JUST FOUND LILLIAN SEABROOK. *ALIVE.*

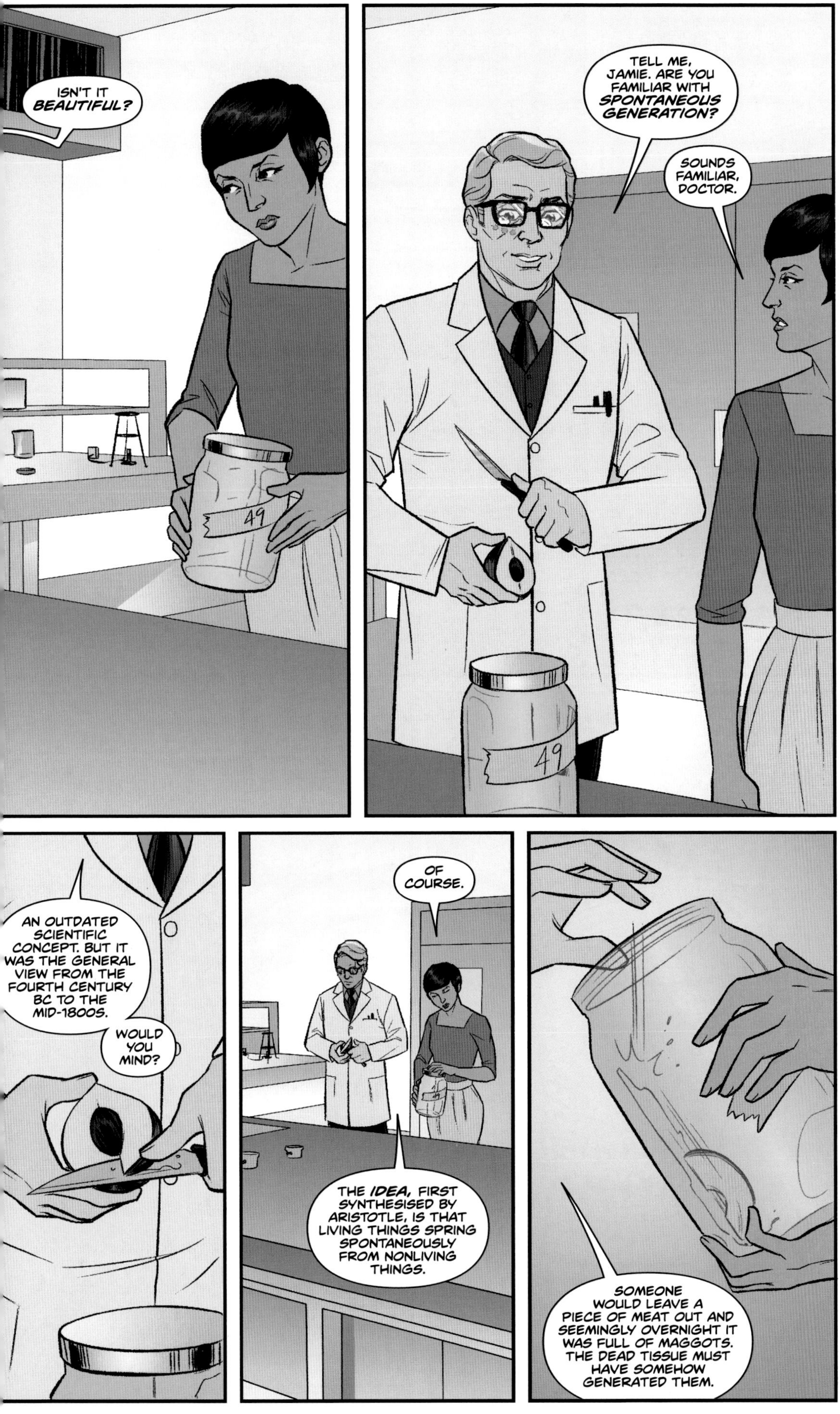
ISN'T IT BEAUTIFUL?
TELL ME, JAMIE. ARE YOU FAMILIAR WITH SPONTANEOUS GENERATION?
SOUNDS FAMILIAR, DOCTOR.
AN OUTDATED SCIENTIFIC CONCEPT. BUT IT WAS THE GENERAL VIEW FROM THE FOURTH CENTURY BC TO THE MID-1800S.
WOULD YOU MIND?
OF COURSE.
THE IDEA, FIRST SYNTHESISED BY ARISTOTLE, IS THAT LIVING THINGS SPRING SPONTANEOUSLY FROM NONLIVING THINGS.
SOMEONE WOULD LEAVE A PIECE OF MEAT OUT AND SEEMINGLY OVERNIGHT IT WAS FULL OF MAGGOTS. THE DEAD TISSUE MUST HAVE SOMEHOW GENERATED THEM.

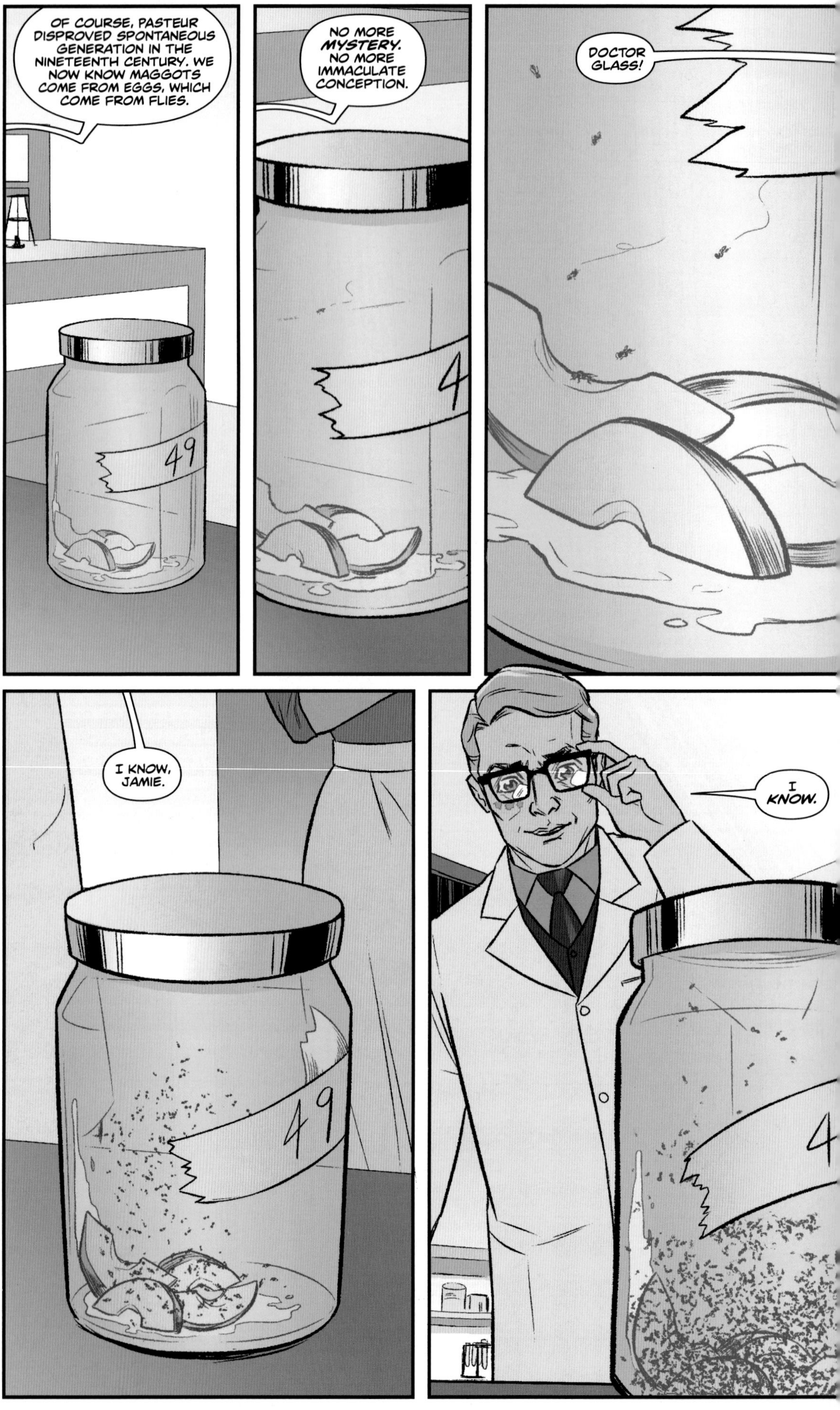
OF COURSE, PASTEUR DISPROVED SPONTANEOUS GENERATION IN THE NINETEENTH CENTURY. WE NOW KNOW MAGGOTS COME FROM EGGS, WHICH COME FROM FLIES.
49
NO MORE *MYSTERY.* NO MORE IMMACULATE CONCEPTION.
DOCTOR GLASS!
I KNOW, JAMIE.
49
I *KNOW.*

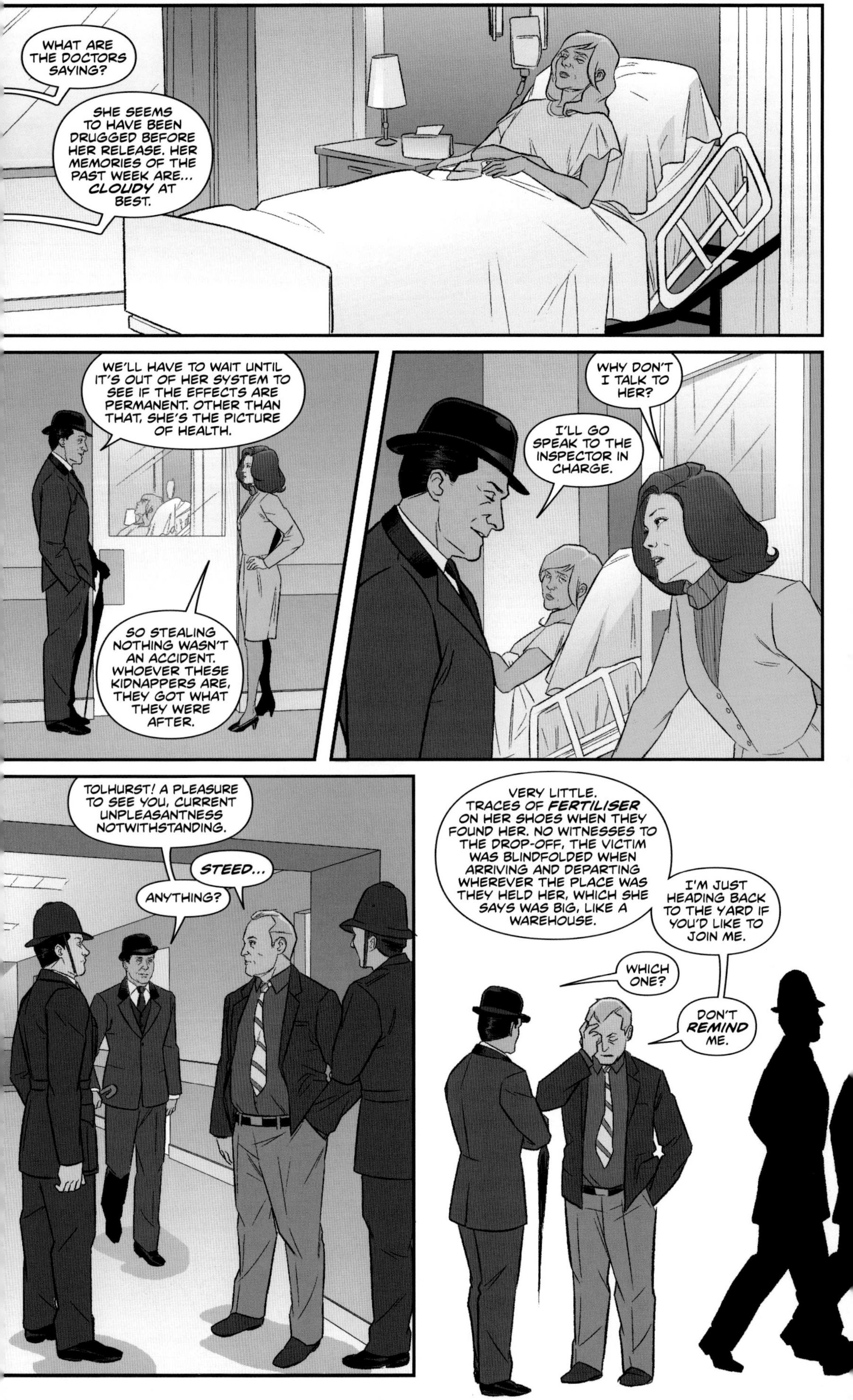
WHAT ARE THE DOCTORS SAYING?
SHE SEEMS TO HAVE BEEN DRUGGED BEFORE HER RELEASE. HER MEMORIES OF THE PAST WEEK ARE... CLOUDY AT BEST.
WE'LL HAVE TO WAIT UNTIL IT'S OUT OF HER SYSTEM TO SEE IF THE EFFECTS ARE PERMANENT. OTHER THAN THAT, SHE'S THE PICTURE OF HEALTH.
SO STEALING NOTHING WASN'T AN ACCIDENT. WHOEVER THESE KIDNAPPERS ARE, THEY GOT WHAT THEY WERE AFTER.
WHY DON'T I TALK TO HER?
I'LL GO SPEAK TO THE INSPECTOR IN CHARGE.
TOLHURST! A PLEASURE TO SEE YOU, CURRENT UNPLEASANTNESS NOTWITHSTANDING.
STEED...
ANYTHING?
VERY LITTLE. TRACES OF FERTILISER ON HER SHOES WHEN THEY FOUND HER. NO WITNESSES TO THE DROP-OFF, THE VICTIM WAS BLINDFOLDED WHEN ARRIVING AND DEPARTING WHEREVER THE PLACE WAS THEY HELD HER, WHICH SHE SAYS WAS BIG, LIKE A WAREHOUSE.
I'M JUST HEADING BACK TO THE YARD IF YOU'D LIKE TO JOIN ME.
WHICH ONE?
DON'T REMIND ME.

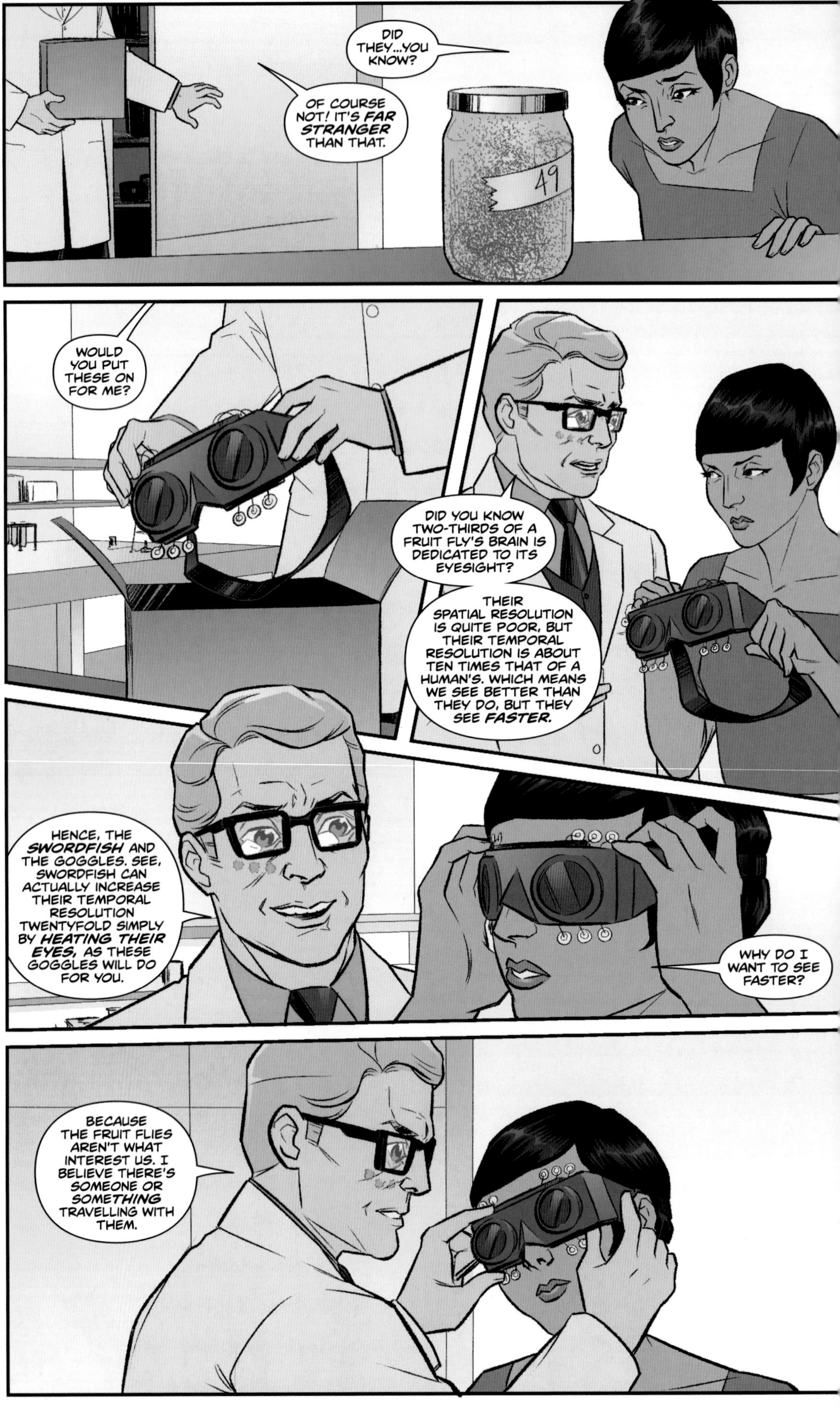
DID THEY...YOU KNOW?
OF COURSE NOT! IT'S FAR STRANGER THAN THAT.
WOULD YOU PUT THESE ON FOR ME?
DID YOU KNOW TWO-THIRDS OF A FRUIT FLY'S BRAIN IS DEDICATED TO ITS EYESIGHT?
THEIR SPATIAL RESOLUTION IS QUITE POOR, BUT THEIR TEMPORAL RESOLUTION IS ABOUT TEN TIMES THAT OF A HUMAN'S. WHICH MEANS WE SEE BETTER THAN THEY DO, BUT THEY SEE FASTER.
HENCE, THE SWORDFISH AND THE GOGGLES. SEE, SWORDFISH CAN ACTUALLY INCREASE THEIR TEMPORAL RESOLUTION TWENTYFOLD SIMPLY BY HEATING THEIR EYES, AS THESE GOGGLES WILL DO FOR YOU.
WHY DO I WANT TO SEE FASTER?
BECAUSE THE FRUIT FLIES AREN'T WHAT INTEREST US. I BELIEVE THERE'S SOMEONE OR SOMETHING TRAVELLING WITH THEM.
49

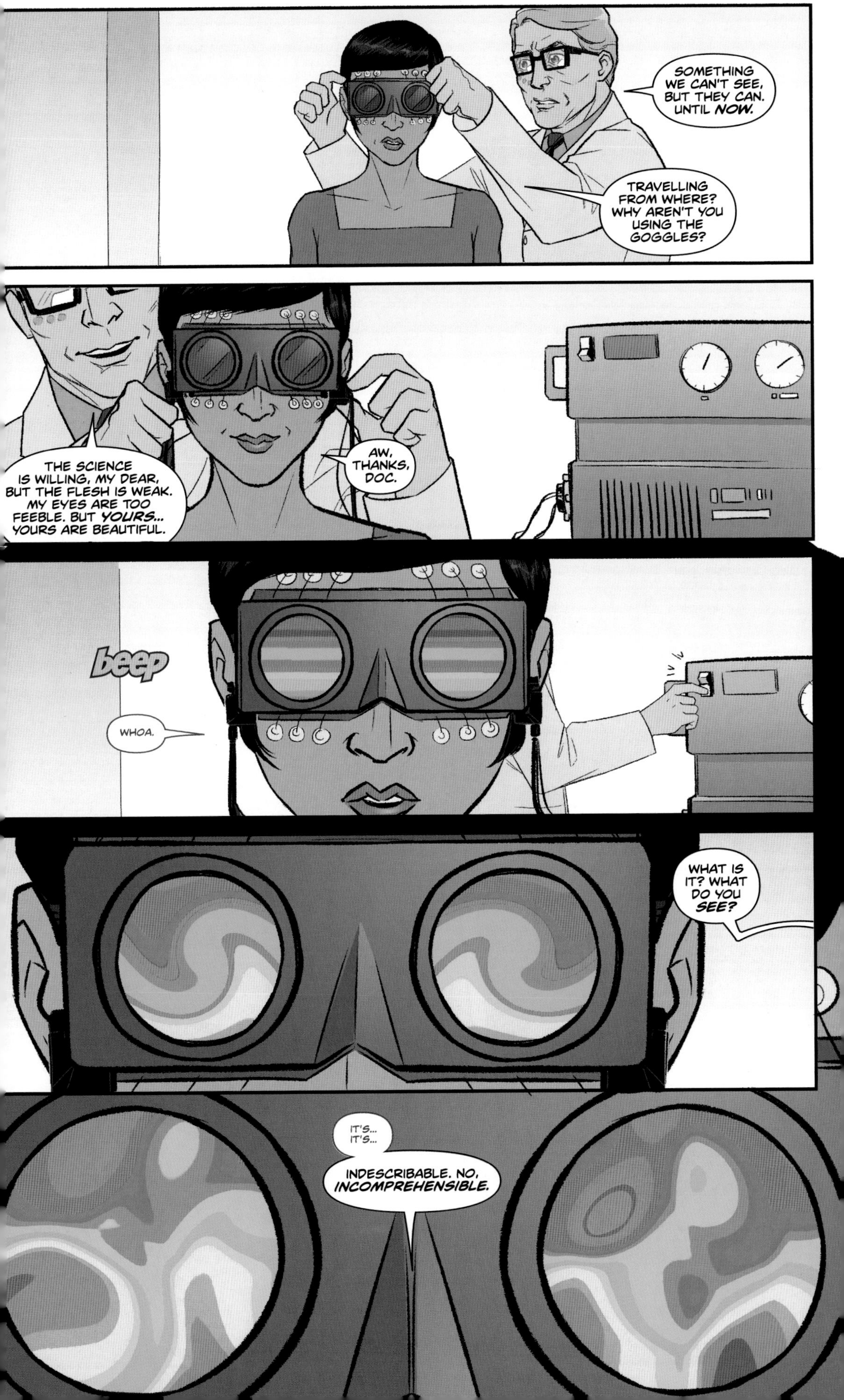
SOMETHING WE CAN'T SEE, BUT THEY CAN. UNTIL NOW.
TRAVELLING FROM WHERE? WHY AREN'T YOU USING THE GOGGLES?
THE SCIENCE IS WILLING, MY DEAR, BUT THE FLESH IS WEAK. MY EYES ARE TOO FEEBLE. BUT YOURS... YOURS ARE BEAUTIFUL.
AW, THANKS, DOC.
beep
WHOA.
WHAT IS IT? WHAT DO YOU SEE?
IT'S... IT'S...
INDESCRIBABLE. NO, INCOMPREHENSIBLE.

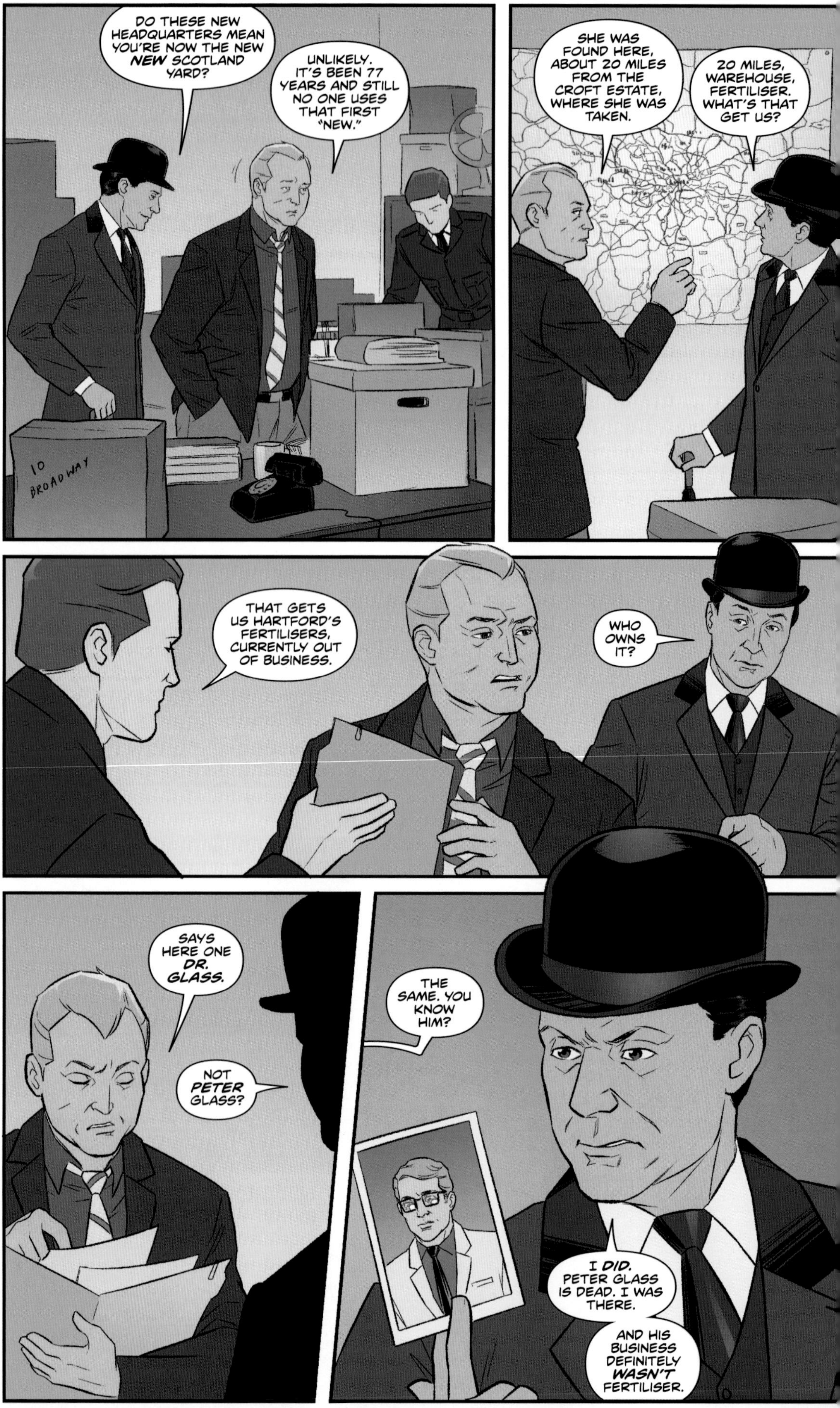
DO THESE NEW HEADQUARTERS MEAN YOU'RE NOW THE NEW *NEW* SCOTLAND YARD?
UNLIKELY. IT'S BEEN 77 YEARS AND STILL NO ONE USES THAT FIRST "NEW."
10 BROADWAY
SHE WAS FOUND HERE, ABOUT 20 MILES FROM THE CROFT ESTATE, WHERE SHE WAS TAKEN.
20 MILES, WAREHOUSE, FERTILISER. WHAT'S THAT GET US?
THAT GETS US HARTFORD'S FERTILISERS, CURRENTLY OUT OF BUSINESS.
WHO OWNS IT?
SAYS HERE ONE *DR. GLASS.*
NOT *PETER* GLASS?
THE SAME. YOU KNOW HIM?
I *DID.* PETER GLASS IS DEAD. I WAS THERE.
AND HIS BUSINESS DEFINITELY *WASN'T* FERTILISER.

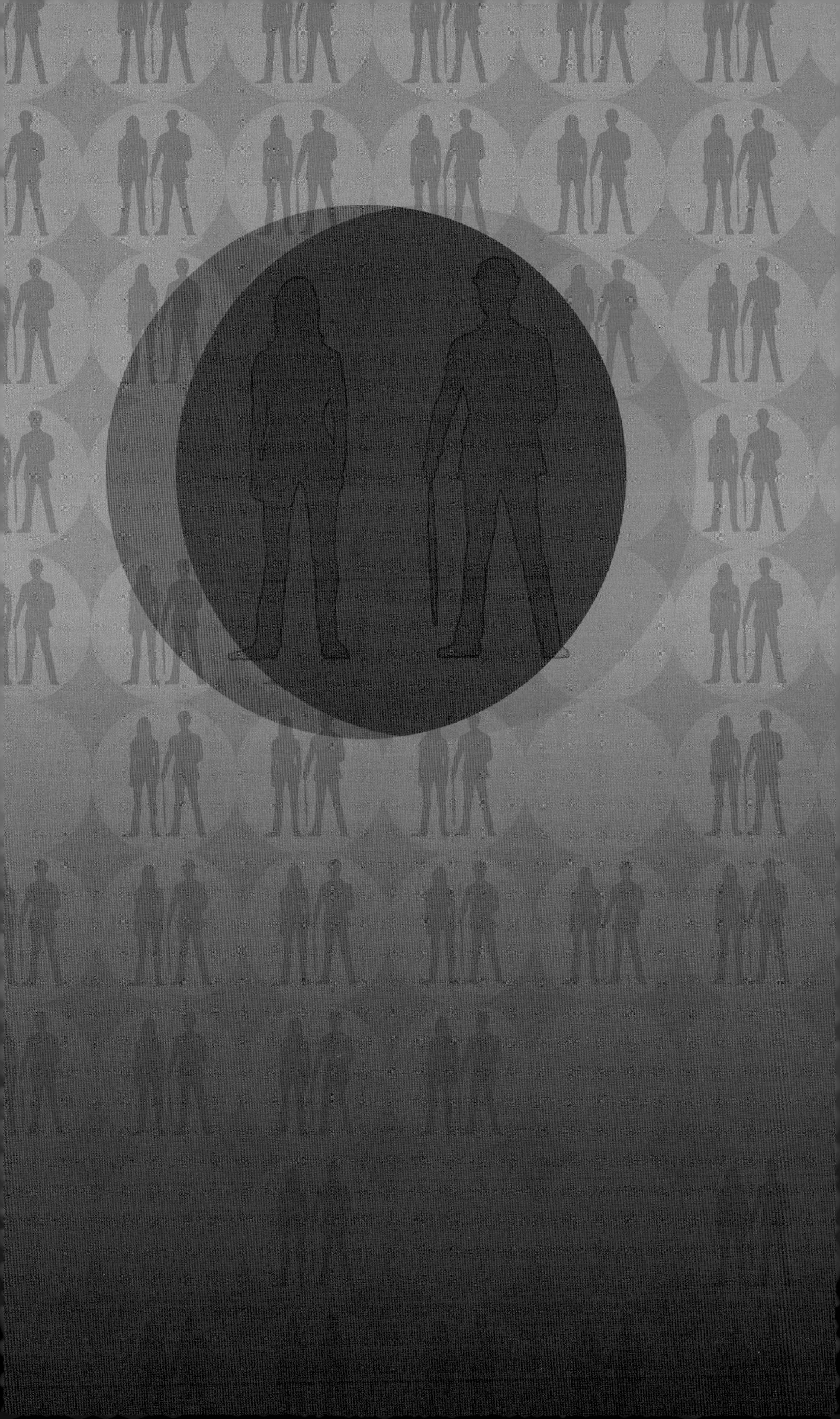

CHAPTER SIX

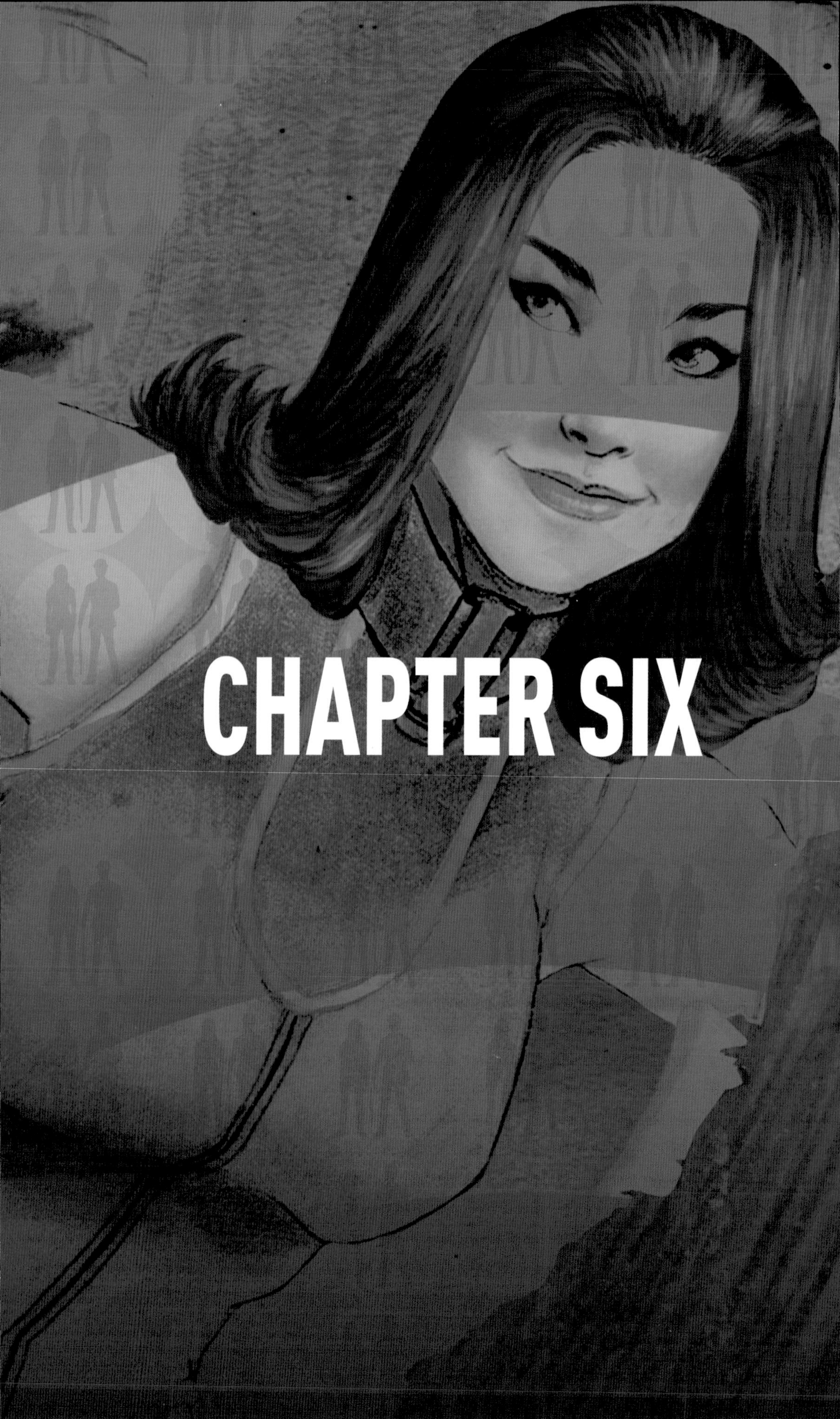

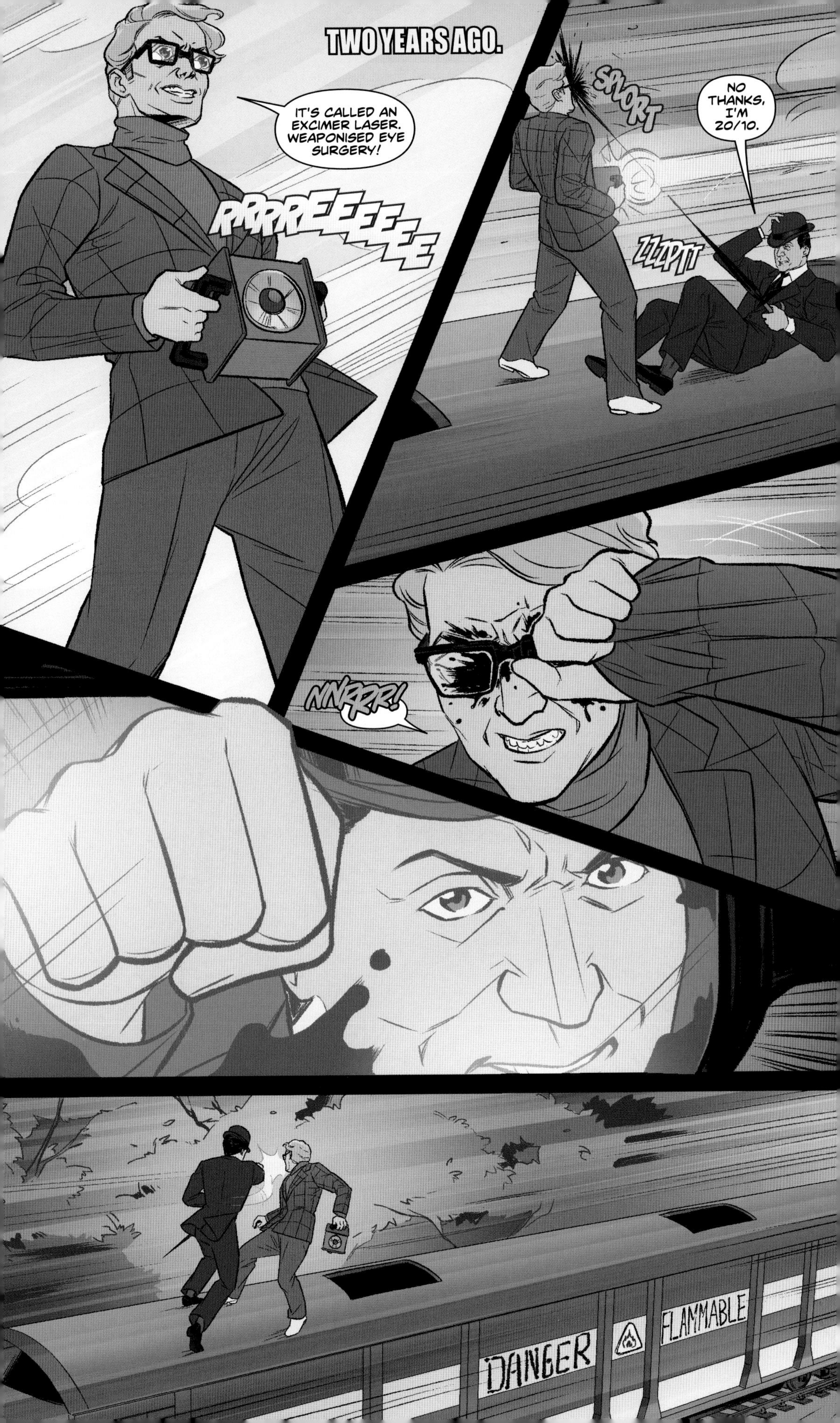
TWO YEARS AGO.
IT'S CALLED AN EXCIMER LASER. WEAPONISED EYE SURGERY!
RRRRREEEEEEE
SPLORT
NO THANKS, I'M 20/10.
ZZZAPTT
NNRRR!
DANGER
FLAMMABLE

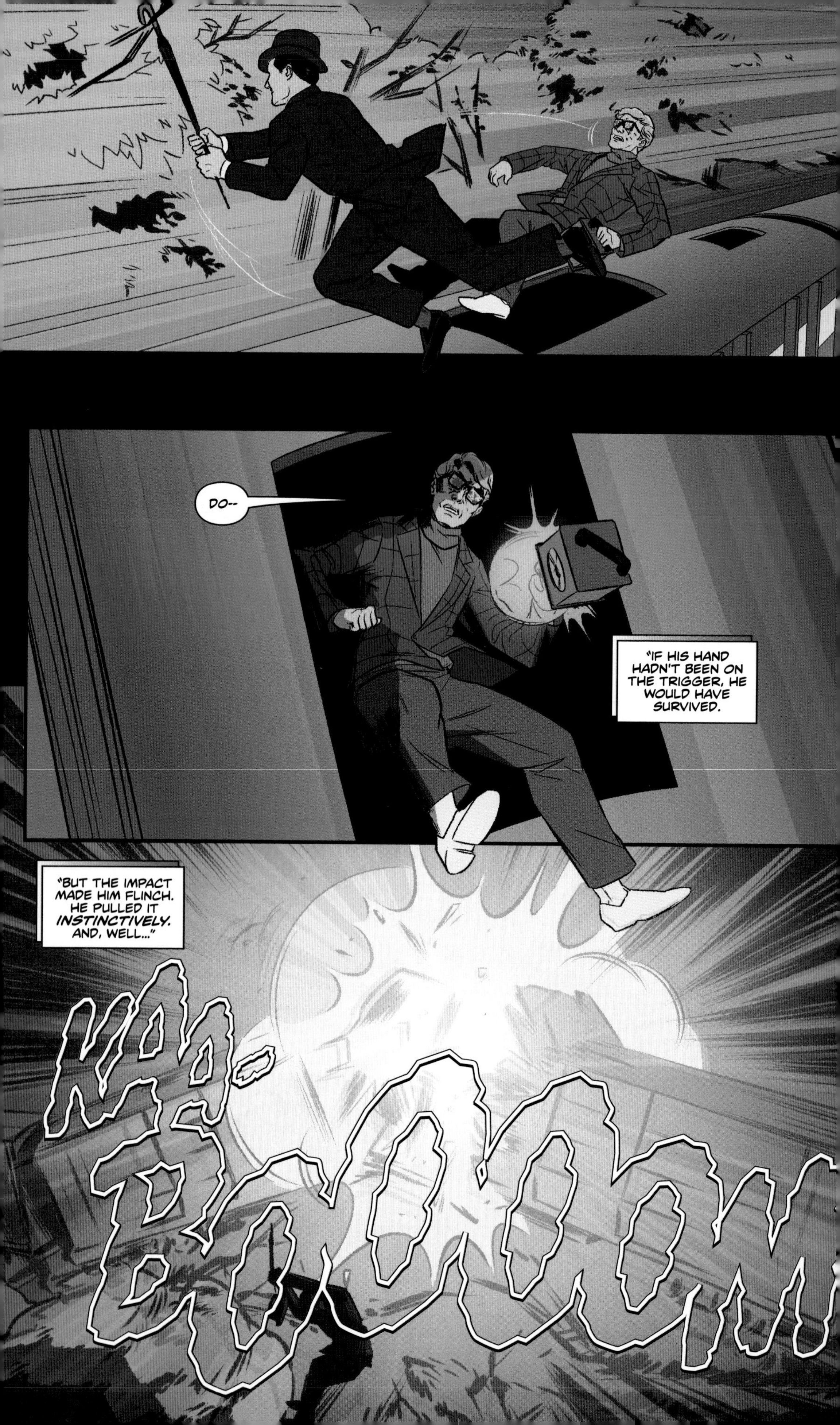
DO--
"IF HIS HAND HADN'T BEEN ON THE TRIGGER, HE WOULD HAVE SURVIVED.
"BUT THE IMPACT MADE HIM FLINCH. HE PULLED IT INSTINCTIVELY. AND, WELL..."

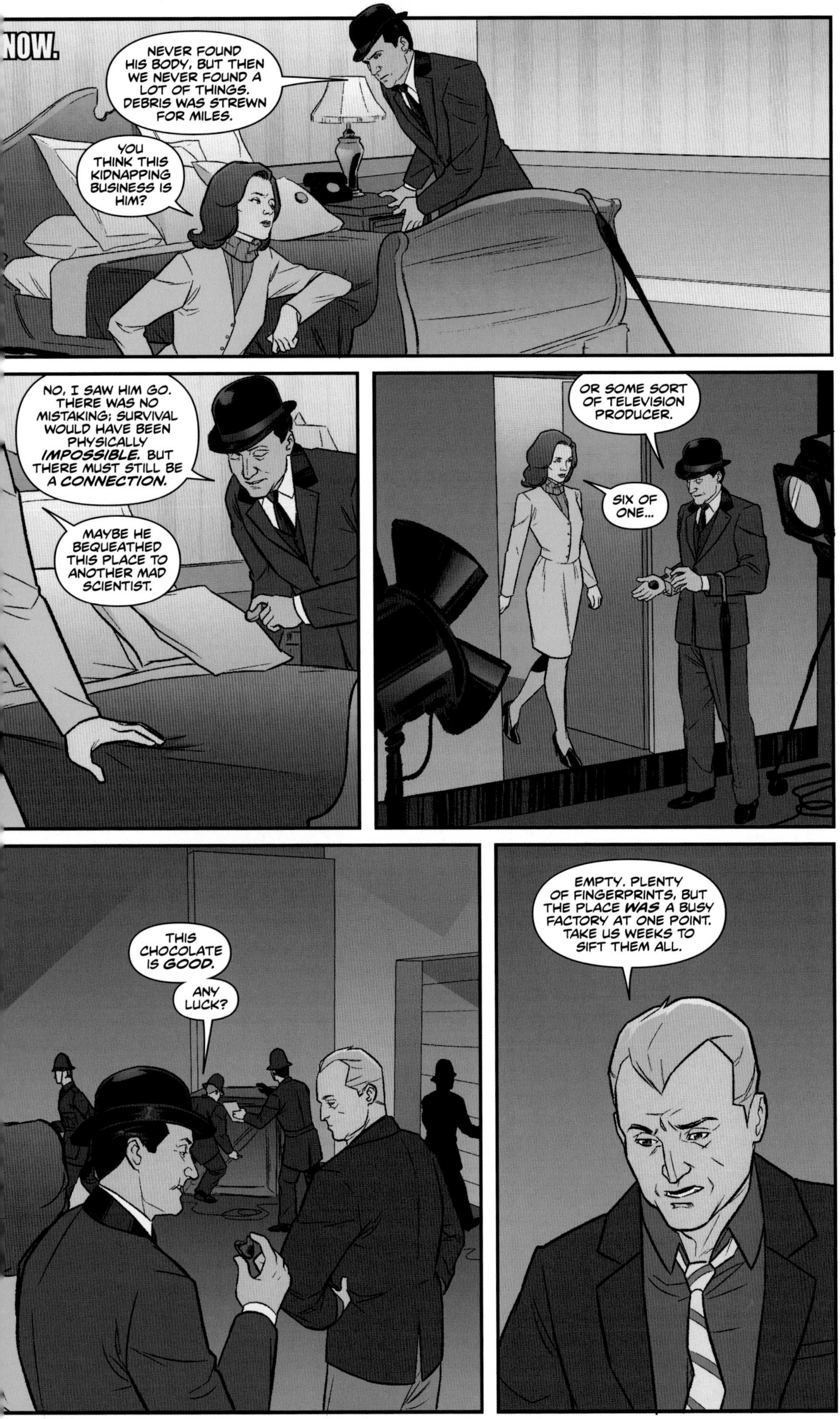
NOW.
NEVER FOUND HIS BODY, BUT THEN WE NEVER FOUND A LOT OF THINGS. DEBRIS WAS STREWN FOR MILES.
YOU THINK THIS KIDNAPPING BUSINESS IS HIM?
NO, I SAW HIM GO. THERE WAS NO MISTAKING; SURVIVAL WOULD HAVE BEEN PHYSICALLY *IMPOSSIBLE.* BUT THERE MUST STILL BE A *CONNECTION.*
MAYBE HE BEQUEATHED THIS PLACE TO ANOTHER MAD SCIENTIST.
OR SOME SORT OF TELEVISION PRODUCER.
SIX OF ONE...
THIS CHOCOLATE IS *GOOD.*
ANY LUCK?
EMPTY. PLENTY OF FINGERPRINTS, BUT THE PLACE *WAS* A BUSY FACTORY AT ONE POINT. TAKE US WEEKS TO SIFT THEM ALL.

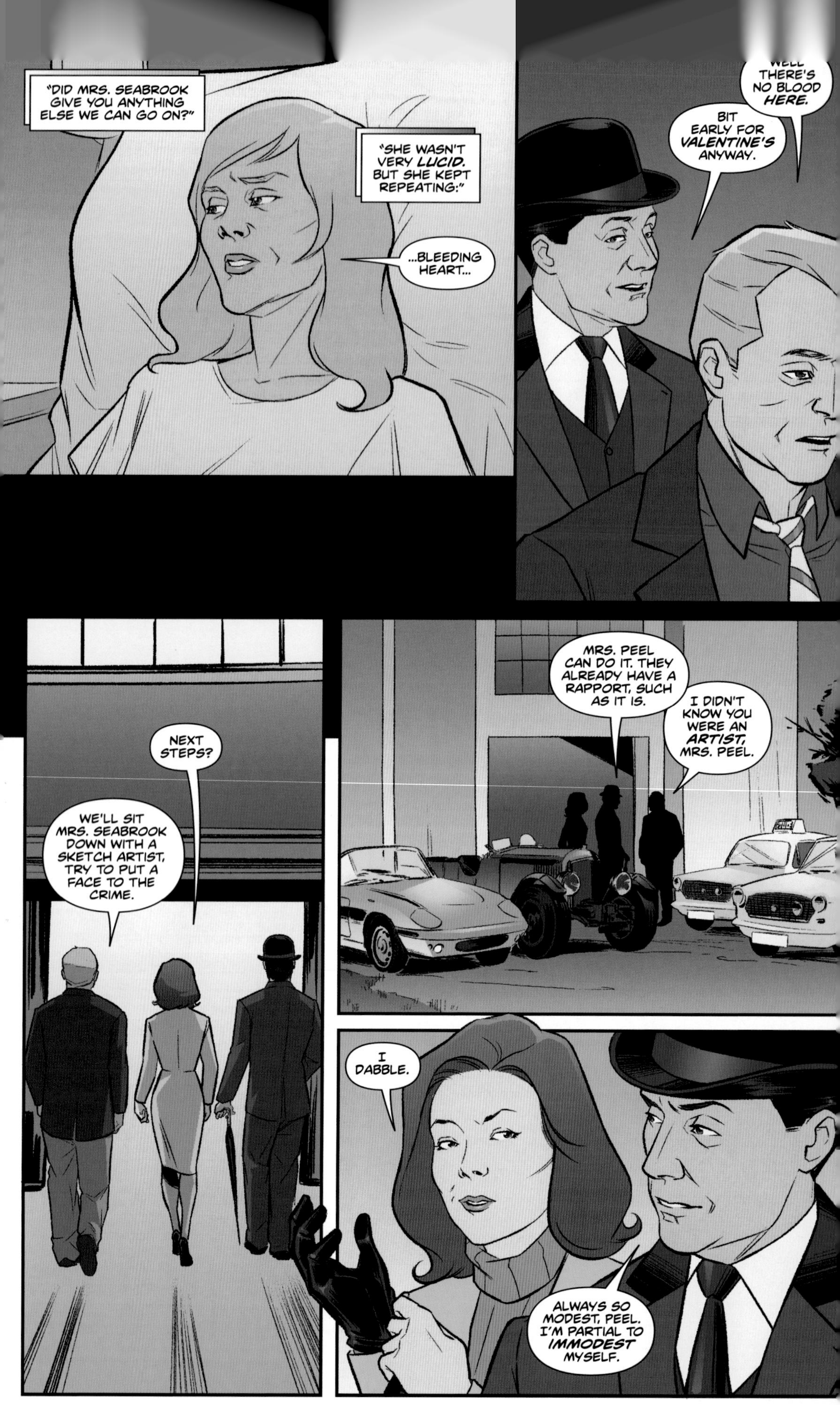
"DID MRS. SEABROOK GIVE YOU ANYTHING ELSE WE CAN GO ON?"
"SHE WASN'T VERY LUCID. BUT SHE KEPT REPEATING:"
...BLEEDING HEART...
WELL THERE'S NO BLOOD HERE.
BIT EARLY FOR VALENTINE'S ANYWAY.
NEXT STEPS?
WE'LL SIT MRS. SEABROOK DOWN WITH A SKETCH ARTIST, TRY TO PUT A FACE TO THE CRIME.
MRS. PEEL CAN DO IT. THEY ALREADY HAVE A RAPPORT, SUCH AS IT IS.
I DIDN'T KNOW YOU WERE AN ARTIST, MRS. PEEL.
I DABBLE.
ALWAYS SO MODEST, PEEL. I'M PARTIAL TO IMMODEST MYSELF.

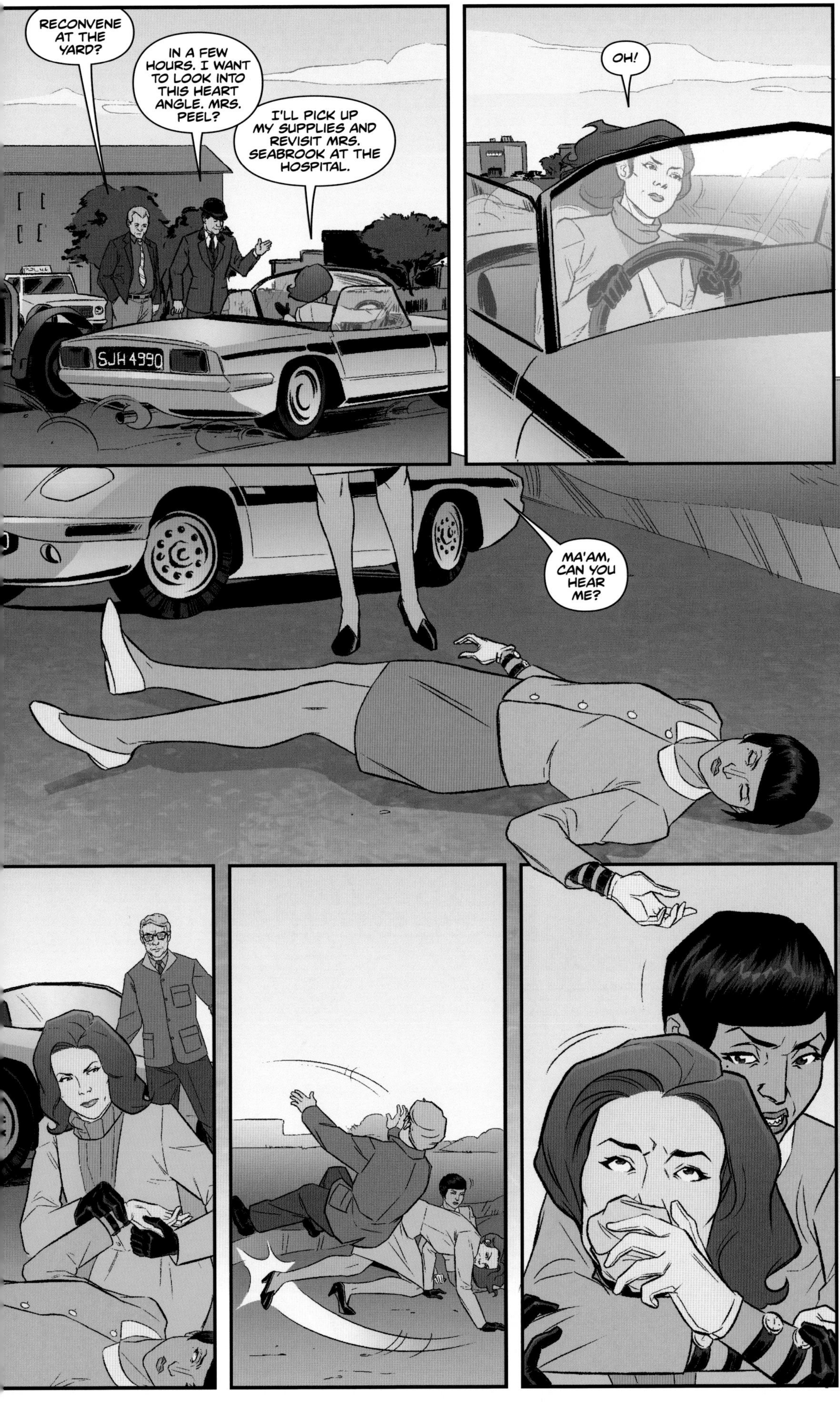
RECONVENE AT THE YARD?
IN A FEW HOURS. I WANT TO LOOK INTO THIS HEART ANGLE. MRS. PEEL?
I'LL PICK UP MY SUPPLIES AND REVISIT MRS. SEABROOK AT THE HOSPITAL.
SJH 499G
OH!
MA'AM, CAN YOU HEAR ME?

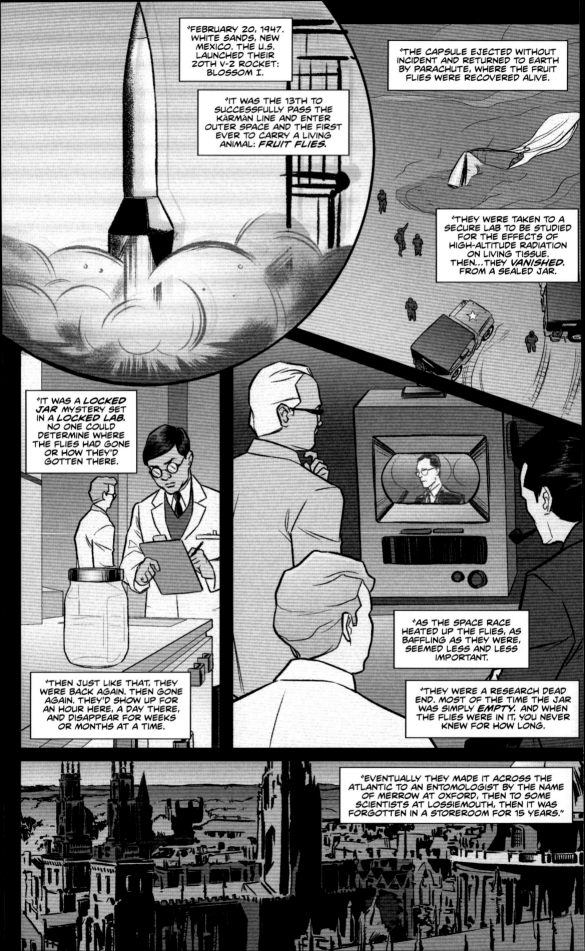

"FEBRUARY 20, 1947. WHITE SANDS, NEW MEXICO. THE U.S. LAUNCHED THEIR 20TH V-2 ROCKET: BLOSSOM I.

"IT WAS THE 13TH TO SUCCESSFULLY PASS THE KÁRMÁN LINE AND ENTER OUTER SPACE AND THE FIRST EVER TO CARRY A LIVING ANIMAL: *FRUIT FLIES*.

"THE CAPSULE EJECTED WITHOUT INCIDENT AND RETURNED TO EARTH BY PARACHUTE, WHERE THE FRUIT FLIES WERE RECOVERED ALIVE.

"THEY WERE TAKEN TO A SECURE LAB TO BE STUDIED FOR THE EFFECTS OF HIGH-ALTITUDE RADIATION ON LIVING TISSUE. THEN...THEY *VANISHED.* FROM A SEALED JAR.

"IT WAS A *LOCKED JAR* MYSTERY SET IN A *LOCKED LAB.* NO ONE COULD DETERMINE WHERE THE FLIES HAD GONE OR HOW THEY'D GOTTEN THERE.

"THEN JUST LIKE THAT, THEY WERE BACK AGAIN. THEN GONE AGAIN. THEY'D SHOW UP FOR AN HOUR HERE, A DAY THERE, AND DISAPPEAR FOR WEEKS OR MONTHS AT A TIME.

"AS THE SPACE RACE HEATED UP THE FLIES, AS BAFFLING AS THEY WERE, SEEMED LESS AND LESS IMPORTANT.

"THEY WERE A RESEARCH DEAD END. MOST OF THE TIME THE JAR WAS SIMPLY *EMPTY.* AND WHEN THE FLIES WERE IN IT, YOU NEVER KNEW FOR HOW LONG.

"EVENTUALLY THEY MADE IT ACROSS THE ATLANTIC TO AN ENTOMOLOGIST BY THE NAME OF MERROW AT OXFORD, THEN TO SOME SCIENTISTS AT LOSSIEMOUTH, THEN IT WAS FORGOTTEN IN A STOREROOM FOR 15 YEARS."

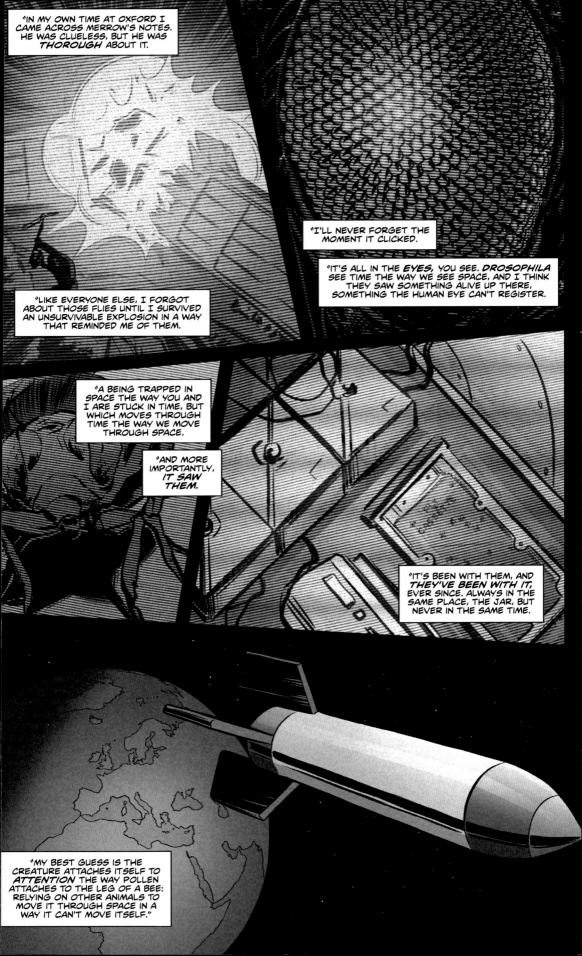

"IN MY OWN TIME AT OXFORD I CAME ACROSS MERROW'S NOTES. HE WAS CLUELESS, BUT HE WAS *THOROUGH* ABOUT IT.

"I'LL NEVER FORGET THE MOMENT IT CLICKED.

"IT'S ALL IN THE *EYES*, YOU SEE. *DROSOPHILA* SEE TIME THE WAY WE SEE SPACE, AND I THINK THEY SAW SOMETHING ALIVE UP THERE, SOMETHING THE HUMAN EYE CAN'T REGISTER.

"LIKE EVERYONE ELSE, I FORGOT ABOUT THOSE FLIES UNTIL I SURVIVED AN UNSURVIVABLE EXPLOSION IN A WAY THAT REMINDED ME OF THEM.

"A BEING TRAPPED IN SPACE THE WAY YOU AND I ARE STUCK IN TIME, BUT WHICH MOVES THROUGH TIME THE WAY WE MOVE THROUGH SPACE.

"AND MORE IMPORTANTLY, *IT SAW THEM.*

"IT'S BEEN WITH THEM, AND *THEY'VE BEEN WITH IT,* EVER SINCE. ALWAYS IN THE SAME PLACE, THE JAR, BUT NEVER IN THE SAME TIME.

"MY BEST GUESS IS THE CREATURE ATTACHES ITSELF TO *ATTENTION* THE WAY POLLEN ATTACHES TO THE LEG OF A BEE: RELYING ON OTHER ANIMALS TO MOVE IT THROUGH SPACE IN A WAY IT CAN'T MOVE ITSELF."

"IT COULD TAKE US THROUGH TIME, TOO.
"ALL WE'D HAVE TO DO IS SEE IT."
WHAT IS IT? WHAT DO YOU SEE?
IT'S... IT'S...
INDESCRIBABLE. NO, INCOMPREHENSIBLE.
TIME FLIES
STEED LOSES TRACK OF EMMA
EMMA LOSES TRACK OF TIME

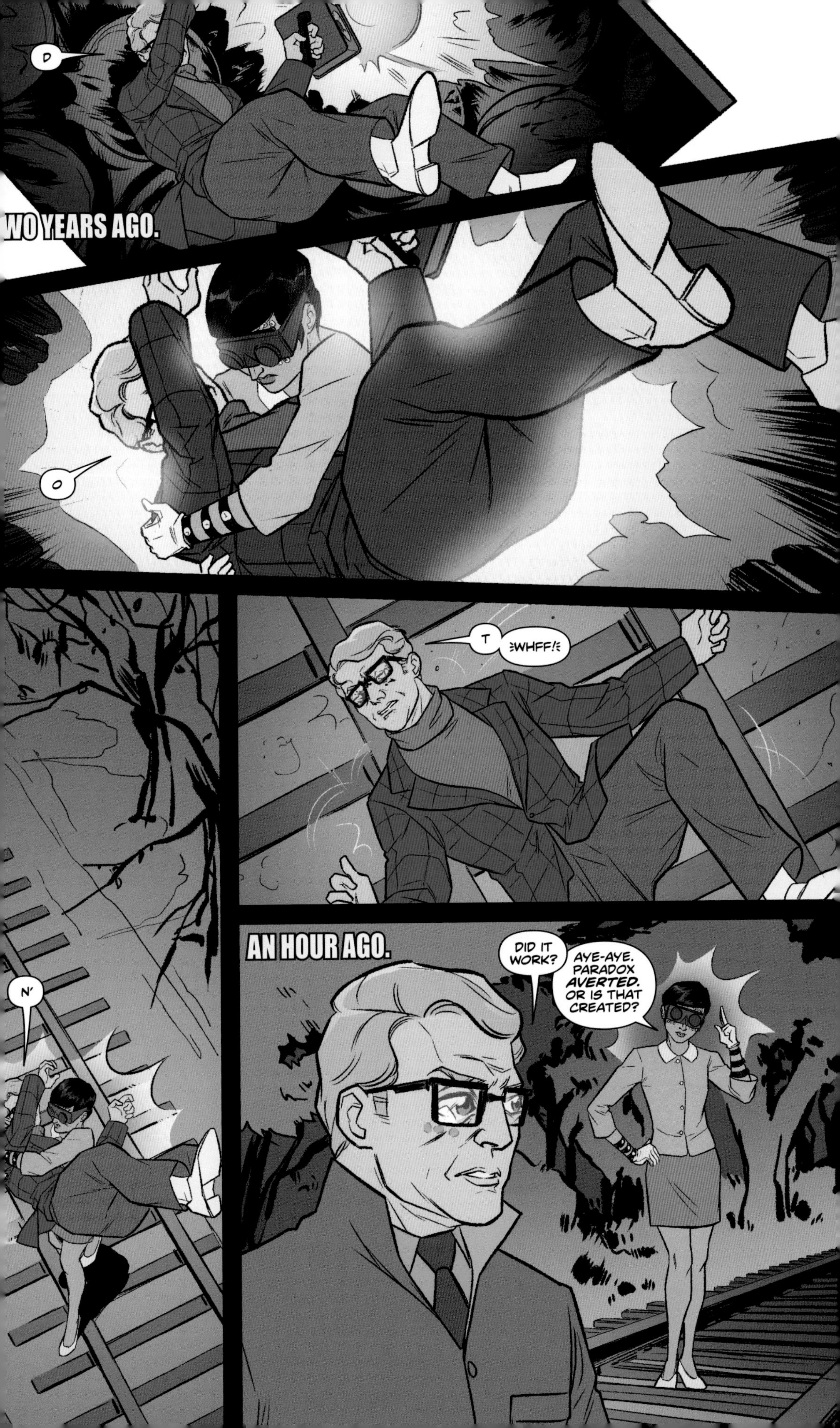
D
WO YEARS AGO.
O
T
WHFF!
N'
AN HOUR AGO.
DID IT WORK?
AYE-AYE. PARADOX AVERTED. OR IS THAT CREATED?

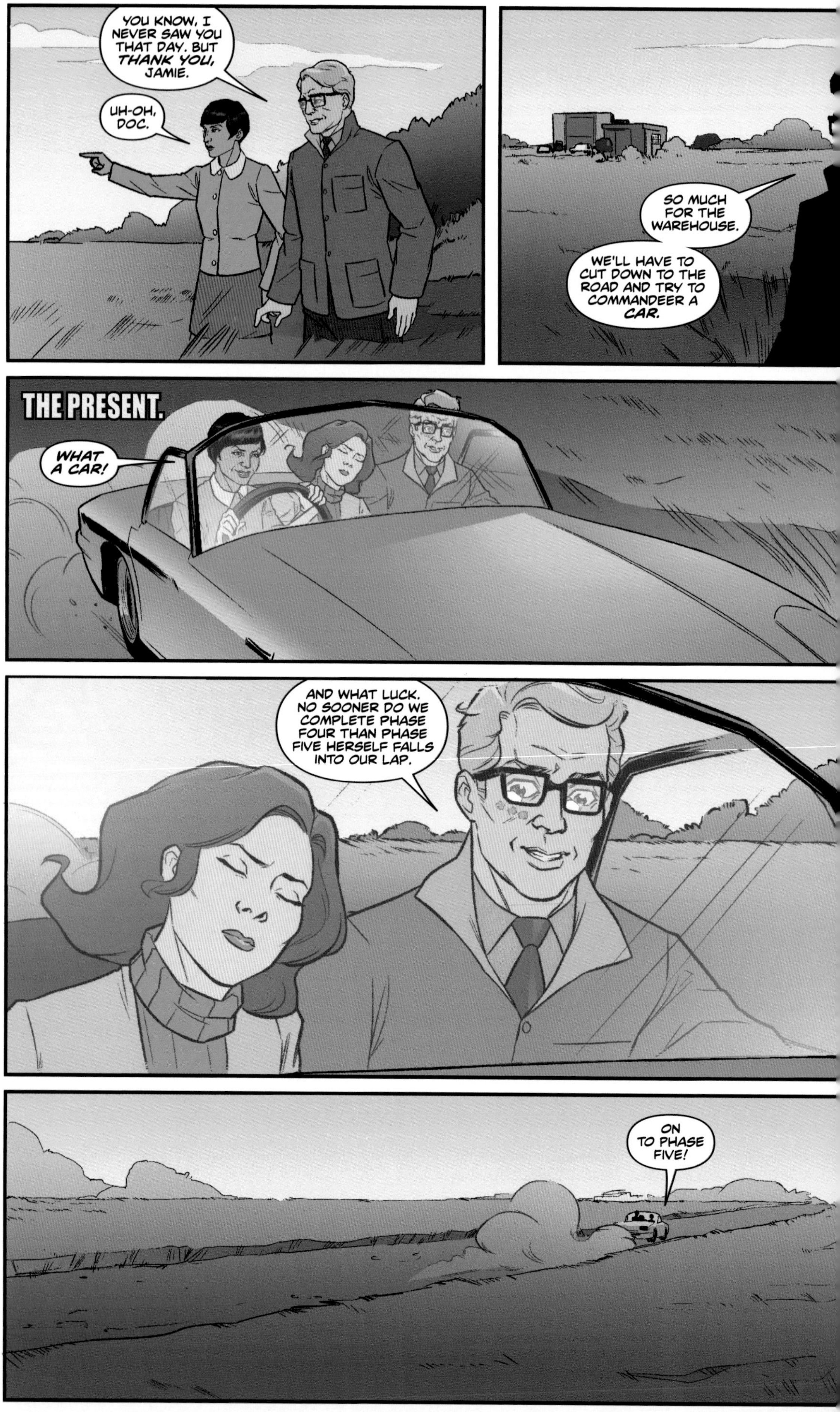
YOU KNOW, I NEVER SAW YOU THAT DAY. BUT THANK YOU, JAMIE.
UH-OH, DOC.
SO MUCH FOR THE WAREHOUSE.
WE'LL HAVE TO CUT DOWN TO THE ROAD AND TRY TO COMMANDEER A CAR.
THE PRESENT.
WHAT A CAR!
AND WHAT LUCK. NO SOONER DO WE COMPLETE PHASE FOUR THAN PHASE FIVE HERSELF FALLS INTO OUR LAP.
ON TO PHASE FIVE!

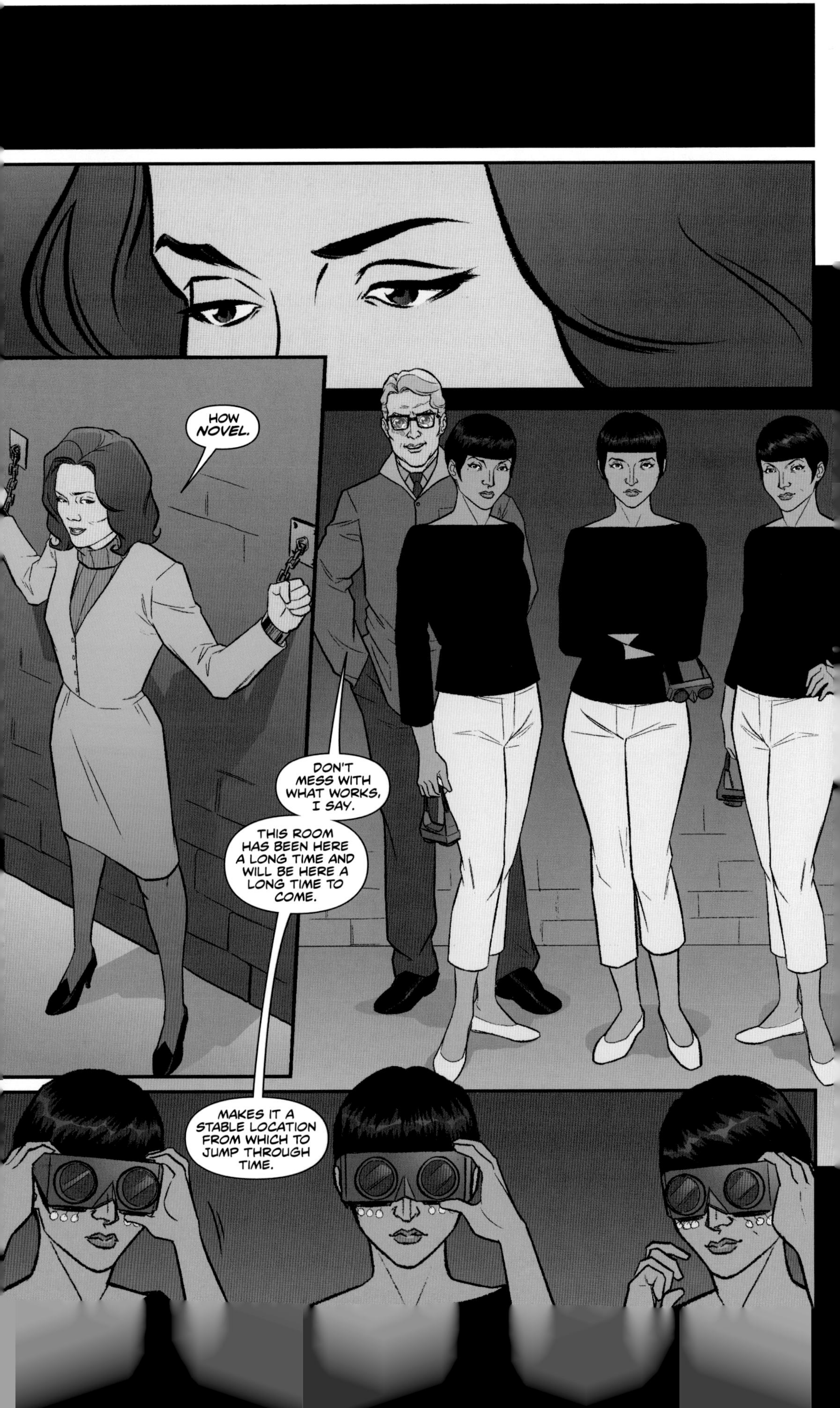
HOW NOVEL.
DON'T MESS WITH WHAT WORKS, I SAY.
THIS ROOM HAS BEEN HERE A LONG TIME AND WILL BE HERE A LONG TIME TO COME.
MAKES IT A STABLE LOCATION FROM WHICH TO JUMP THROUGH TIME.

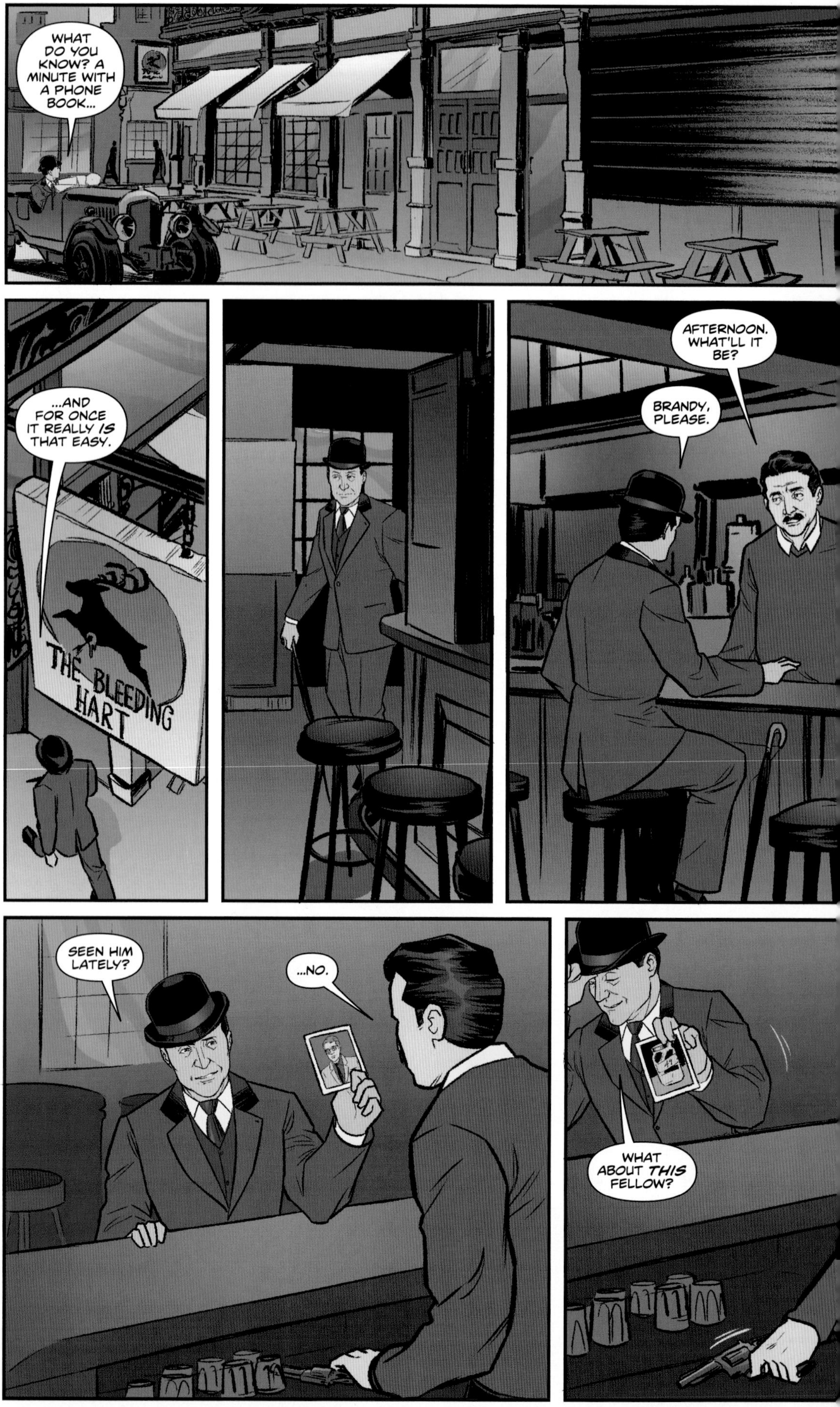
WHAT DO YOU KNOW? A MINUTE WITH A PHONE BOOK...
...AND FOR ONCE IT REALLY *IS* THAT EASY.
THE BLEEDING HART
AFTERNOON. WHAT'LL IT BE?
BRANDY, PLEASE.
SEEN HIM LATELY?
...NO.
WHAT ABOUT *THIS* FELLOW?

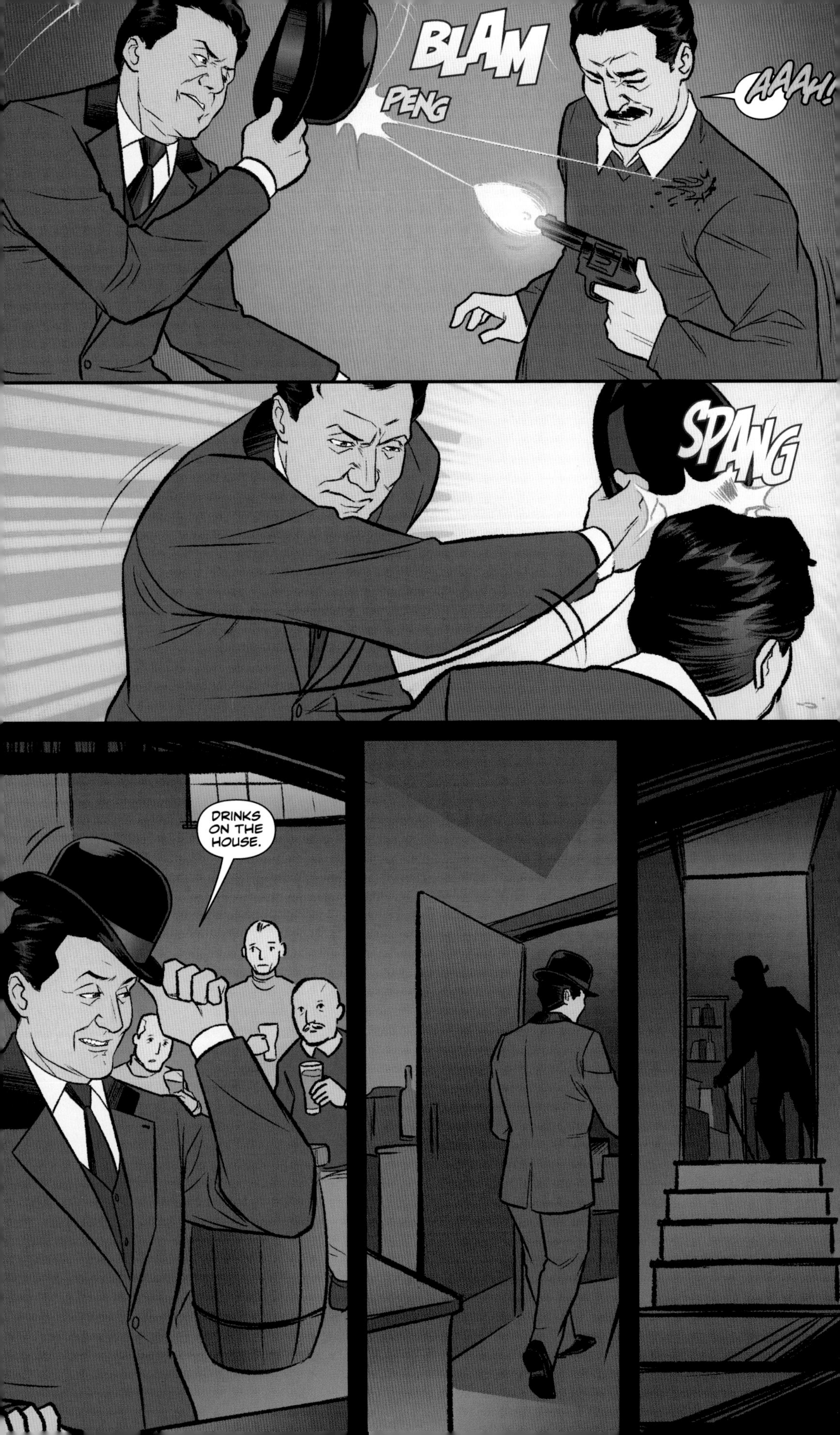
BLAM
PENG
AAAH!
SPANG
DRINKS ON THE HOUSE.

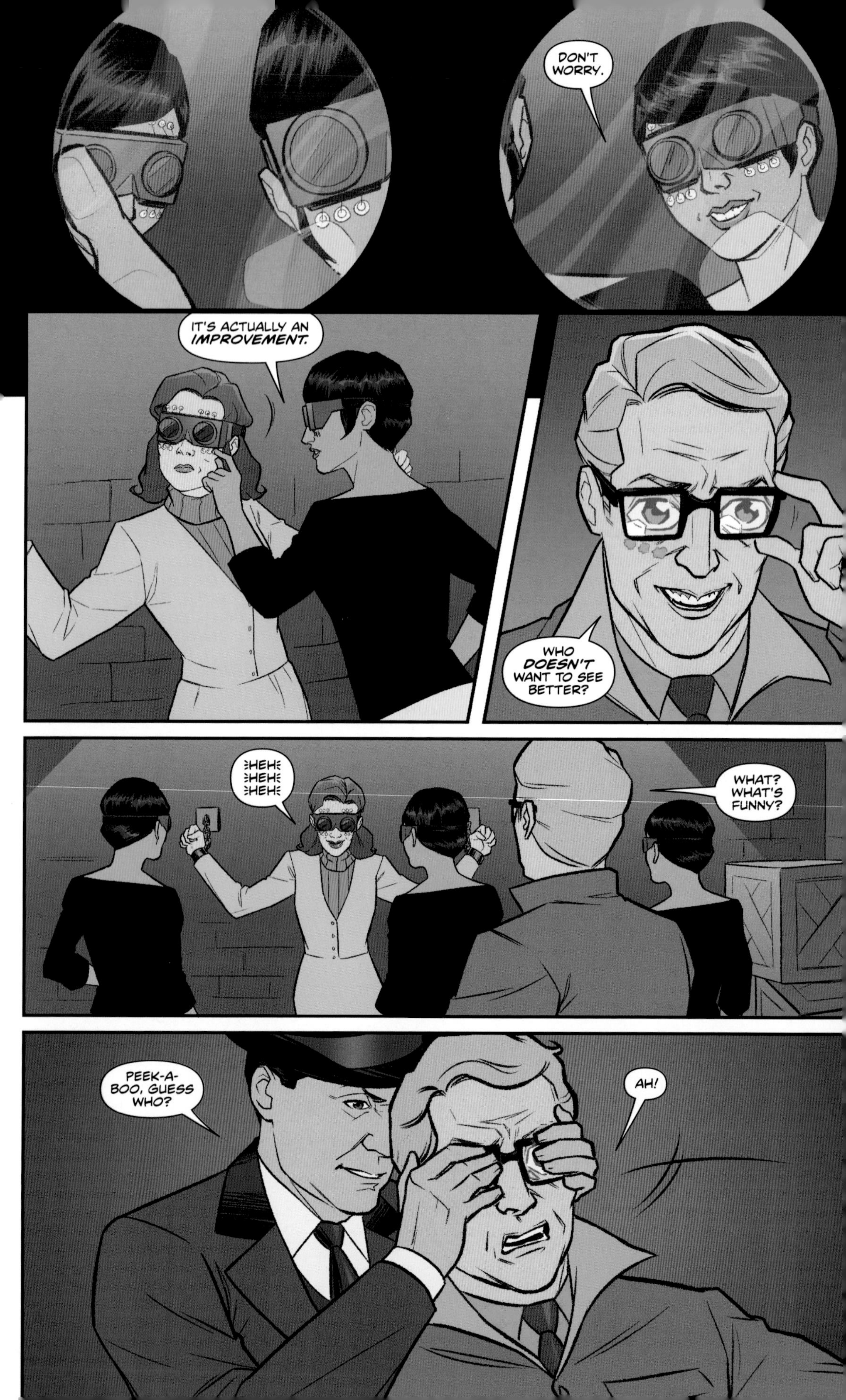
DON'T WORRY.
IT'S ACTUALLY AN *IMPROVEMENT.*
WHO *DOESN'T* WANT TO SEE BETTER?
HEH HEH HEH
WHAT? WHAT'S FUNNY?
PEEK-A-BOO, GUESS WHO?
AH!

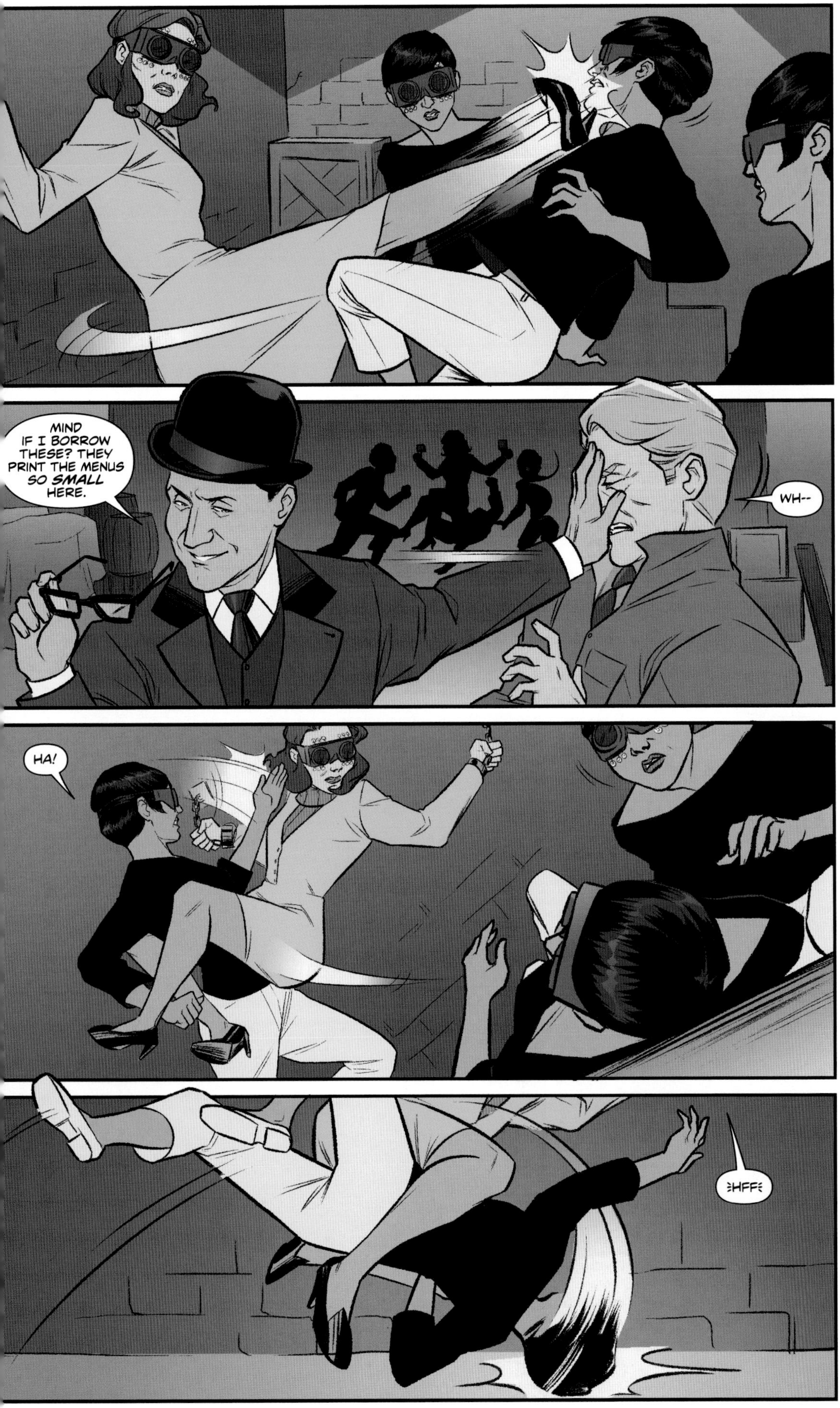
MIND IF I BORROW THESE? THEY PRINT THE MENUS SO *SMALL* HERE.
WH--
HA!
HFF

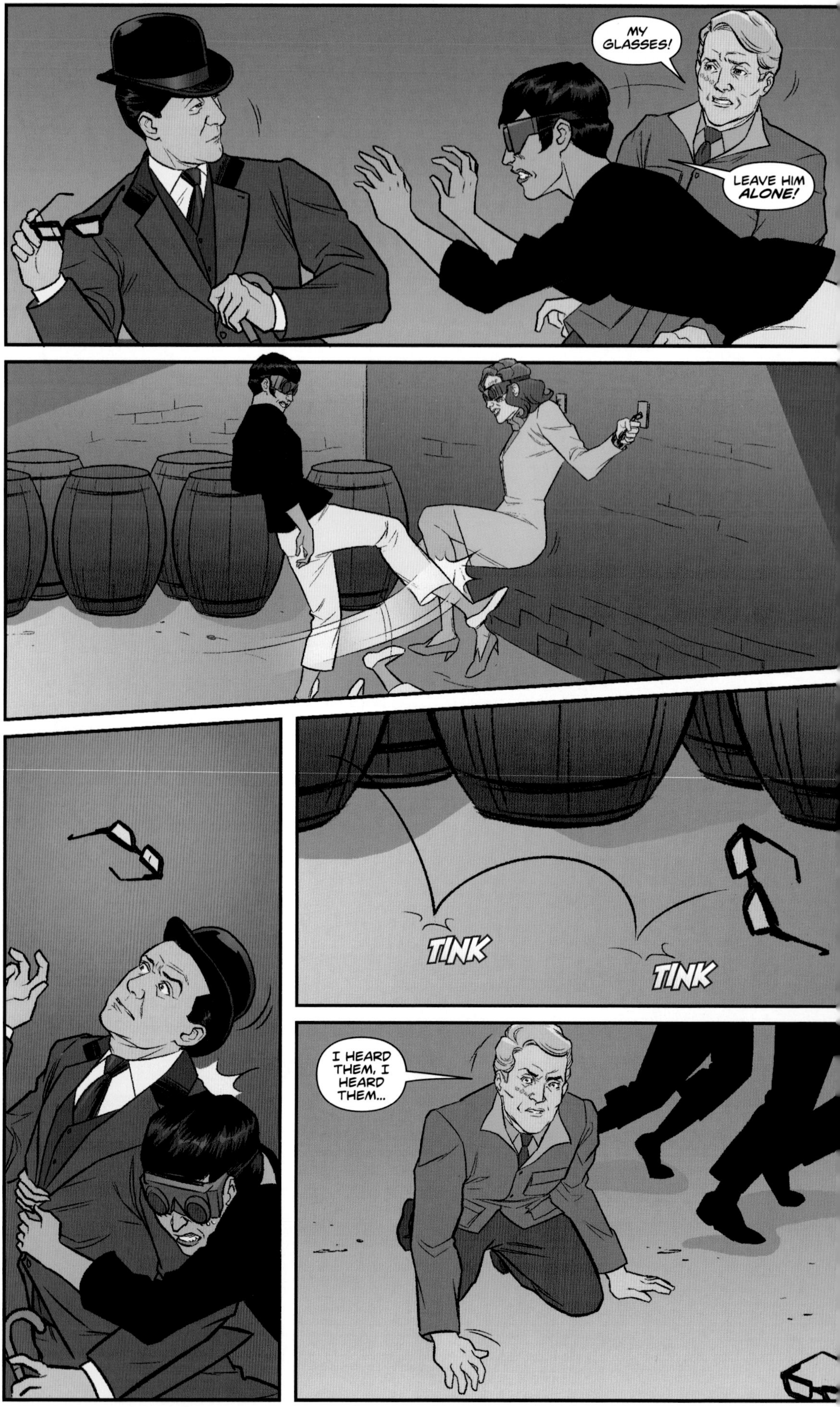
MY GLASSES!
LEAVE HIM ALONE!
TINK
TINK
I HEARD THEM, I HEARD THEM...

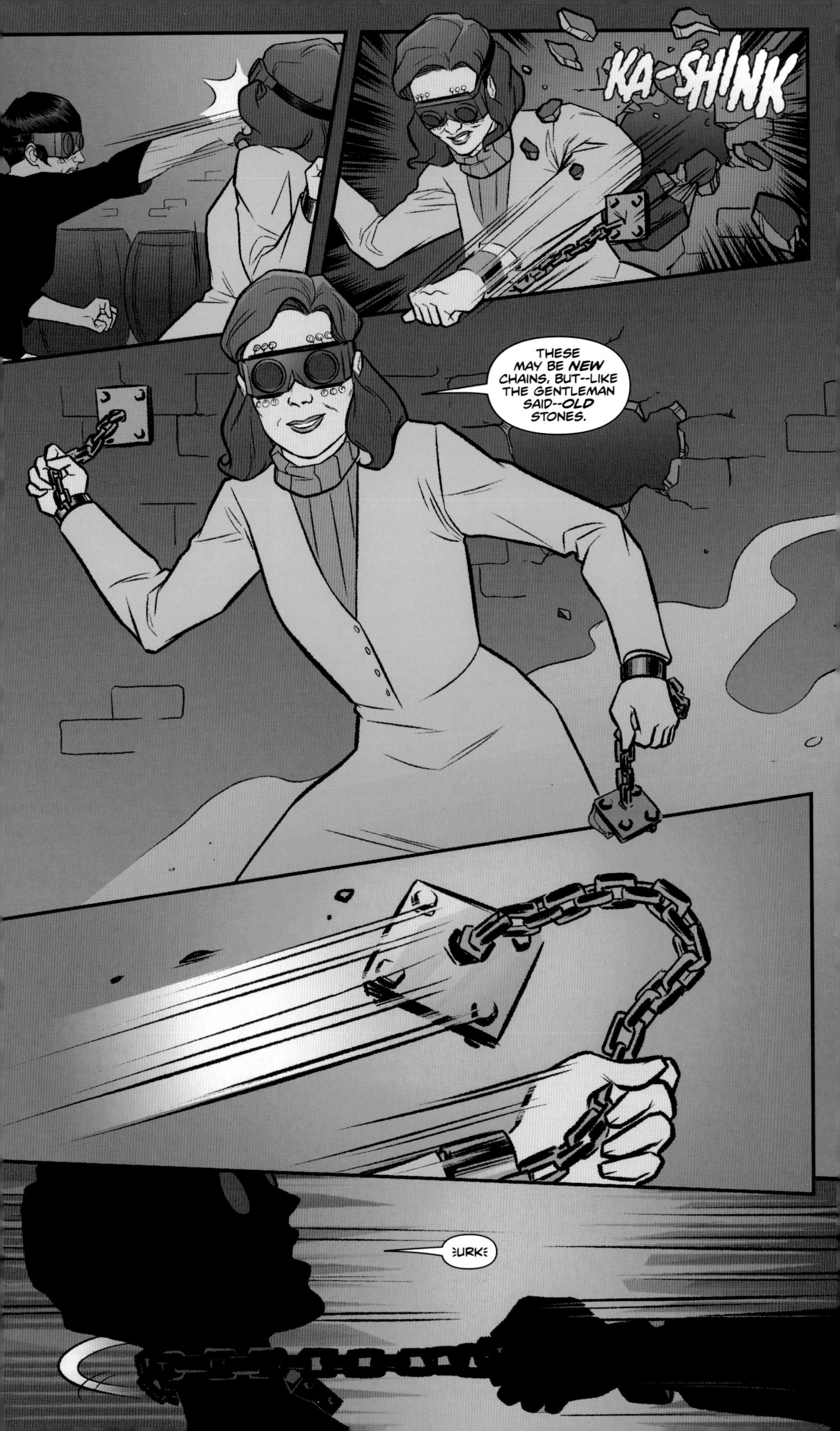
KA-SHINK
THESE MAY BE NEW CHAINS, BUT--LIKE THE GENTLEMAN SAID--OLD STONES.
URK

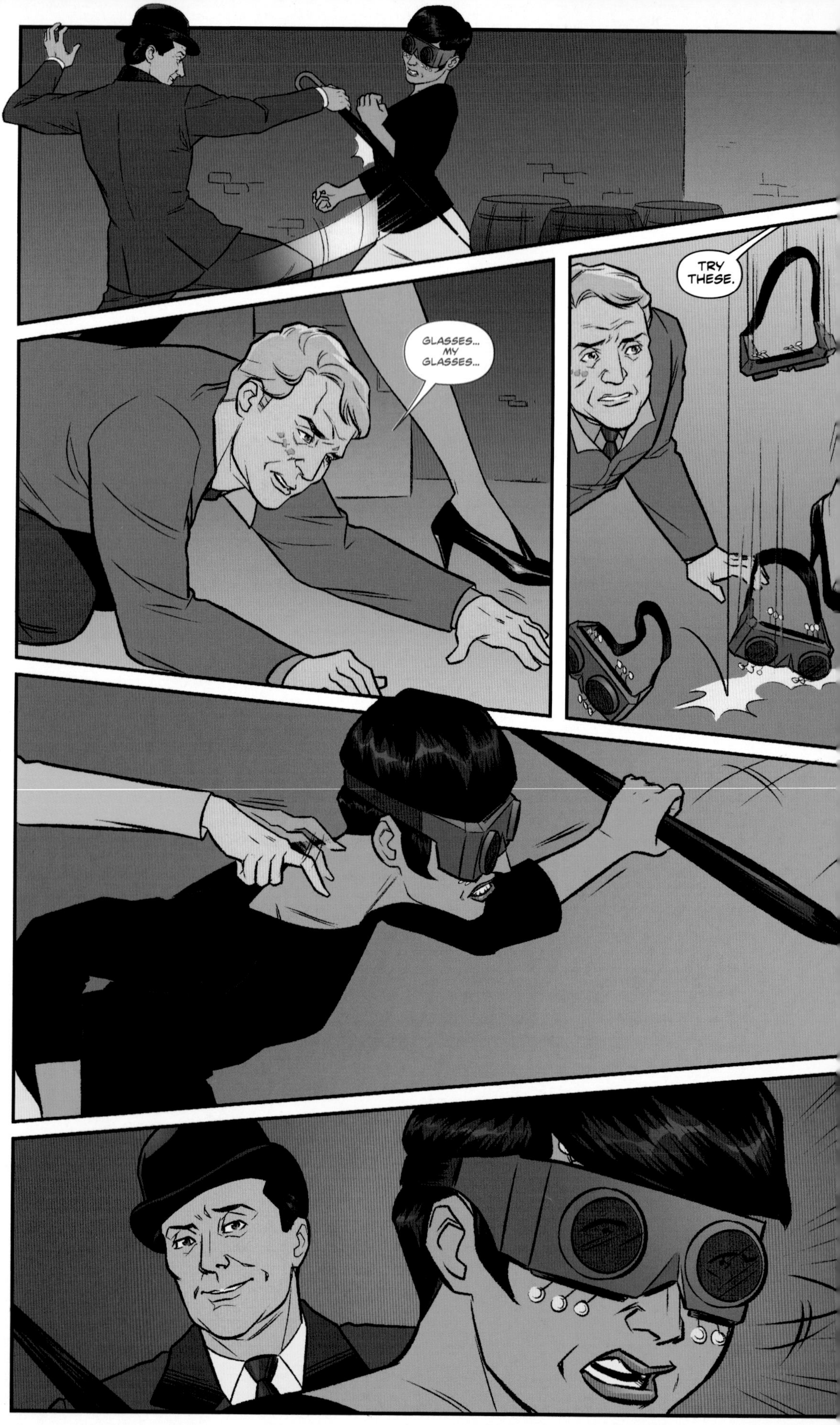
GLASSES... MY GLASSES...
TRY THESE.

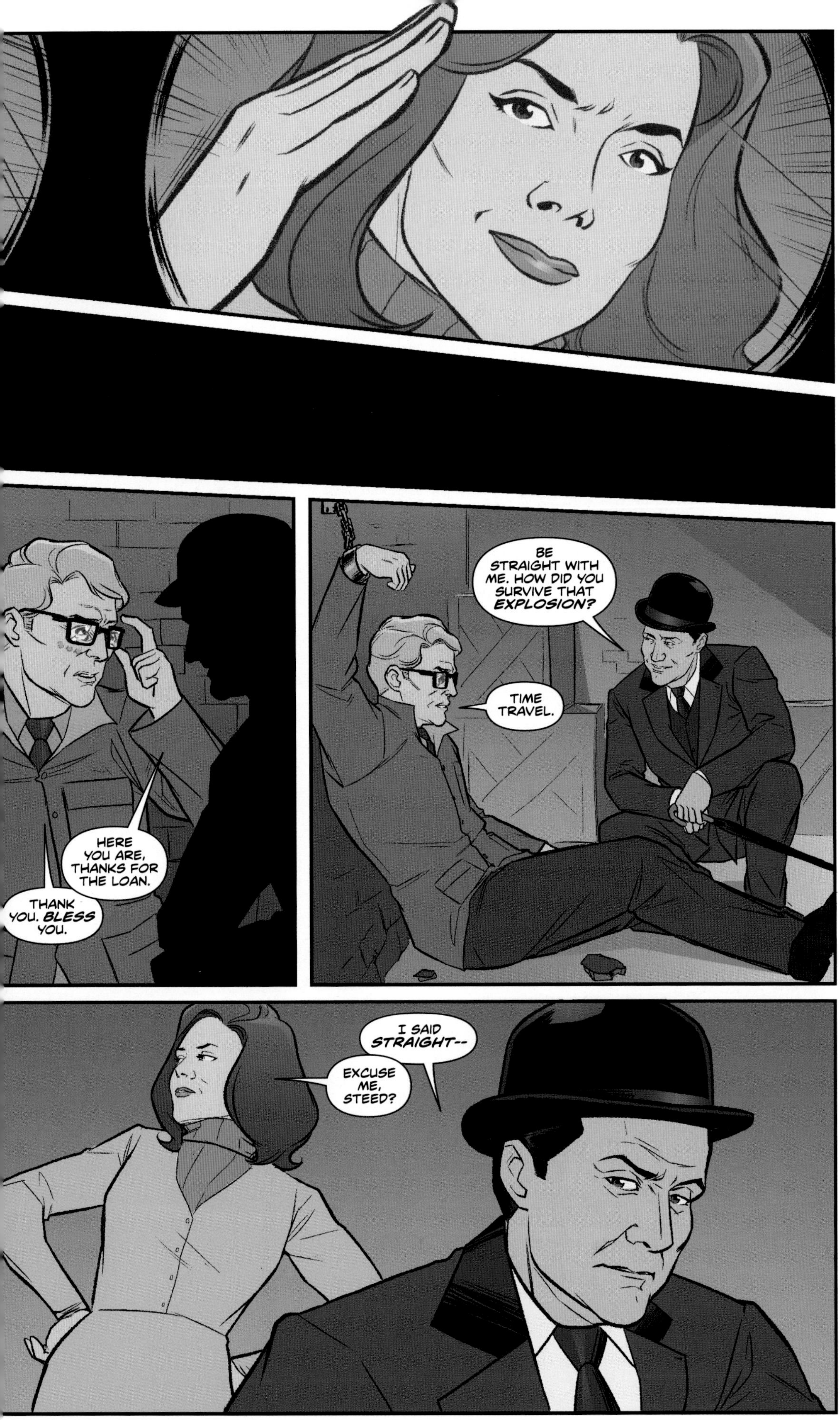
HERE YOU ARE, THANKS FOR THE LOAN.
THANK YOU. BLESS YOU.
BE STRAIGHT WITH ME. HOW DID YOU SURVIVE THAT EXPLOSION?
TIME TRAVEL.
I SAID STRAIGHT--
EXCUSE ME, STEED?

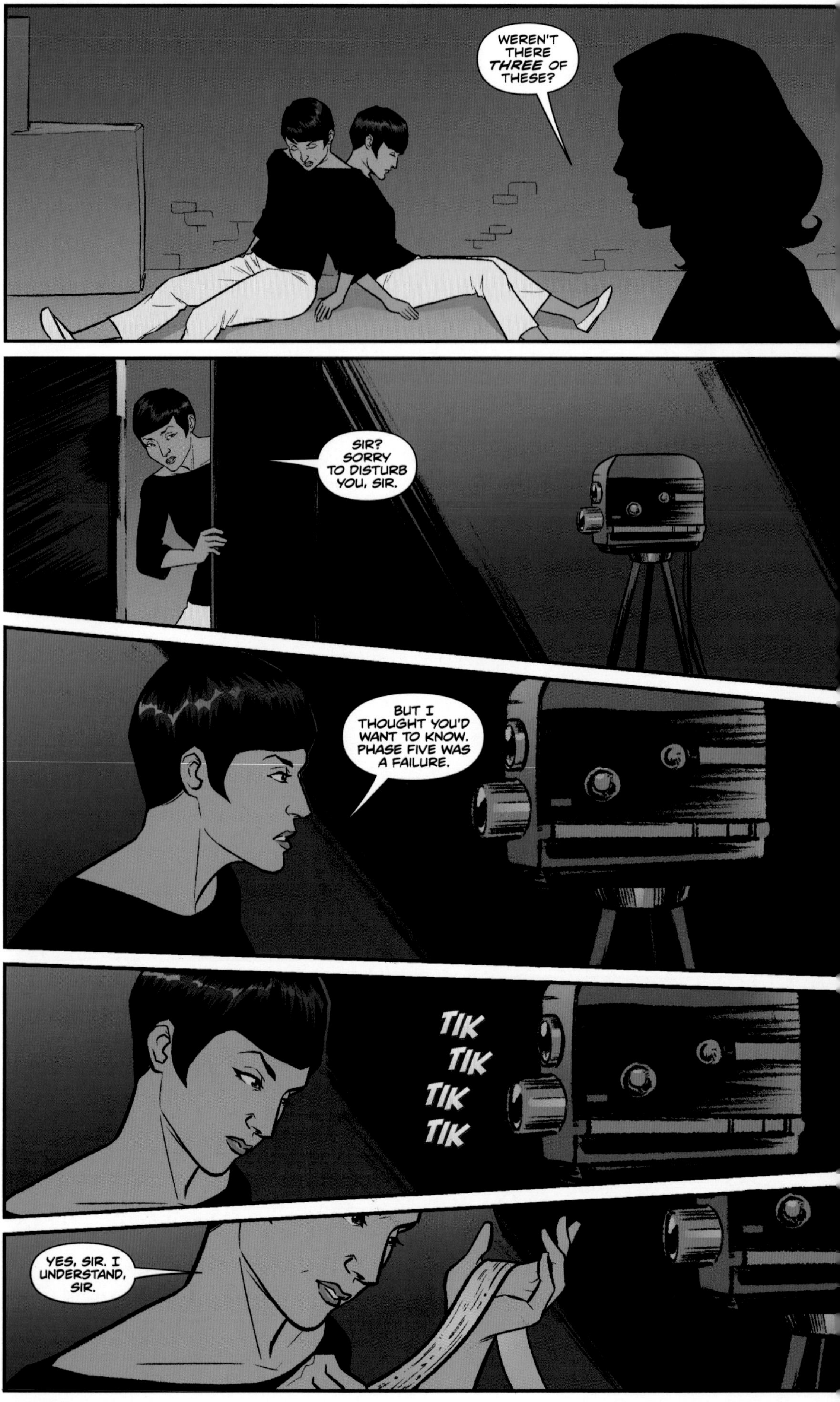
WEREN'T THERE THREE OF THESE?
SIR? SORRY TO DISTURB YOU, SIR.
BUT I THOUGHT YOU'D WANT TO KNOW. PHASE FIVE WAS A FAILURE.
TIK TIK TIK TIK
YES, SIR. I UNDERSTAND, SIR.

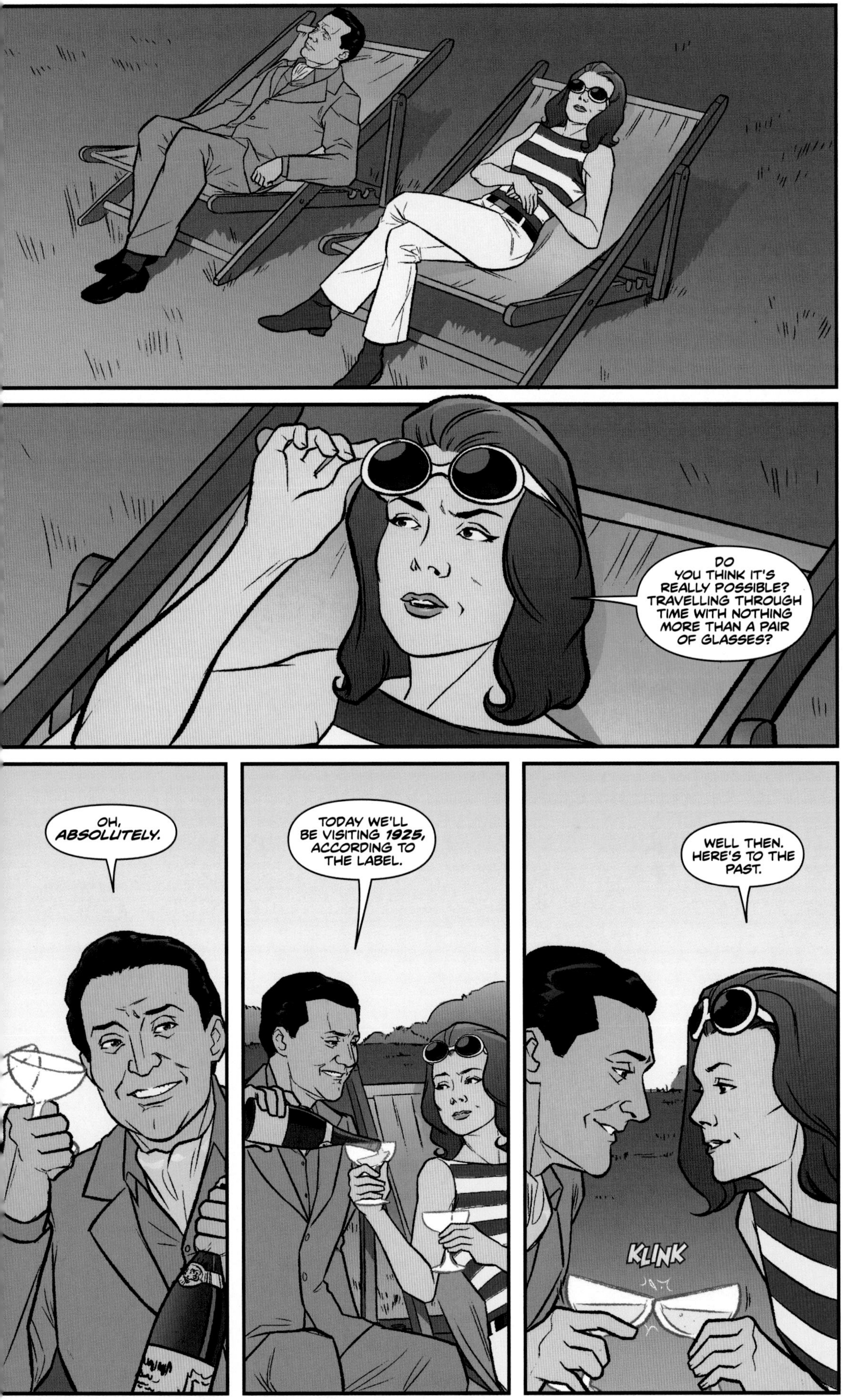
DO YOU THINK IT'S REALLY POSSIBLE? TRAVELLING THROUGH TIME WITH NOTHING MORE THAN A PAIR OF GLASSES?
OH, *ABSOLUTELY.*
TODAY WE'LL BE VISITING *1925,* ACCORDING TO THE LABEL.
WELL THEN. HERE'S TO THE PAST.
KLINK

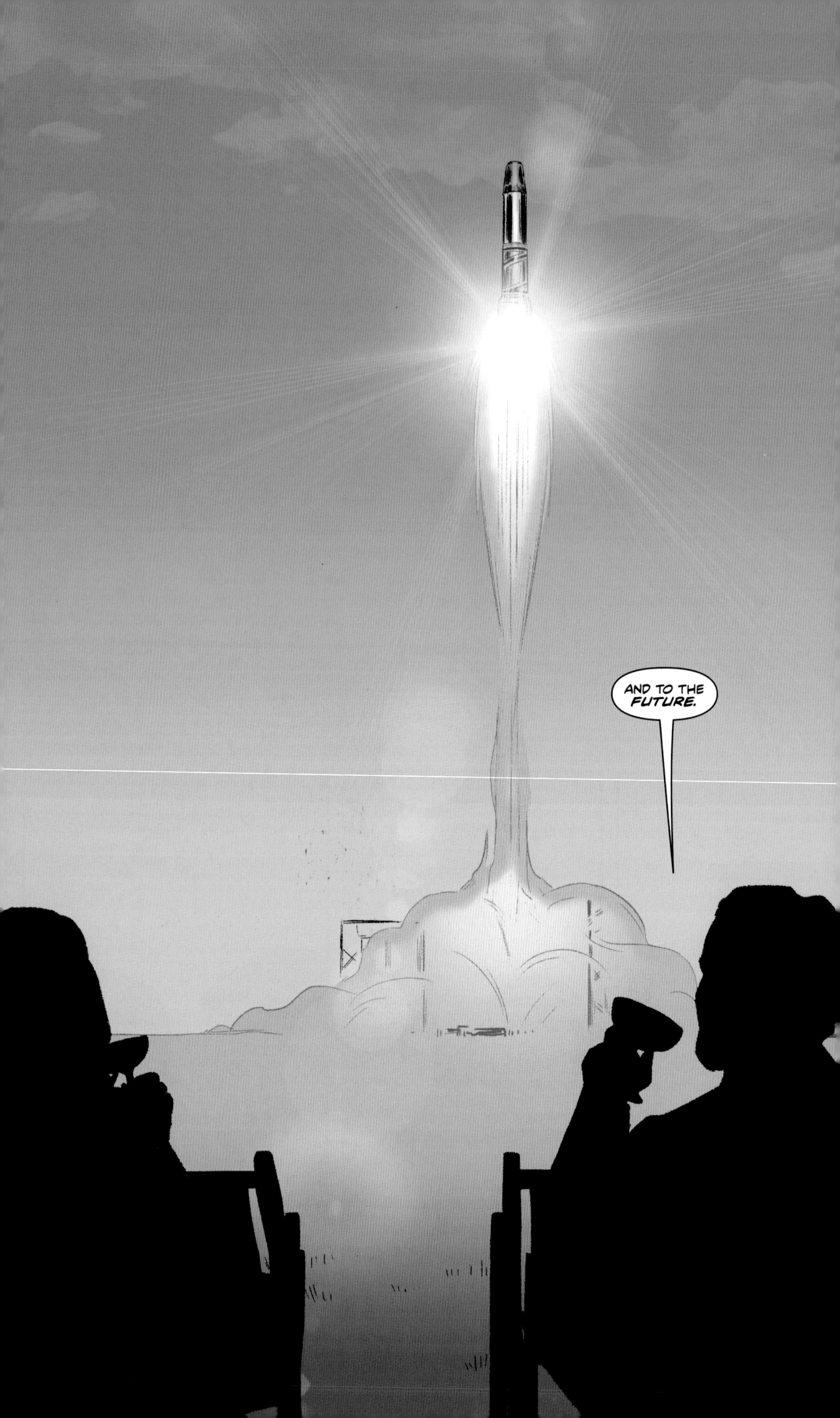
AND TO THE FUTURE.

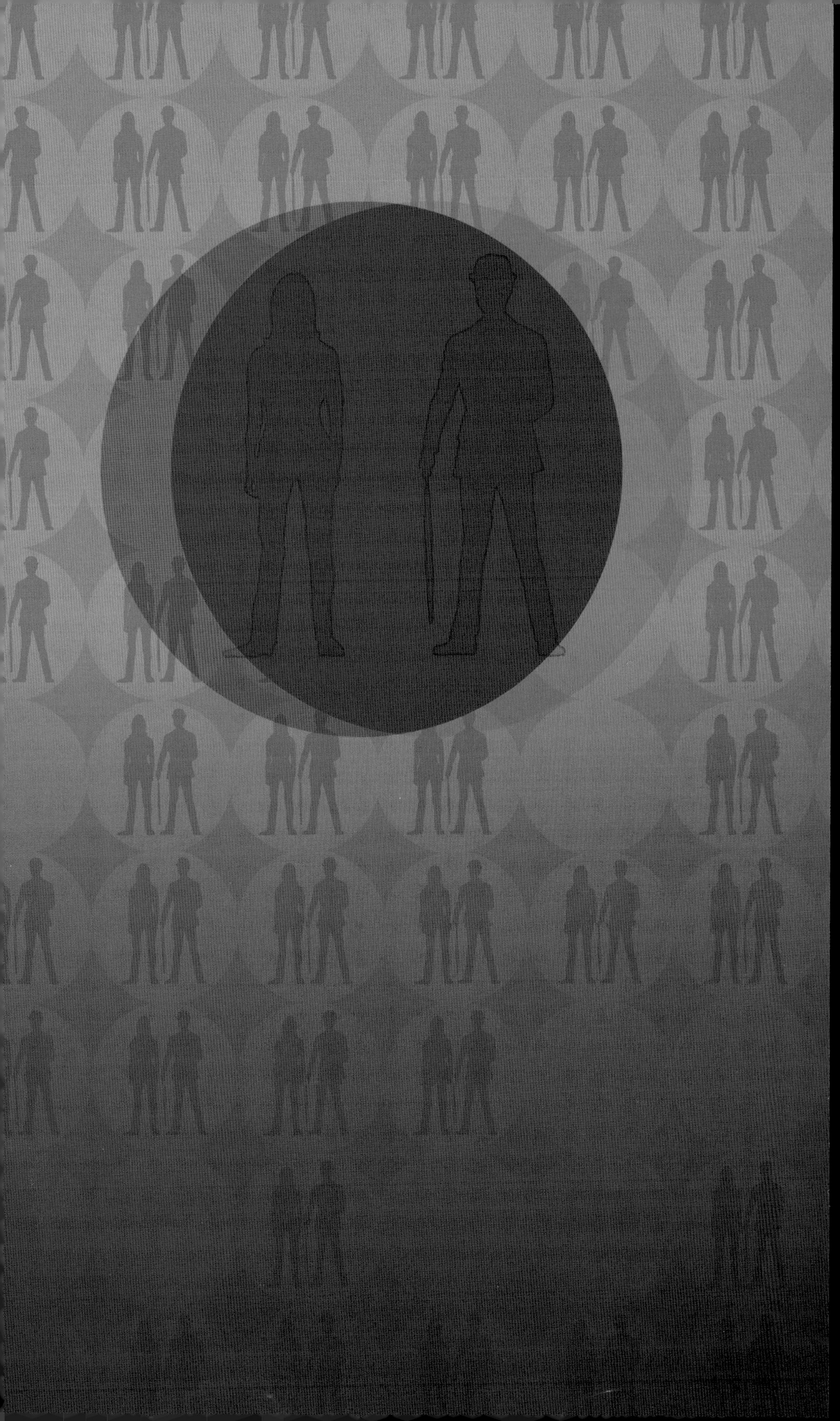

CHAPTER SEVEN

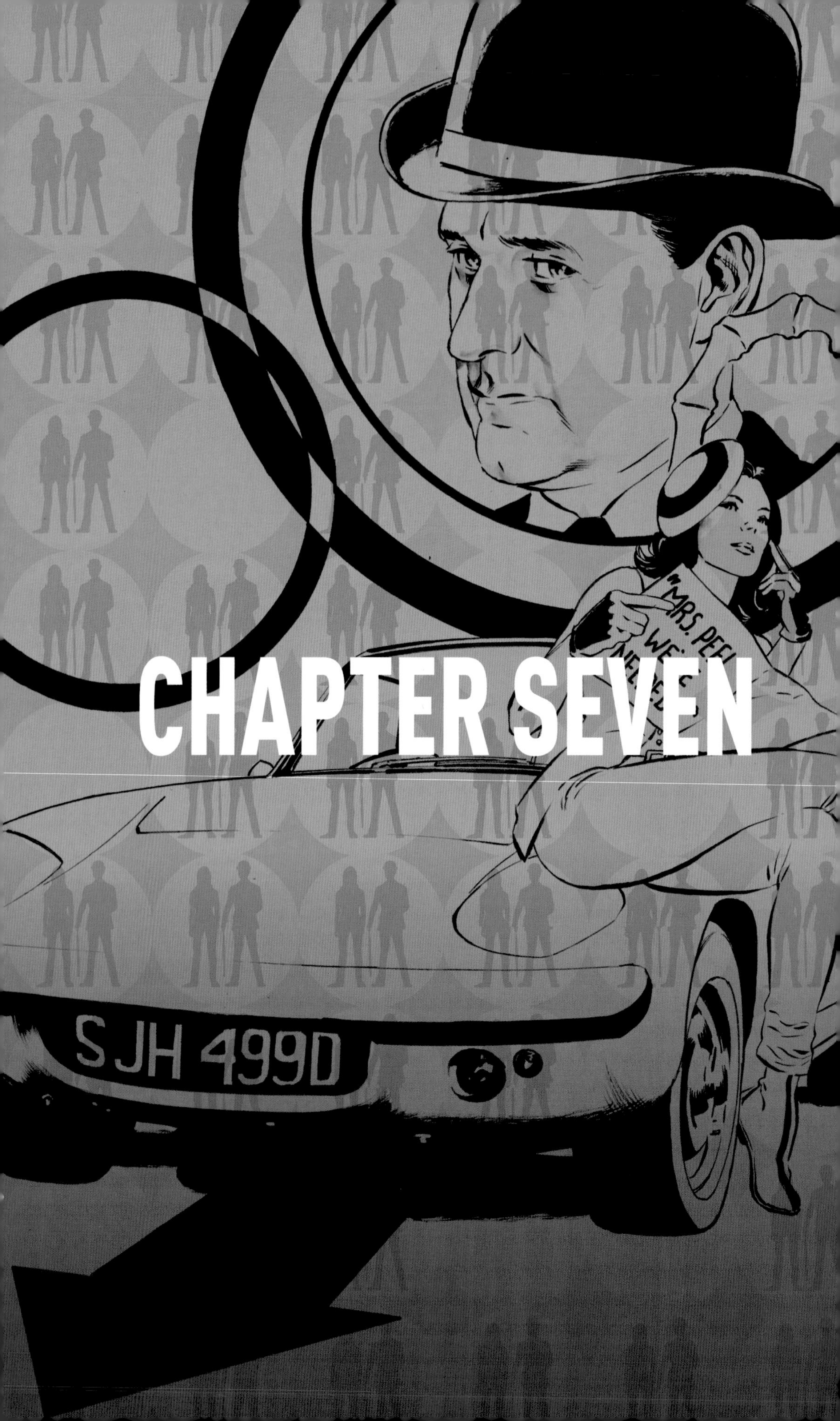
"MRS. PEEL
SJH 499D

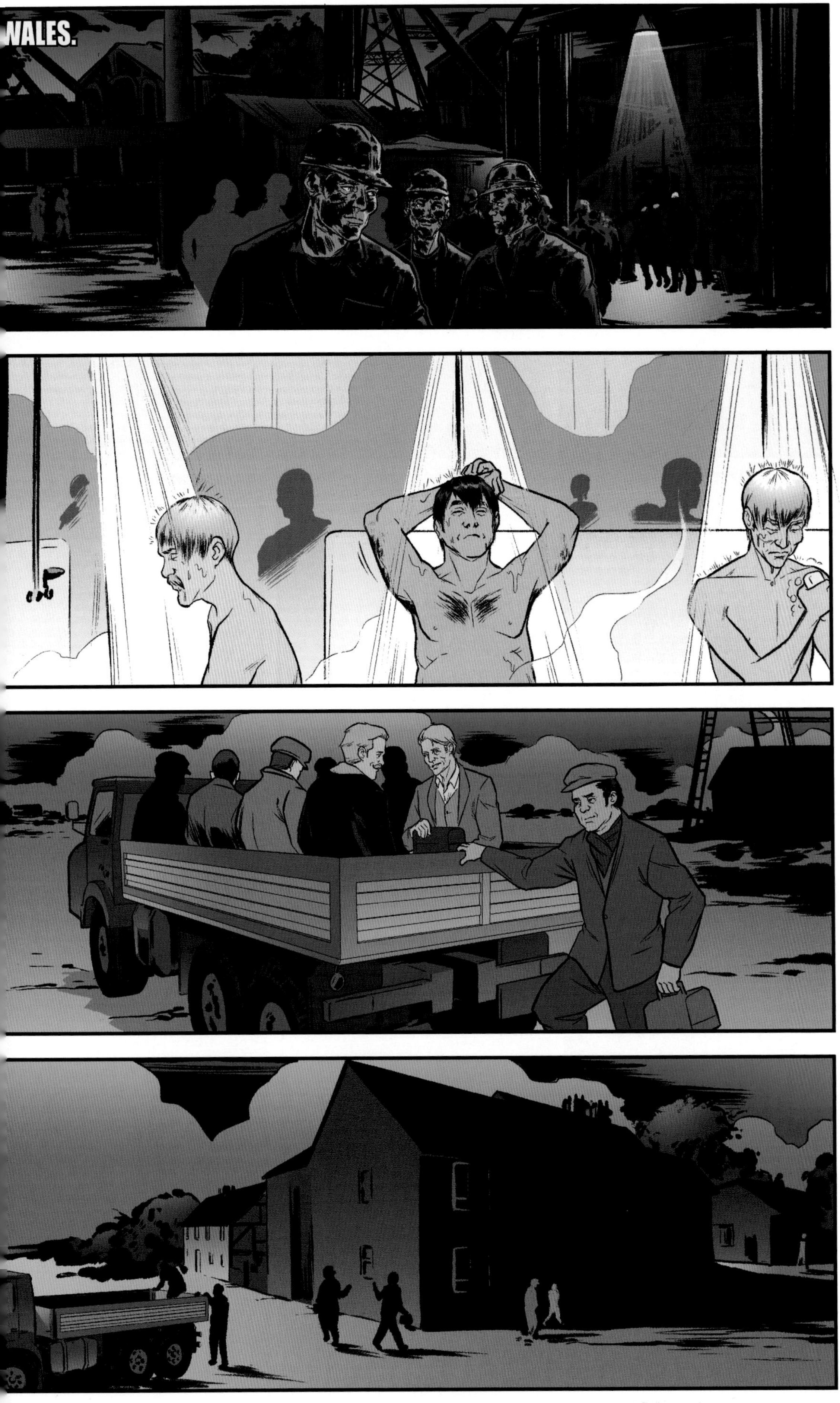
WALES.

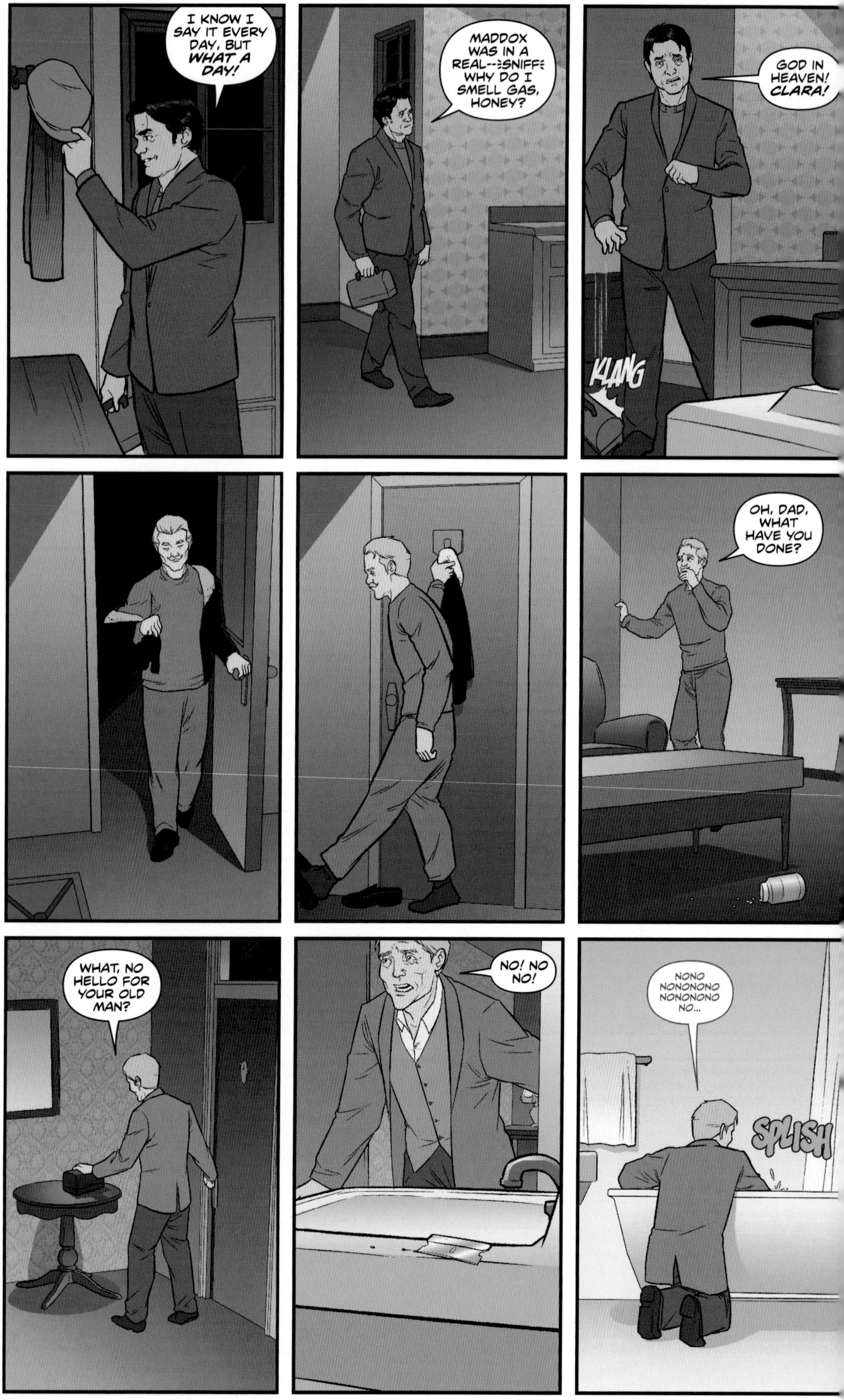
I KNOW I SAY IT EVERY DAY, BUT WHAT A DAY!
MADDOX WAS IN A REAL--SNIFF- WHY DO I SMELL GAS, HONEY?
GOD IN HEAVEN! CLARA!
KLANG
OH, DAD, WHAT HAVE YOU DONE?
WHAT, NO HELLO FOR YOUR OLD MAN?
NO! NO NO!
NONO NONONONO NONONONO NO...
SPLISH

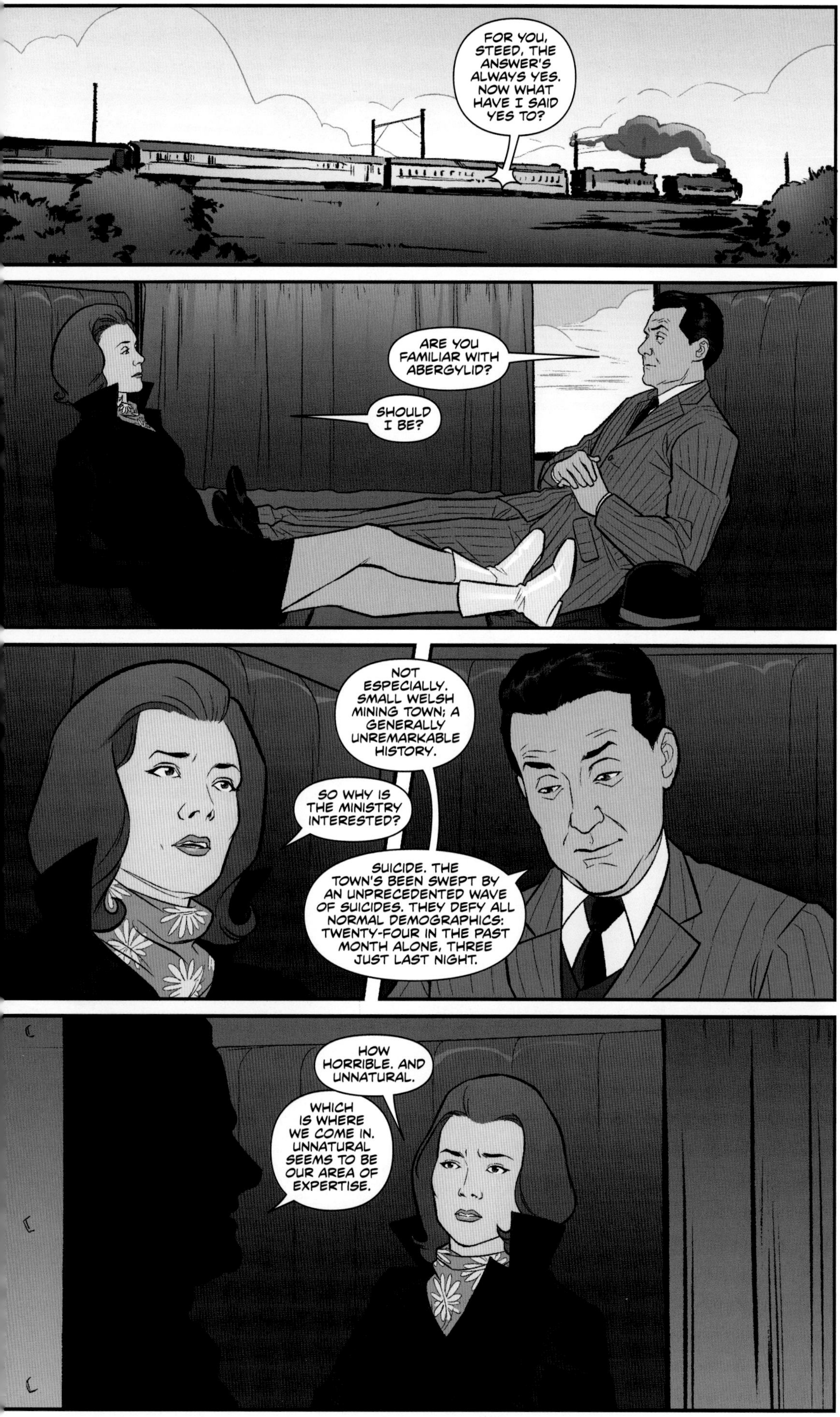
FOR YOU, STEED, THE ANSWER'S ALWAYS YES. NOW WHAT HAVE I SAID YES TO?
ARE YOU FAMILIAR WITH ABERGYLID?
SHOULD I BE?
NOT ESPECIALLY. SMALL WELSH MINING TOWN; A GENERALLY UNREMARKABLE HISTORY.
SO WHY IS THE MINISTRY INTERESTED?
SUICIDE. THE TOWN'S BEEN SWEPT BY AN UNPRECEDENTED WAVE OF SUICIDES. THEY DEFY ALL NORMAL DEMOGRAPHICS: TWENTY-FOUR IN THE PAST MONTH ALONE, THREE JUST LAST NIGHT.
HOW HORRIBLE. AND UNNATURAL.
WHICH IS WHERE WE COME IN. UNNATURAL SEEMS TO BE OUR AREA OF EXPERTISE.

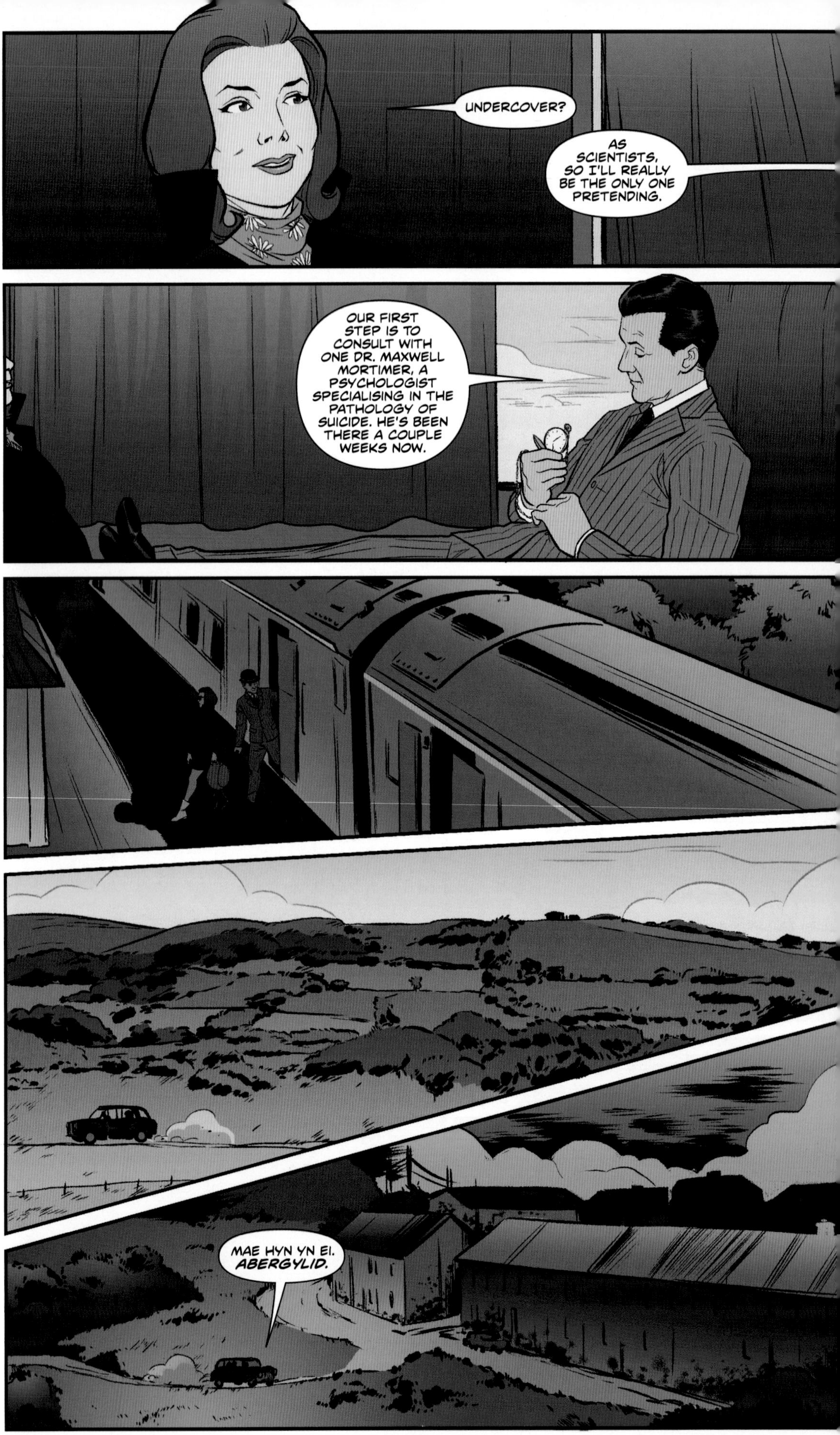
UNDERCOVER?
AS SCIENTISTS, SO I'LL REALLY BE THE ONLY ONE PRETENDING.
OUR FIRST STEP IS TO CONSULT WITH ONE DR. MAXWELL MORTIMER, A PSYCHOLOGIST SPECIALISING IN THE PATHOLOGY OF SUICIDE. HE'S BEEN THERE A COUPLE WEEKS NOW.
MAE HYN YN EI. *ABERGYLID.*

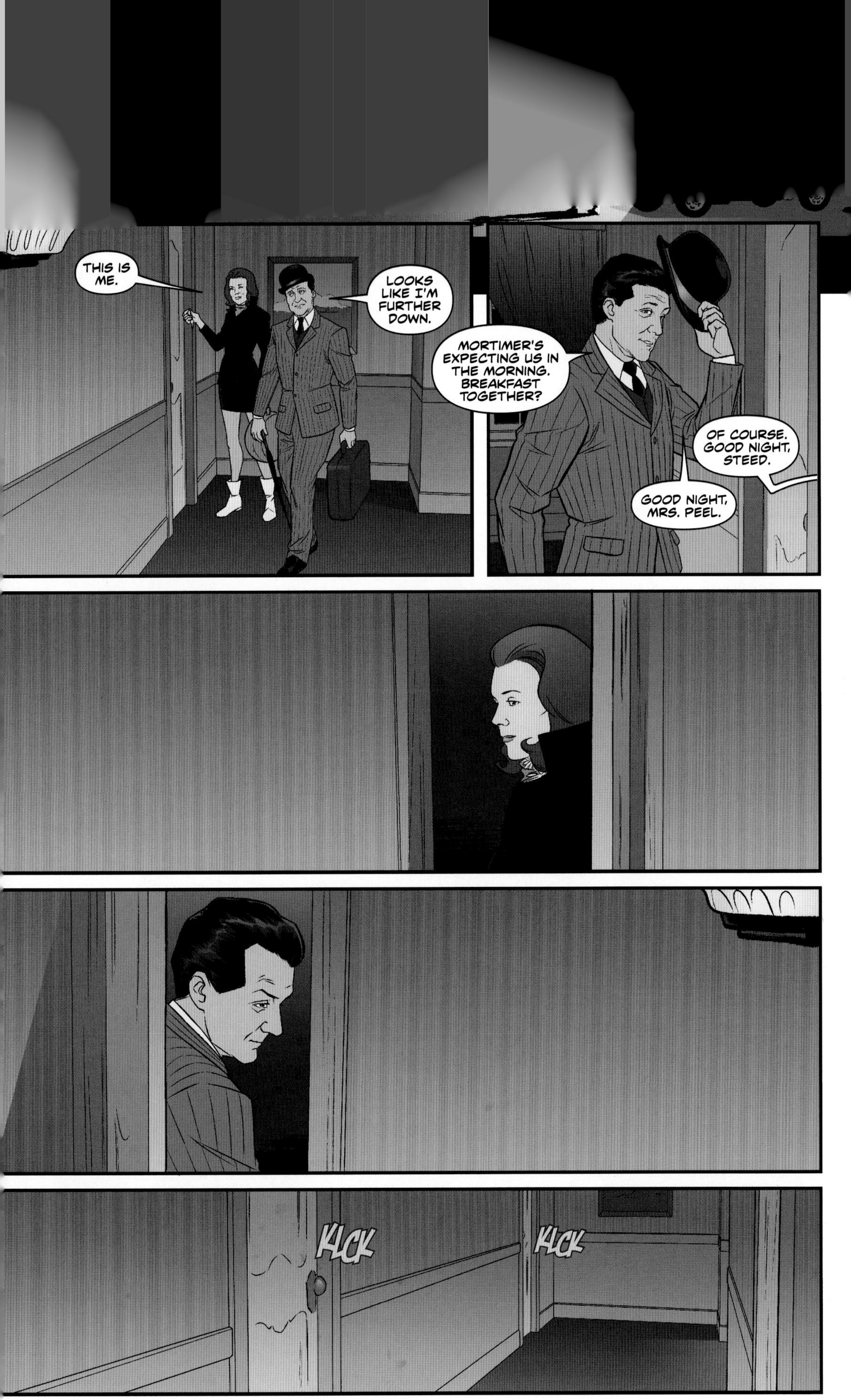
THIS IS ME.
LOOKS LIKE I'M FURTHER DOWN.
MORTIMER'S EXPECTING US IN THE MORNING. BREAKFAST TOGETHER?
OF COURSE. GOOD NIGHT, STEED.
GOOD NIGHT, MRS. PEEL.
KLCK
KLCK

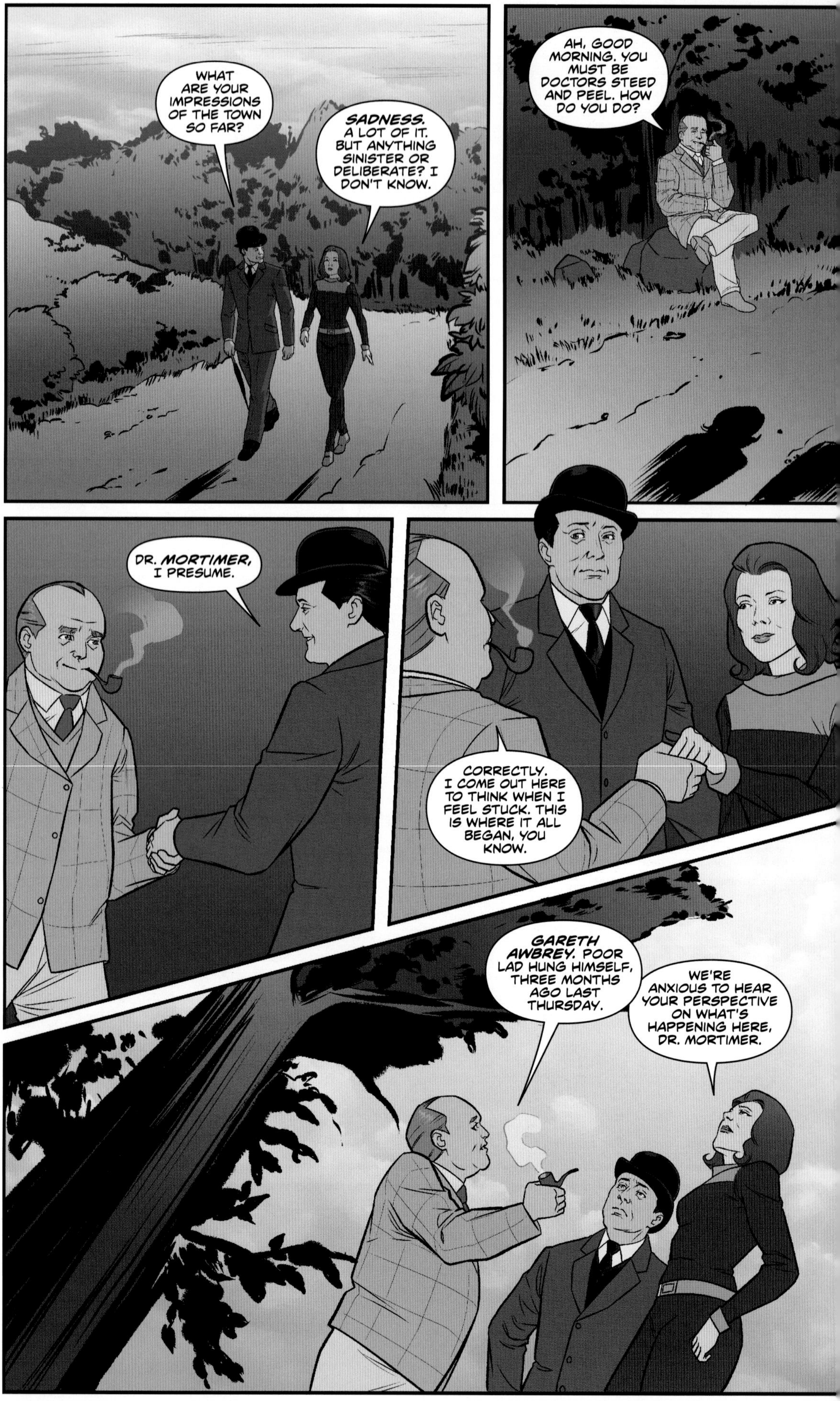
WHAT ARE YOUR IMPRESSIONS OF THE TOWN SO FAR?
SADNESS. A LOT OF IT. BUT ANYTHING SINISTER OR DELIBERATE? I DON'T KNOW.
AH, GOOD MORNING. YOU MUST BE DOCTORS STEED AND PEEL. HOW DO YOU DO?
DR. MORTIMER, I PRESUME.
CORRECTLY. I COME OUT HERE TO THINK WHEN I FEEL STUCK. THIS IS WHERE IT ALL BEGAN, YOU KNOW.
GARETH AWBREY. POOR LAD HUNG HIMSELF, THREE MONTHS AGO LAST THURSDAY.
WE'RE ANXIOUS TO HEAR YOUR PERSPECTIVE ON WHAT'S HAPPENING HERE, DR. MORTIMER.

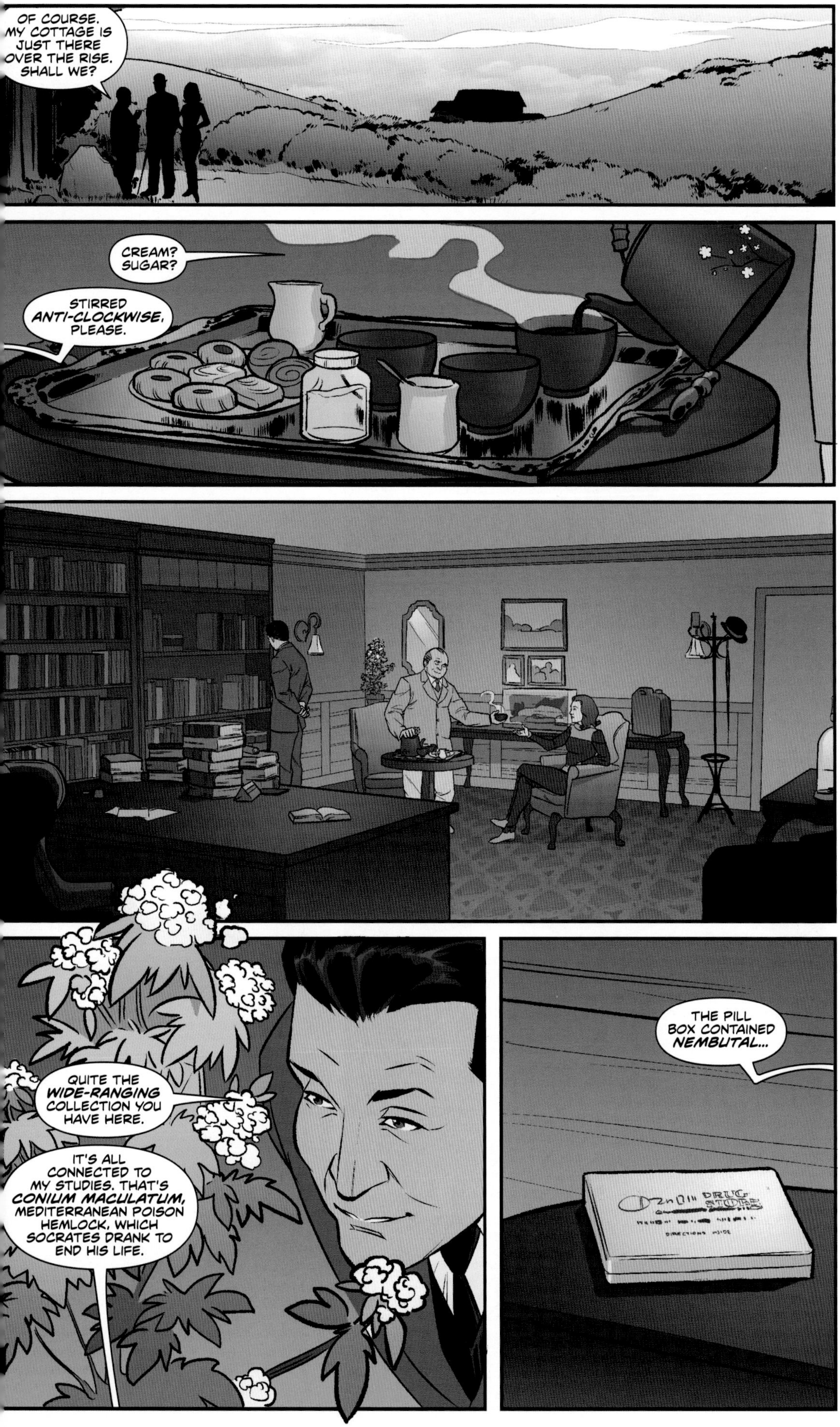

OF COURSE. MY COTTAGE IS JUST THERE OVER THE RISE. SHALL WE?
CREAM? SUGAR?
STIRRED *ANTI-CLOCKWISE*, PLEASE.
QUITE THE *WIDE-RANGING* COLLECTION YOU HAVE HERE.
IT'S ALL CONNECTED TO MY STUDIES. THAT'S *CONIUM MACULATUM*, MEDITERRANEAN POISON HEMLOCK, WHICH SOCRATES DRANK TO END HIS LIFE.
THE PILL BOX CONTAINED *NEMBUTAL*...

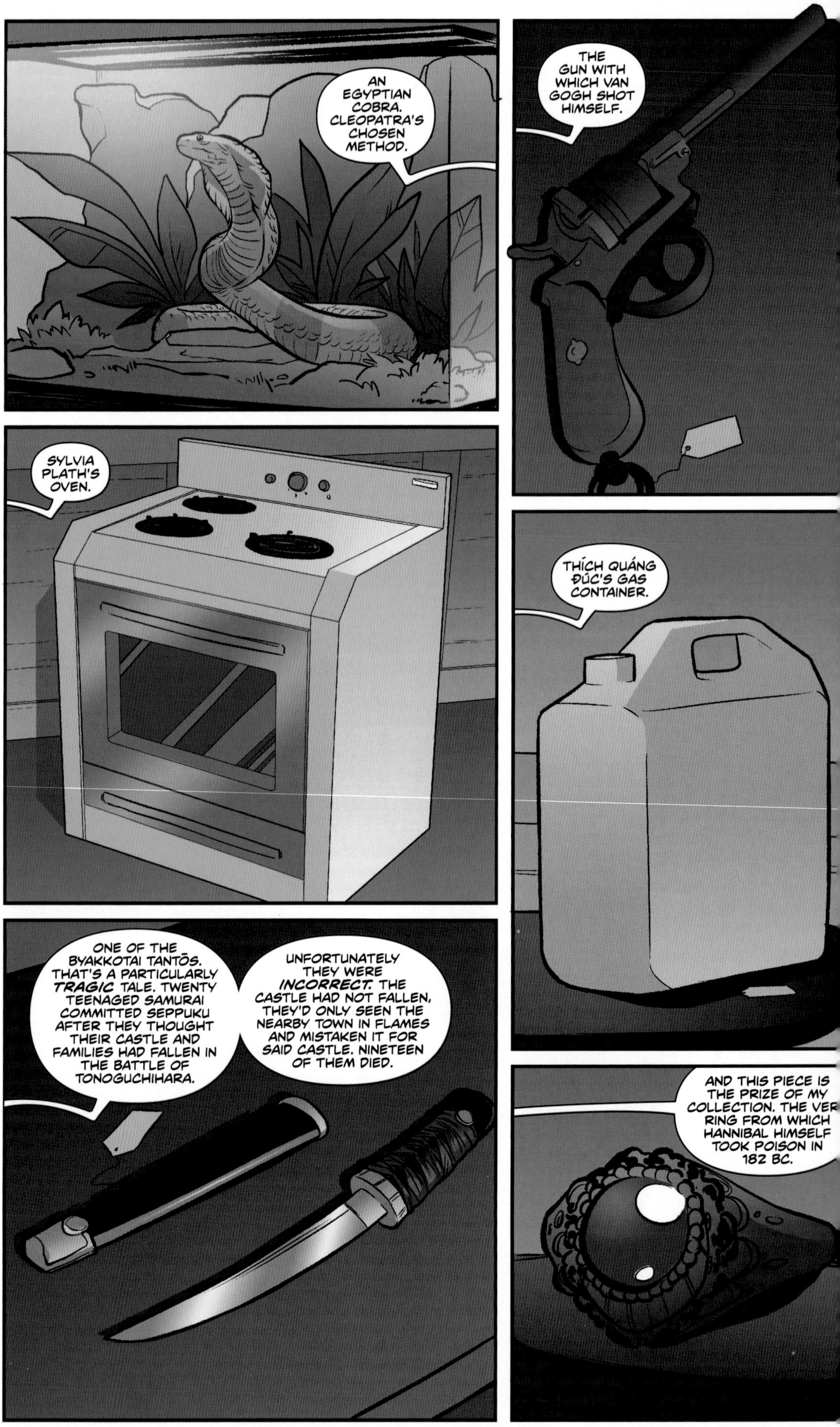
AN EGYPTIAN COBRA. CLEOPATRA'S CHOSEN METHOD.
THE GUN WITH WHICH VAN GOGH SHOT HIMSELF.
SYLVIA PLATH'S OVEN.
THÍCH QUẢNG ĐỨC'S GAS CONTAINER.
ONE OF THE BYAKKOTAI TANTŌS. THAT'S A PARTICULARLY *TRAGIC* TALE. TWENTY TEENAGED SAMURAI COMMITTED SEPPUKU AFTER THEY THOUGHT THEIR CASTLE AND FAMILIES HAD FALLEN IN THE BATTLE OF TONOGUCHIHARA.
UNFORTUNATELY THEY WERE *INCORRECT.* THE CASTLE HAD NOT FALLEN, THEY'D ONLY SEEN THE NEARBY TOWN IN FLAMES AND MISTAKEN IT FOR SAID CASTLE. NINETEEN OF THEM DIED.
AND THIS PIECE IS THE PRIZE OF MY COLLECTION. THE VER RING FROM WHICH HANNIBAL HIMSELF TOOK POISON IN 182 BC.

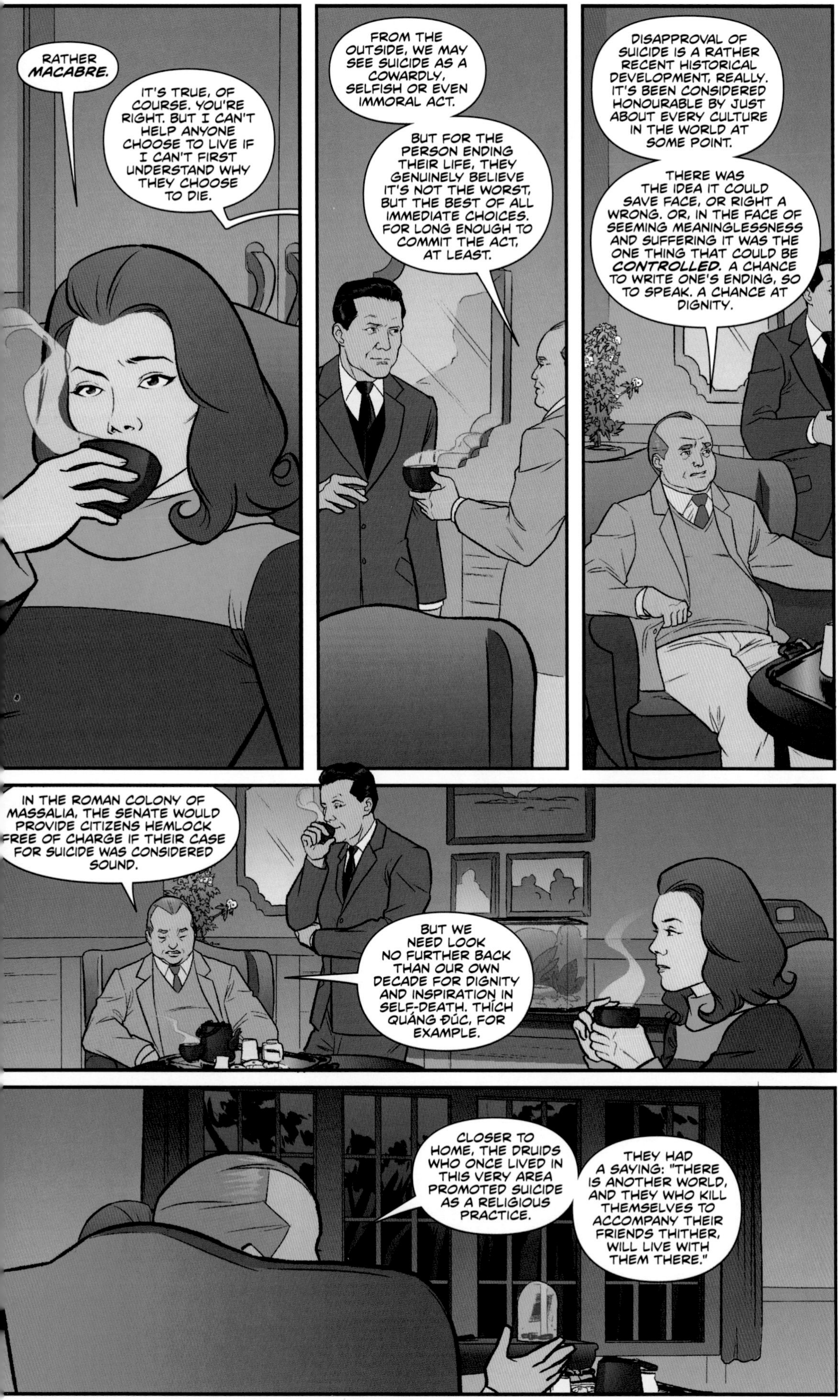
RATHER *MACABRE.*
IT'S TRUE, OF COURSE. YOU'RE RIGHT. BUT I CAN'T HELP ANYONE CHOOSE TO LIVE IF I CAN'T FIRST UNDERSTAND WHY THEY CHOOSE TO DIE.
FROM THE OUTSIDE, WE MAY SEE SUICIDE AS A COWARDLY, SELFISH OR EVEN IMMORAL ACT.
BUT FOR THE PERSON ENDING THEIR LIFE, THEY GENUINELY BELIEVE IT'S NOT THE WORST, BUT THE BEST OF ALL IMMEDIATE CHOICES. FOR LONG ENOUGH TO COMMIT THE ACT, AT LEAST.
DISAPPROVAL OF SUICIDE IS A RATHER RECENT HISTORICAL DEVELOPMENT, REALLY. IT'S BEEN CONSIDERED HONOURABLE BY JUST ABOUT EVERY CULTURE IN THE WORLD AT SOME POINT.
THERE WAS THE IDEA IT COULD SAVE FACE, OR RIGHT A WRONG. OR, IN THE FACE OF SEEMING MEANINGLESSNESS AND SUFFERING IT WAS THE ONE THING THAT COULD BE ***CONTROLLED.*** A CHANCE TO WRITE ONE'S ENDING, SO TO SPEAK. A CHANCE AT DIGNITY.
IN THE ROMAN COLONY OF MASSALIA, THE SENATE WOULD PROVIDE CITIZENS HEMLOCK FREE OF CHARGE IF THEIR CASE FOR SUICIDE WAS CONSIDERED SOUND.
BUT WE NEED LOOK NO FURTHER BACK THAN OUR OWN DECADE FOR DIGNITY AND INSPIRATION IN SELF-DEATH. THÍCH QUẢNG ĐỨC, FOR EXAMPLE.
CLOSER TO HOME, THE DRUIDS WHO ONCE LIVED IN THIS VERY AREA PROMOTED SUICIDE AS A RELIGIOUS PRACTICE.
THEY HAD A SAYING: "THERE IS ANOTHER WORLD, AND THEY WHO KILL THEMSELVES TO ACCOMPANY THEIR FRIENDS THITHER, WILL LIVE WITH THEM THERE."

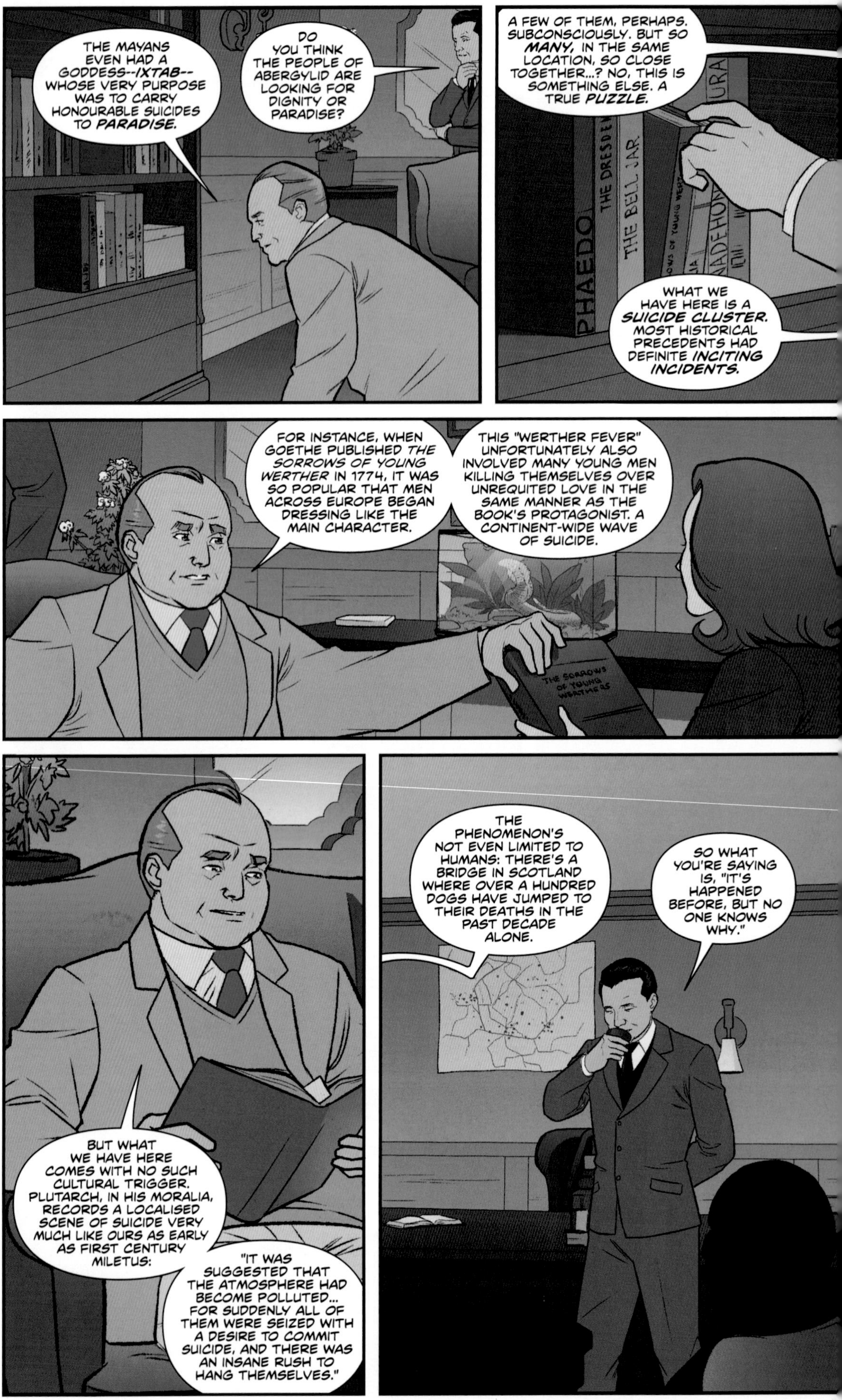
THE MAYANS EVEN HAD A GODDESS--*IXTAB*--WHOSE VERY PURPOSE WAS TO CARRY HONOURABLE SUICIDES TO *PARADISE.*
DO YOU THINK THE PEOPLE OF ABERGYLID ARE LOOKING FOR DIGNITY OR PARADISE?
A FEW OF THEM, PERHAPS. SUBCONSCIOUSLY. BUT SO *MANY,* IN THE SAME LOCATION, SO CLOSE TOGETHER...? NO, THIS IS SOMETHING ELSE. A TRUE *PUZZLE.*
PHAEDO
THE DRESDEN
THE BELL JAR
WHAT WE HAVE HERE IS A *SUICIDE CLUSTER.* MOST HISTORICAL PRECEDENTS HAD DEFINITE *INCITING INCIDENTS.*
FOR INSTANCE, WHEN GOETHE PUBLISHED *THE SORROWS OF YOUNG WERTHER* IN 1774, IT WAS SO POPULAR THAT MEN ACROSS EUROPE BEGAN DRESSING LIKE THE MAIN CHARACTER.
THIS "WERTHER FEVER" UNFORTUNATELY ALSO INVOLVED MANY YOUNG MEN KILLING THEMSELVES OVER UNREQUITED LOVE IN THE SAME MANNER AS THE BOOK'S PROTAGONIST. A CONTINENT-WIDE WAVE OF SUICIDE.
THE SORROWS OF YOUNG WERTHERS
BUT WHAT WE HAVE HERE COMES WITH NO SUCH CULTURAL TRIGGER. PLUTARCH, IN HIS MORALIA, RECORDS A LOCALISED SCENE OF SUICIDE VERY MUCH LIKE OURS AS EARLY AS FIRST CENTURY MILETUS:
"IT WAS SUGGESTED THAT THE ATMOSPHERE HAD BECOME POLLUTED... FOR SUDDENLY ALL OF THEM WERE SEIZED WITH A DESIRE TO COMMIT SUICIDE, AND THERE WAS AN INSANE RUSH TO HANG THEMSELVES."
THE PHENOMENON'S NOT EVEN LIMITED TO HUMANS: THERE'S A BRIDGE IN SCOTLAND WHERE OVER A HUNDRED DOGS HAVE JUMPED TO THEIR DEATHS IN THE PAST DECADE ALONE.
SO WHAT YOU'RE SAYING IS, "IT'S HAPPENED BEFORE, BUT NO ONE KNOWS WHY."

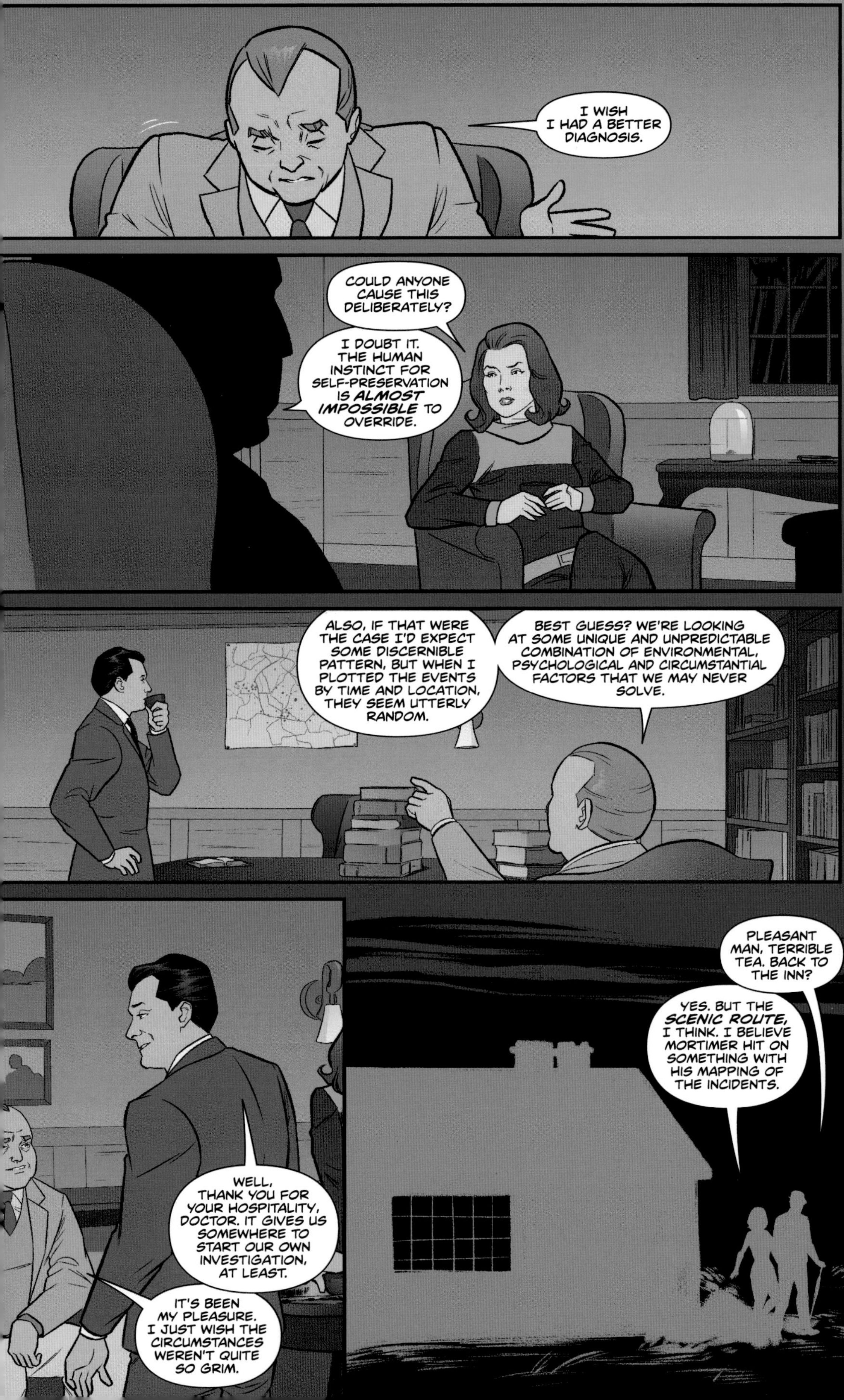
I WISH I HAD A BETTER DIAGNOSIS.
COULD ANYONE CAUSE THIS DELIBERATELY?
I DOUBT IT. THE HUMAN INSTINCT FOR SELF-PRESERVATION IS ALMOST IMPOSSIBLE TO OVERRIDE.
ALSO, IF THAT WERE THE CASE I'D EXPECT SOME DISCERNIBLE PATTERN, BUT WHEN I PLOTTED THE EVENTS BY TIME AND LOCATION, THEY SEEM UTTERLY RANDOM.
BEST GUESS? WE'RE LOOKING AT SOME UNIQUE AND UNPREDICTABLE COMBINATION OF ENVIRONMENTAL, PSYCHOLOGICAL AND CIRCUMSTANTIAL FACTORS THAT WE MAY NEVER SOLVE.
WELL, THANK YOU FOR YOUR HOSPITALITY, DOCTOR. IT GIVES US SOMEWHERE TO START OUR OWN INVESTIGATION, AT LEAST.
IT'S BEEN MY PLEASURE. I JUST WISH THE CIRCUMSTANCES WEREN'T QUITE SO GRIM.
PLEASANT MAN, TERRIBLE TEA. BACK TO THE INN?
YES. BUT THE SCENIC ROUTE, I THINK. I BELIEVE MORTIMER HIT ON SOMETHING WITH HIS MAPPING OF THE INCIDENTS.

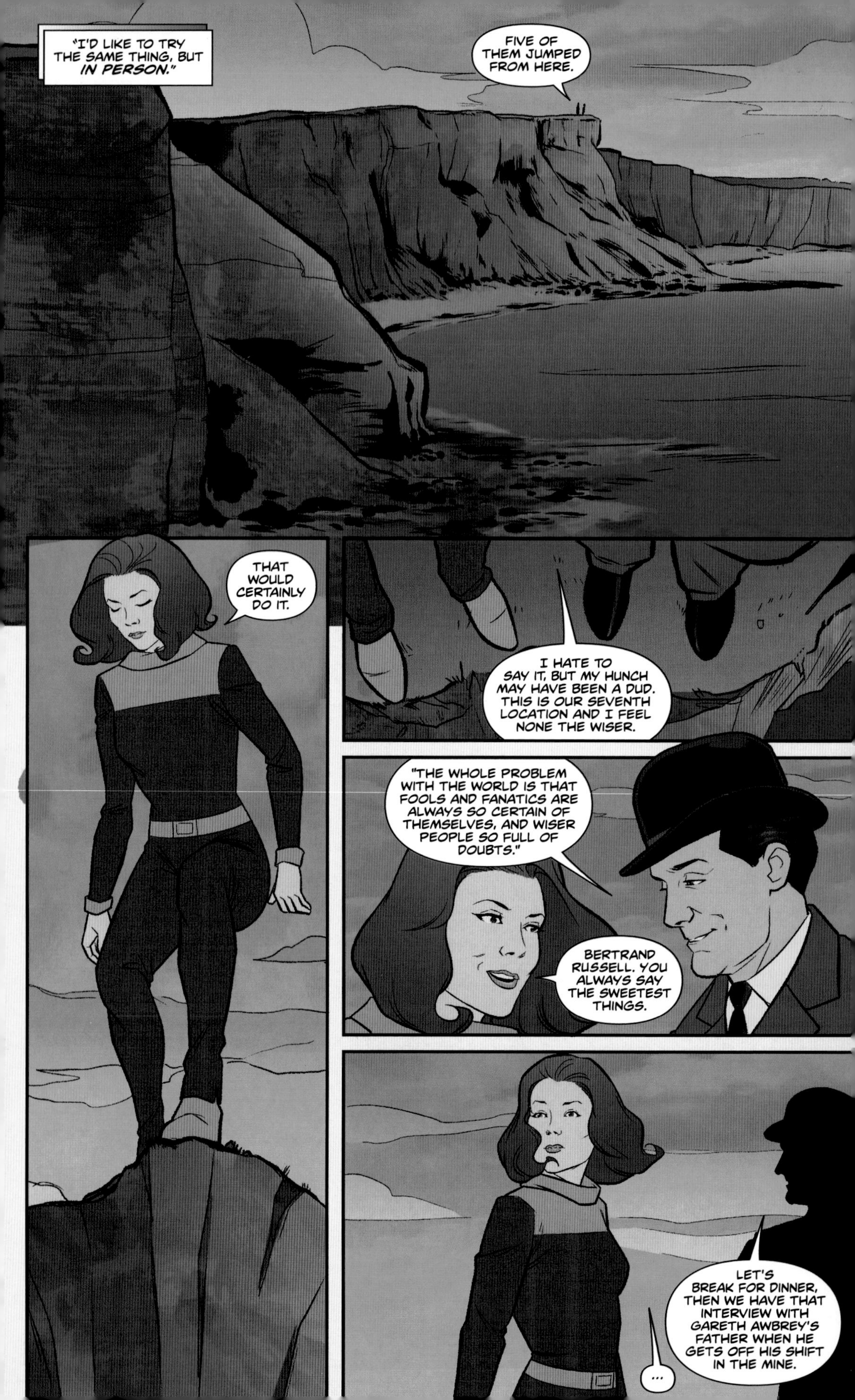

"I'D LIKE TO TRY THE SAME THING, BUT *IN PERSON*."
FIVE OF THEM JUMPED FROM HERE.
THAT WOULD CERTAINLY DO IT.
I HATE TO SAY IT, BUT MY HUNCH MAY HAVE BEEN A DUD. THIS IS OUR SEVENTH LOCATION AND I FEEL NONE THE WISER.
"THE WHOLE PROBLEM WITH THE WORLD IS THAT FOOLS AND FANATICS ARE ALWAYS SO CERTAIN OF THEMSELVES, AND WISER PEOPLE SO FULL OF DOUBTS."
BERTRAND RUSSELL. YOU ALWAYS SAY THE SWEETEST THINGS.
LET'S BREAK FOR DINNER, THEN WE HAVE THAT INTERVIEW WITH GARETH AWBREY'S FATHER WHEN HE GETS OFF HIS SHIFT IN THE MINE.
...

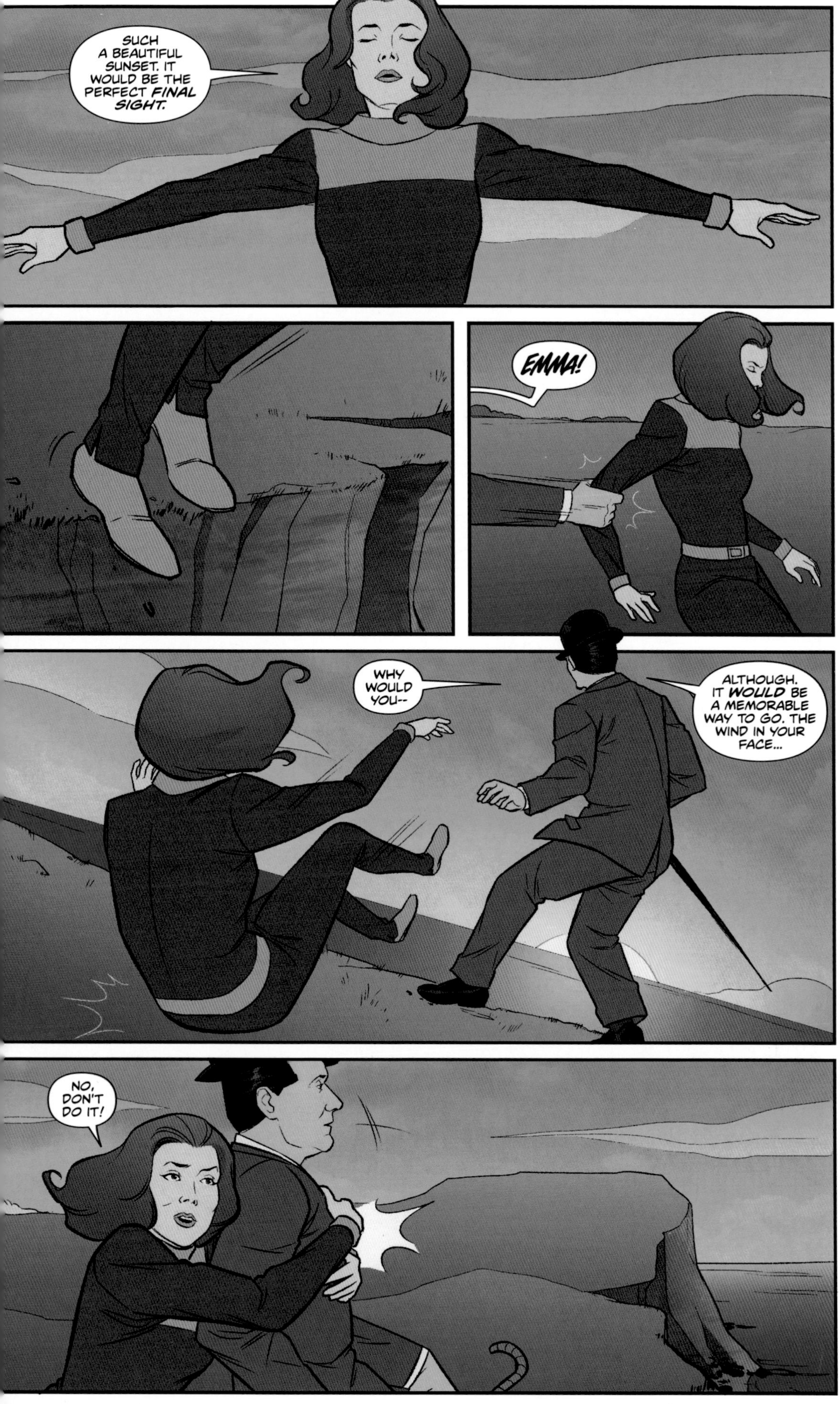
SUCH A BEAUTIFUL SUNSET. IT WOULD BE THE PERFECT *FINAL SIGHT.*
EMMA!
WHY WOULD YOU--
ALTHOUGH. IT ***WOULD*** BE A MEMORABLE WAY TO GO. THE WIND IN YOUR FACE...
NO, DON'T DO IT!

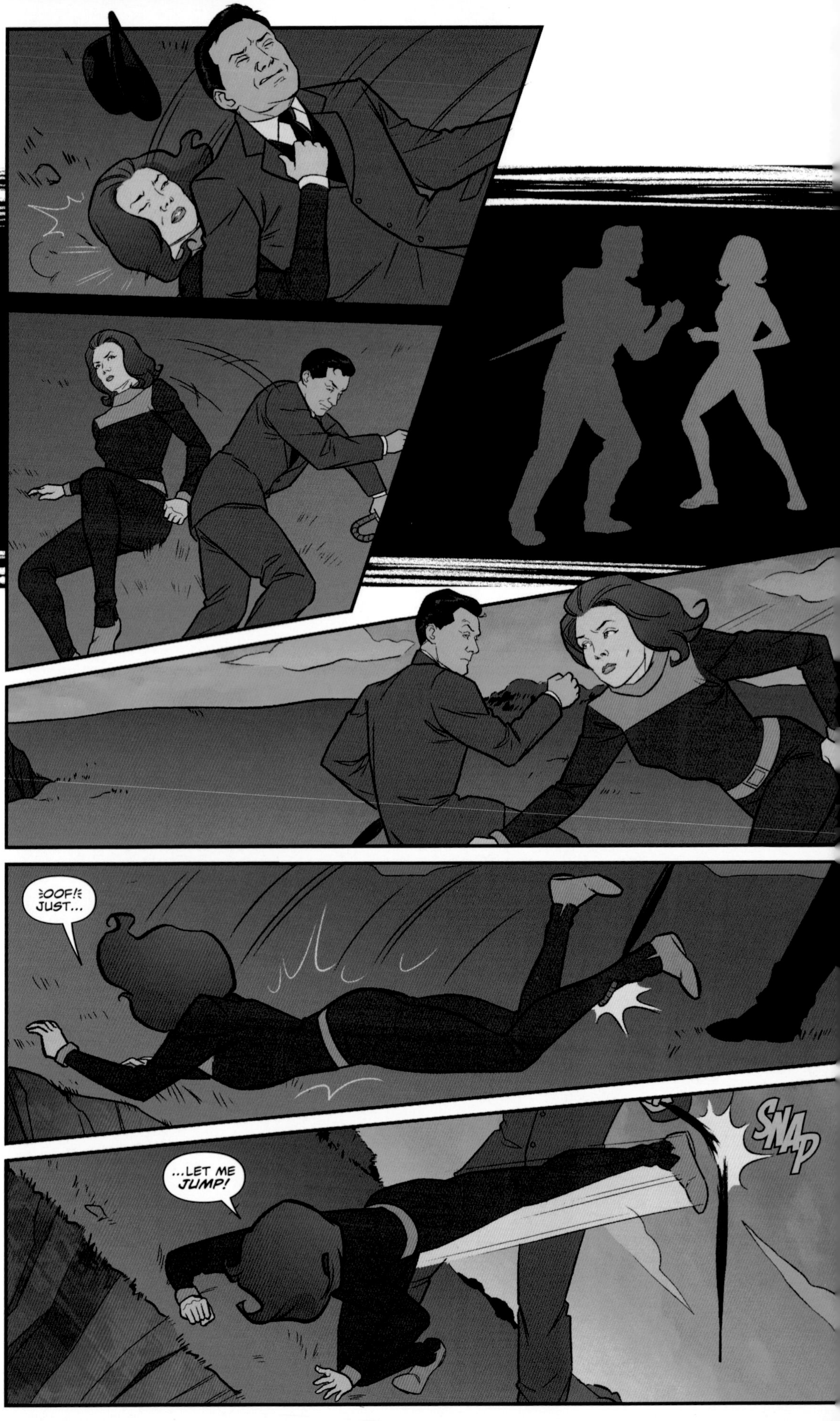
OOF! JUST...
...LET ME JUMP!
SNAP

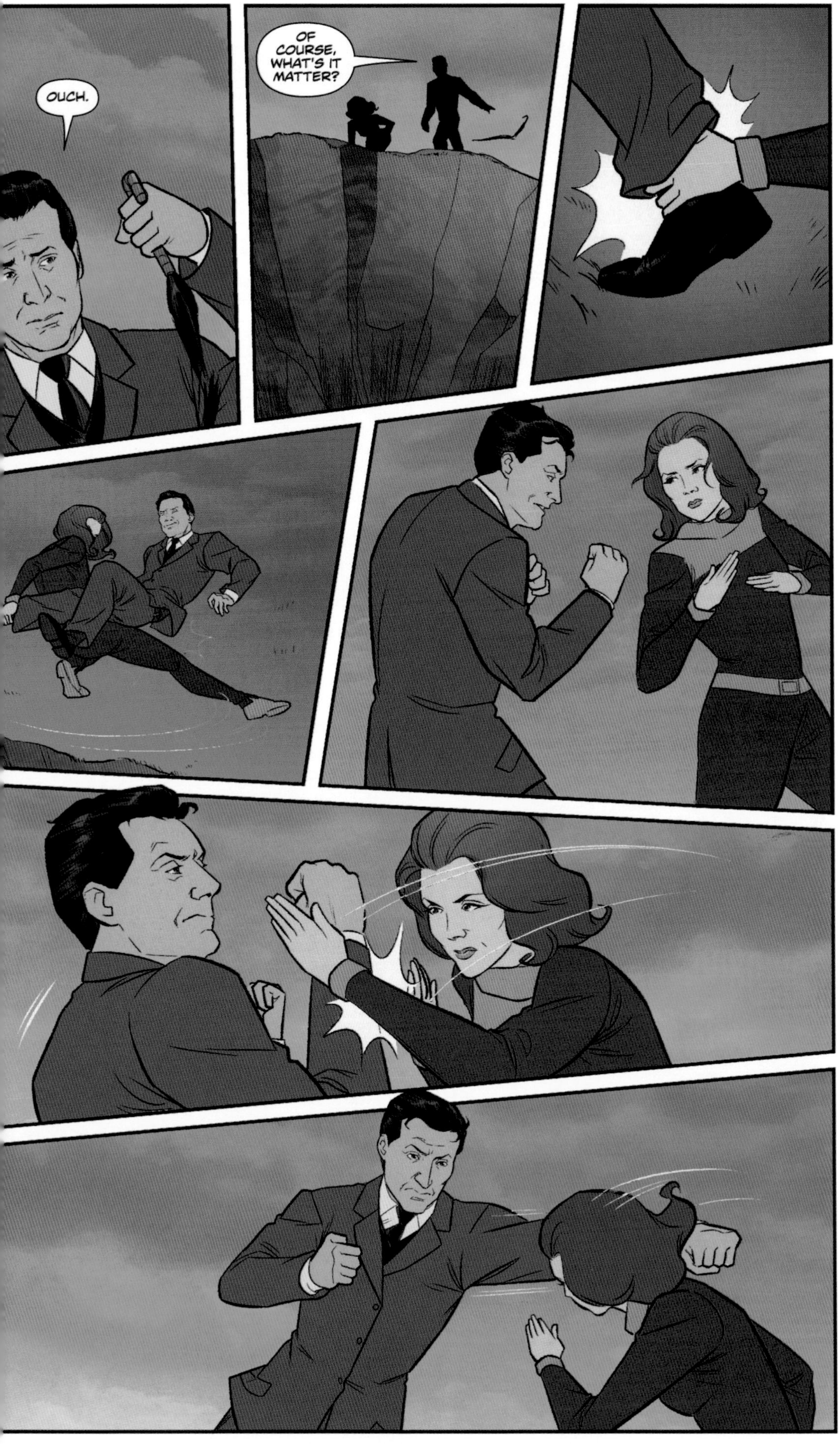
OUCH.
OF COURSE, WHAT'S IT MATTER?

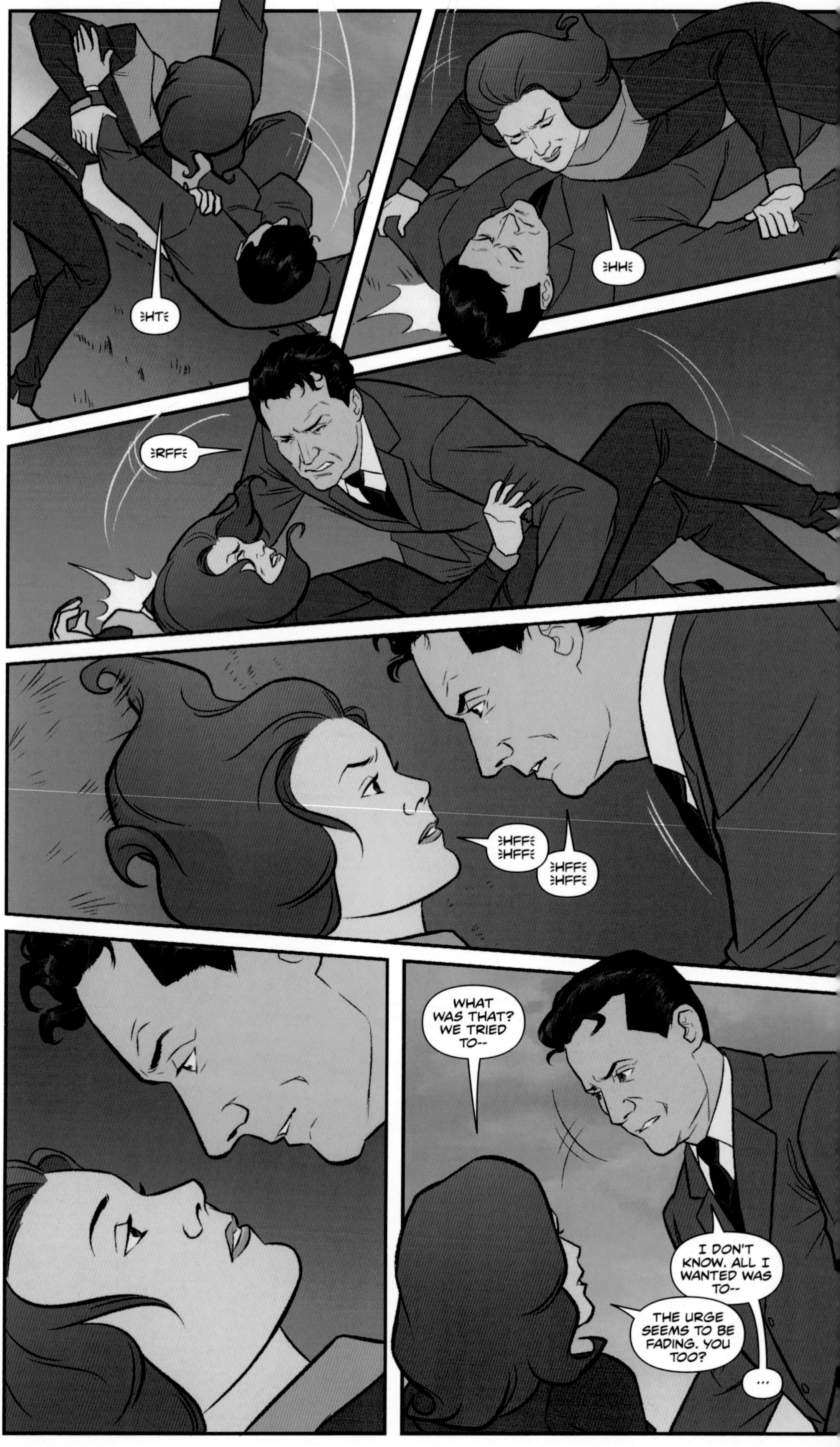
HT
HH
RFF
HFF HFF
HFF HFF
WHAT WAS THAT? WE TRIED TO--
I DON'T KNOW. ALL I WANTED WAS TO--
THE URGE SEEMS TO BE FADING. YOU TOO?
...

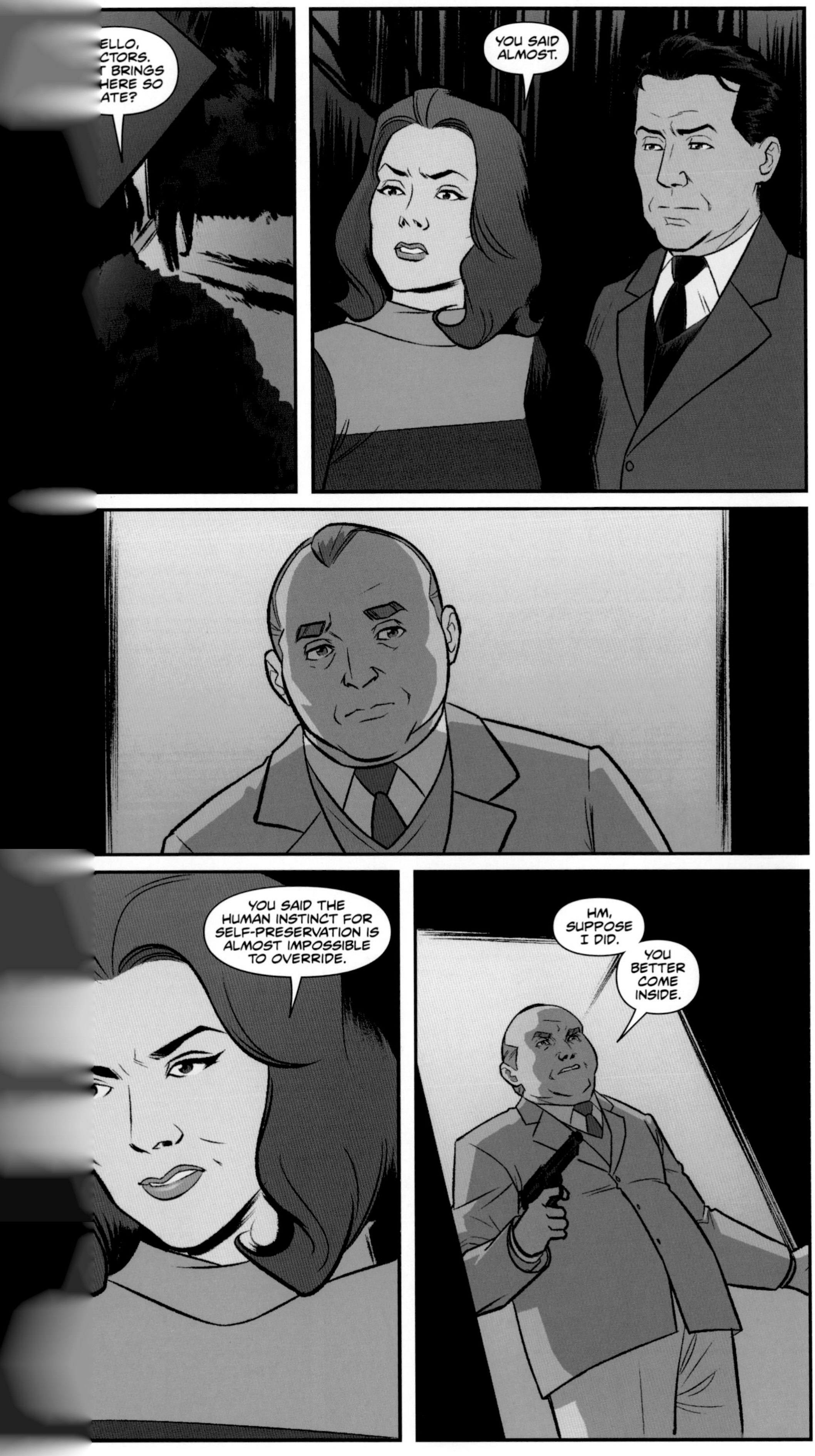
ELLO, CTORS. T BRINGS HERE SO ATE?
YOU SAID ALMOST.
YOU SAID THE HUMAN INSTINCT FOR SELF-PRESERVATION IS ALMOST IMPOSSIBLE TO OVERRIDE.
HM, SUPPOSE I DID.
YOU BETTER COME INSIDE.

JUST TWO MORE SUICIDES, EH? BY GUNSHOT THIS TIME.

A TRAGEDY INDEED. BUT FIRST I'M GOING TO DRAW SOME BLOOD.

THAT DOSE I GAVE YOU WAS MY STRONGEST FORMULATION YET. I NEED TO UNDERSTAND WHY IT DIDN'T WORK.

OH, IT WORKED *FINE.*

WE WERE JUST *TOGETHER* AT THE TIME. TURNS OUT EACH OF OUR DRIVES TO SAVE THE OTHER WAS STRONGER THAN OUR DRIVE TO END OUR OWN LIFE.

FASCINATING. TRULY.

WHAT'S THE END GAME IN SUICIDE ON DEMAND?

WEAPONISED SUICIDE. IMAGINE DROPPING MY FORMULA IN THE ENEMY'S WATER SUPPLY. THEY'LL KILL THEMSELVES *FOR* YOU!

CONFLICTS OV WITHIN WEEKS MESSY NUCLE OPTION. IT'D THE NEW AR RACE!

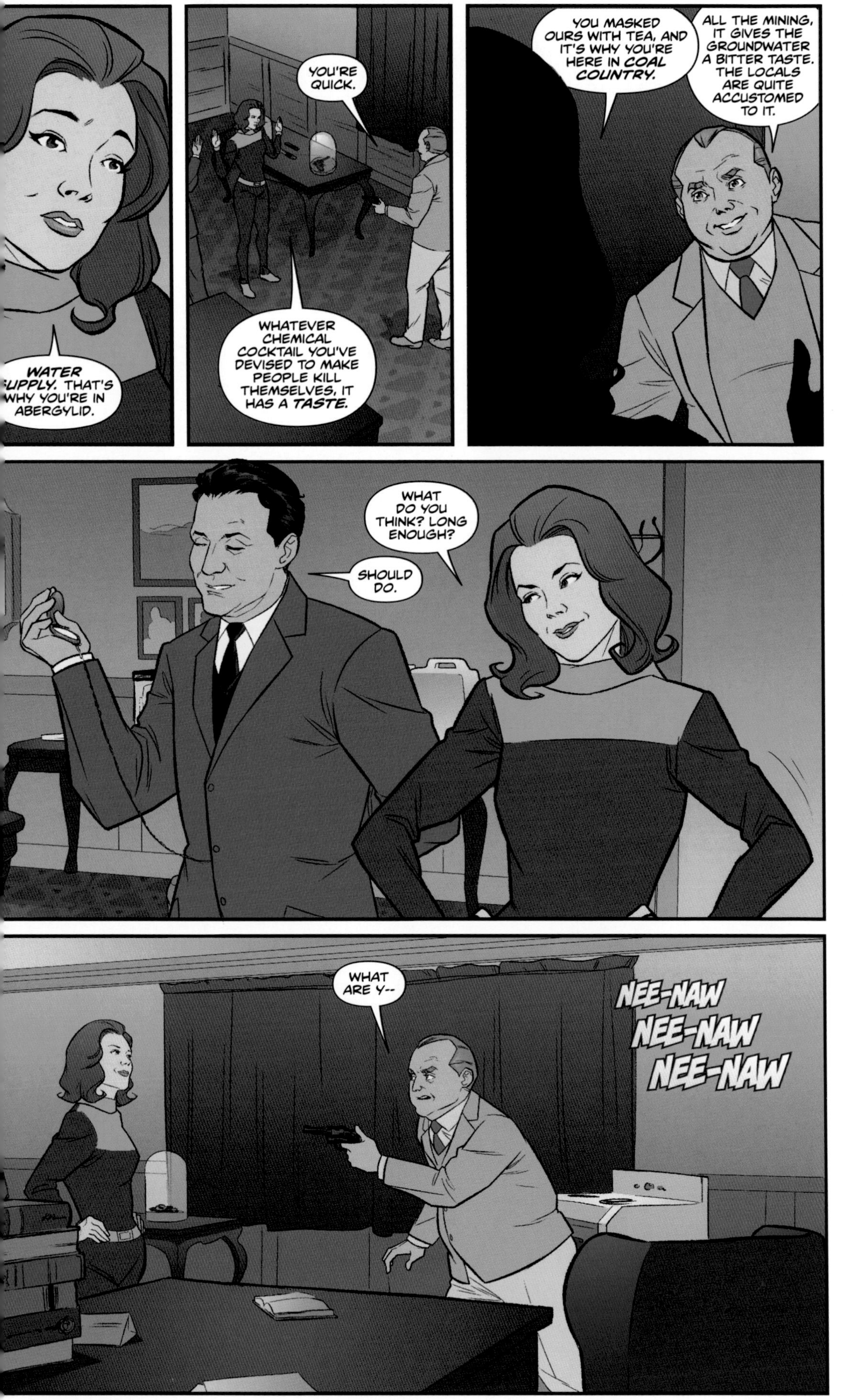
WATER SUPPLY. THAT'S WHY YOU'RE IN ABERGYLID.
YOU'RE QUICK.
WHATEVER CHEMICAL COCKTAIL YOU'VE DEVISED TO MAKE PEOPLE KILL THEMSELVES, IT HAS A TASTE.
YOU MASKED OURS WITH TEA, AND IT'S WHY YOU'RE HERE IN COAL COUNTRY.
ALL THE MINING, IT GIVES THE GROUNDWATER A BITTER TASTE. THE LOCALS ARE QUITE ACCUSTOMED TO IT.
WHAT DO YOU THINK? LONG ENOUGH?
SHOULD DO.
WHAT ARE Y--
NEE-NAW
NEE-NAW
NEE-NAW

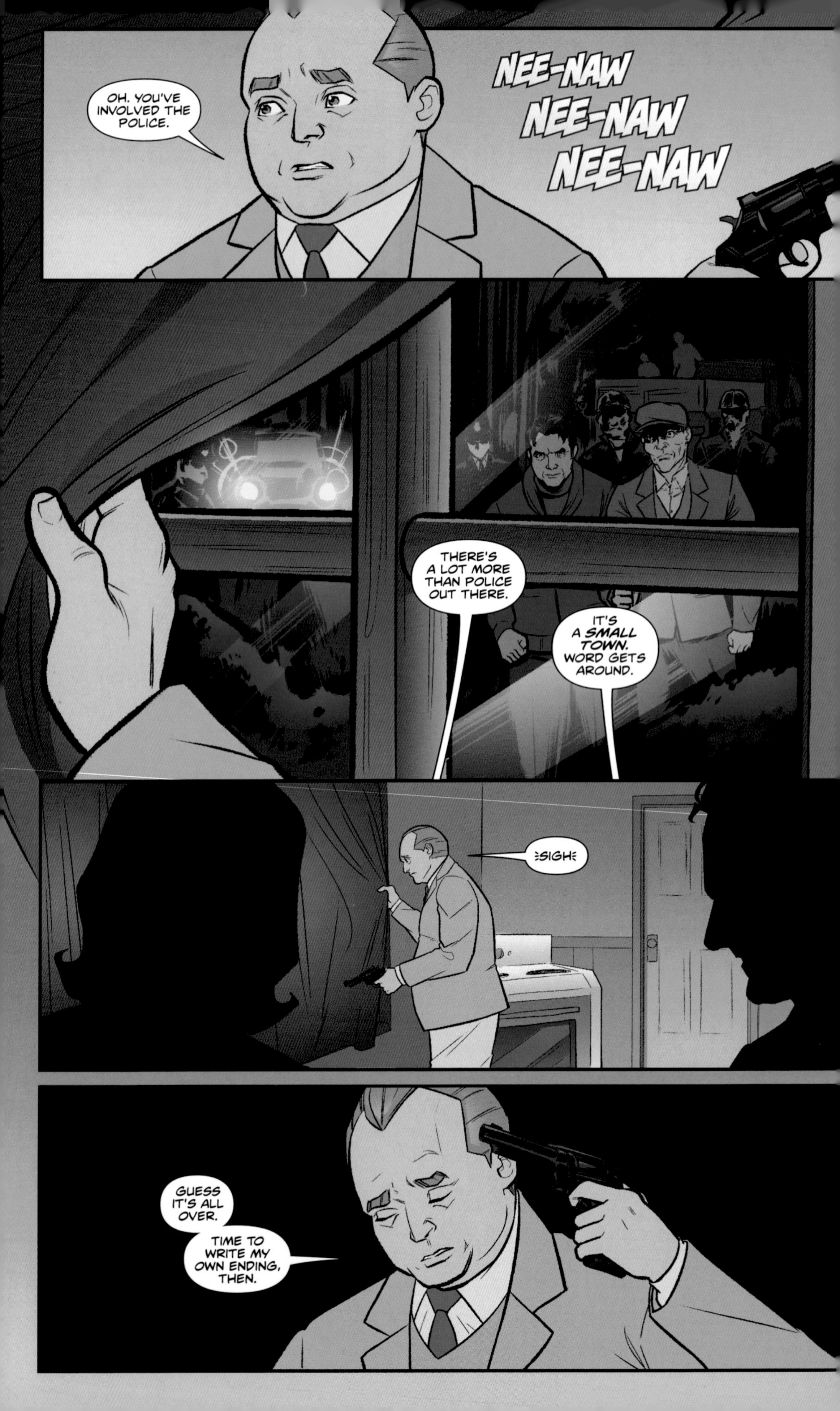
OH. YOU'VE INVOLVED THE POLICE.
NEE-NAW
NEE-NAW
NEE-NAW
THERE'S A LOT MORE THAN POLICE OUT THERE.
IT'S A *SMALL TOWN.* WORD GETS AROUND.
SIGH
GUESS IT'S ALL OVER.
TIME TO WRITE MY OWN ENDING, THEN.

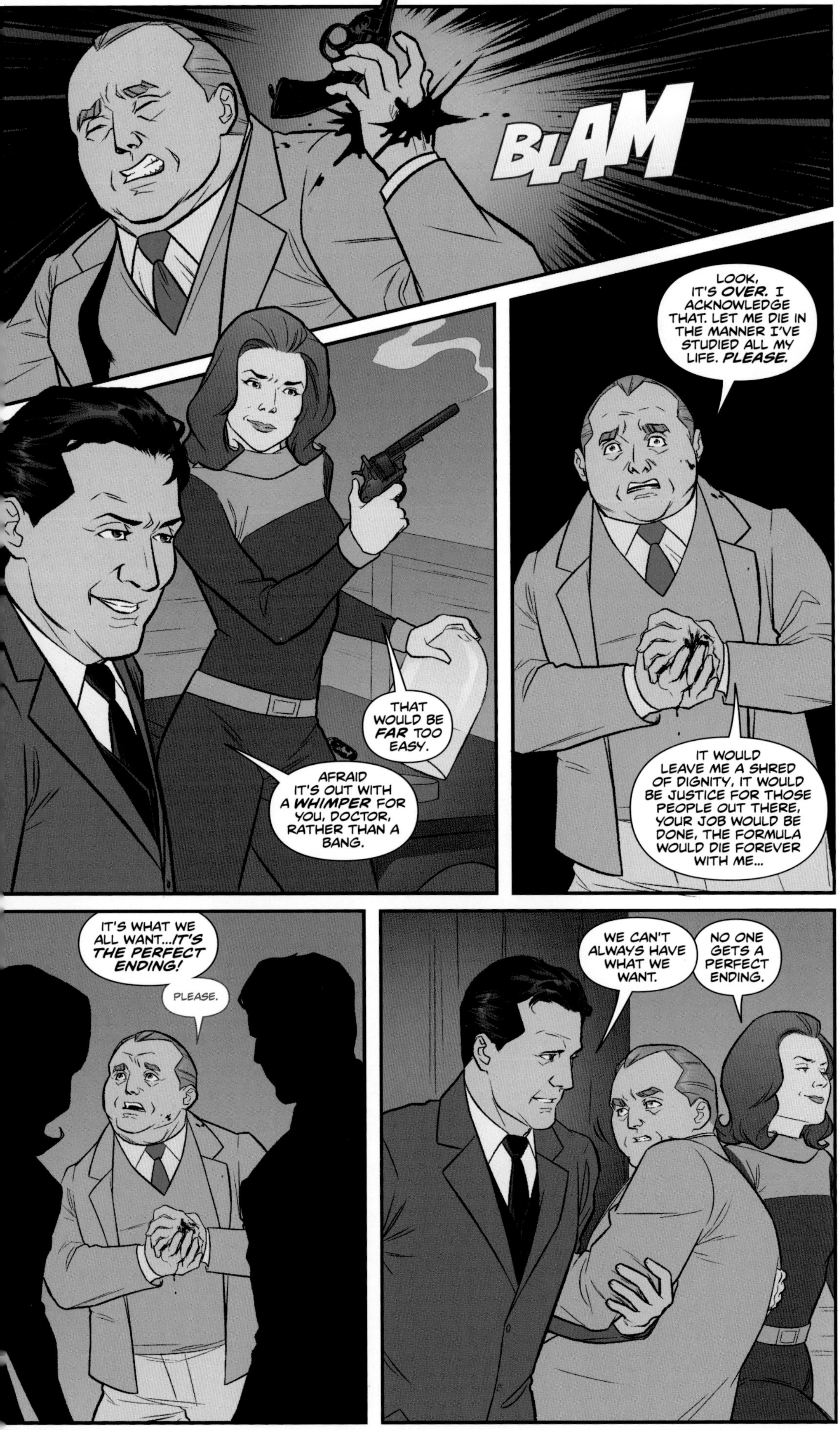
BLAM
LOOK, IT'S OVER. I ACKNOWLEDGE THAT. LET ME DIE IN THE MANNER I'VE STUDIED ALL MY LIFE. PLEASE.
THAT WOULD BE FAR TOO EASY.
AFRAID IT'S OUT WITH A WHIMPER FOR YOU, DOCTOR, RATHER THAN A BANG.
IT WOULD LEAVE ME A SHRED OF DIGNITY, IT WOULD BE JUSTICE FOR THOSE PEOPLE OUT THERE, YOUR JOB WOULD BE DONE, THE FORMULA WOULD DIE FOREVER WITH ME...
IT'S WHAT WE ALL WANT...IT'S THE PERFECT ENDING!
PLEASE.
WE CAN'T ALWAYS HAVE WHAT WE WANT.
NO ONE GETS A PERFECT ENDING.

TAWDR

LITTL

ENDINGS

STEED SUBDUED BY EMM
EMMA SUBDUED BY STEE

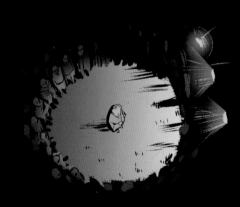

NEXT:
RETURN OF THE MONST

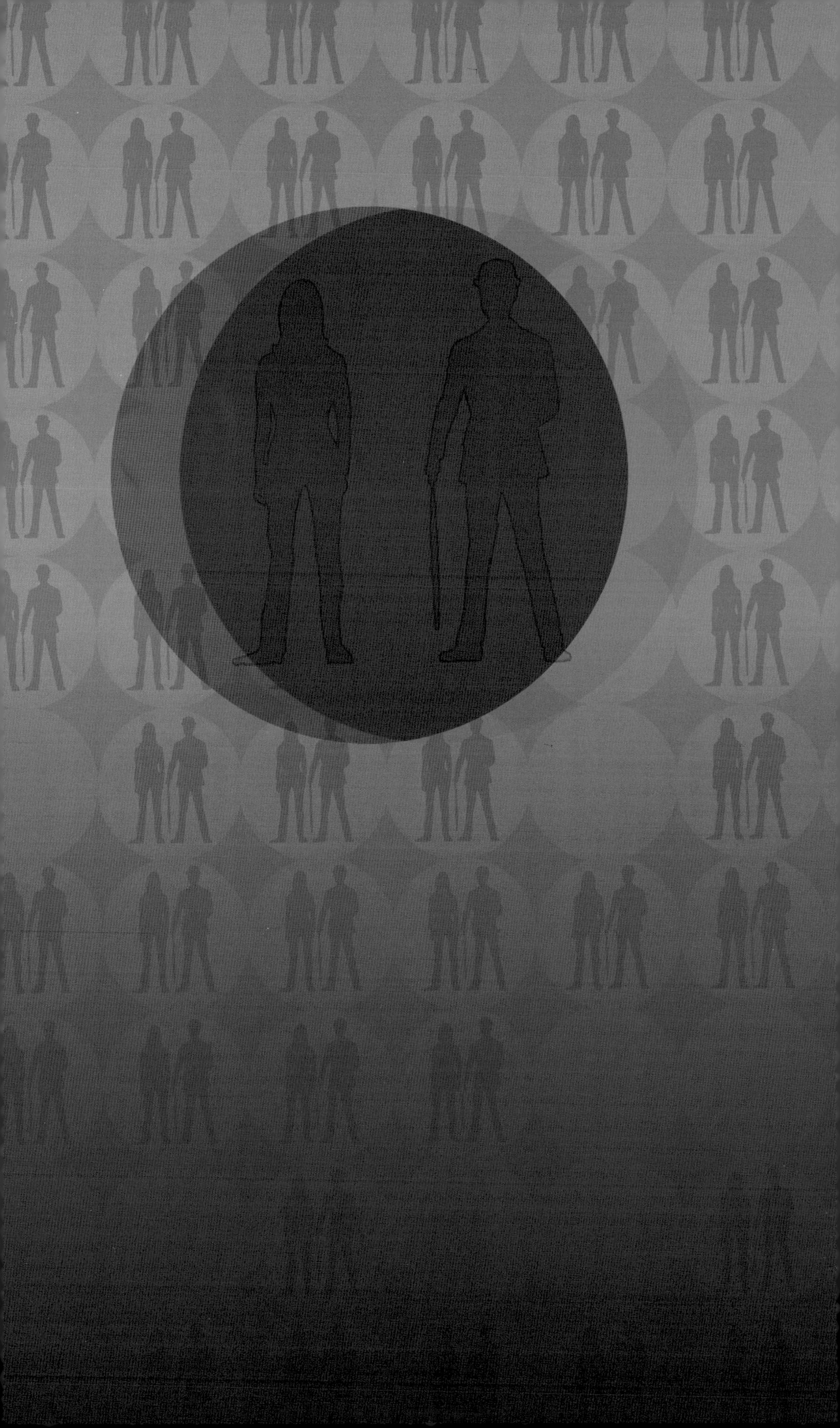

COVER GALLERY

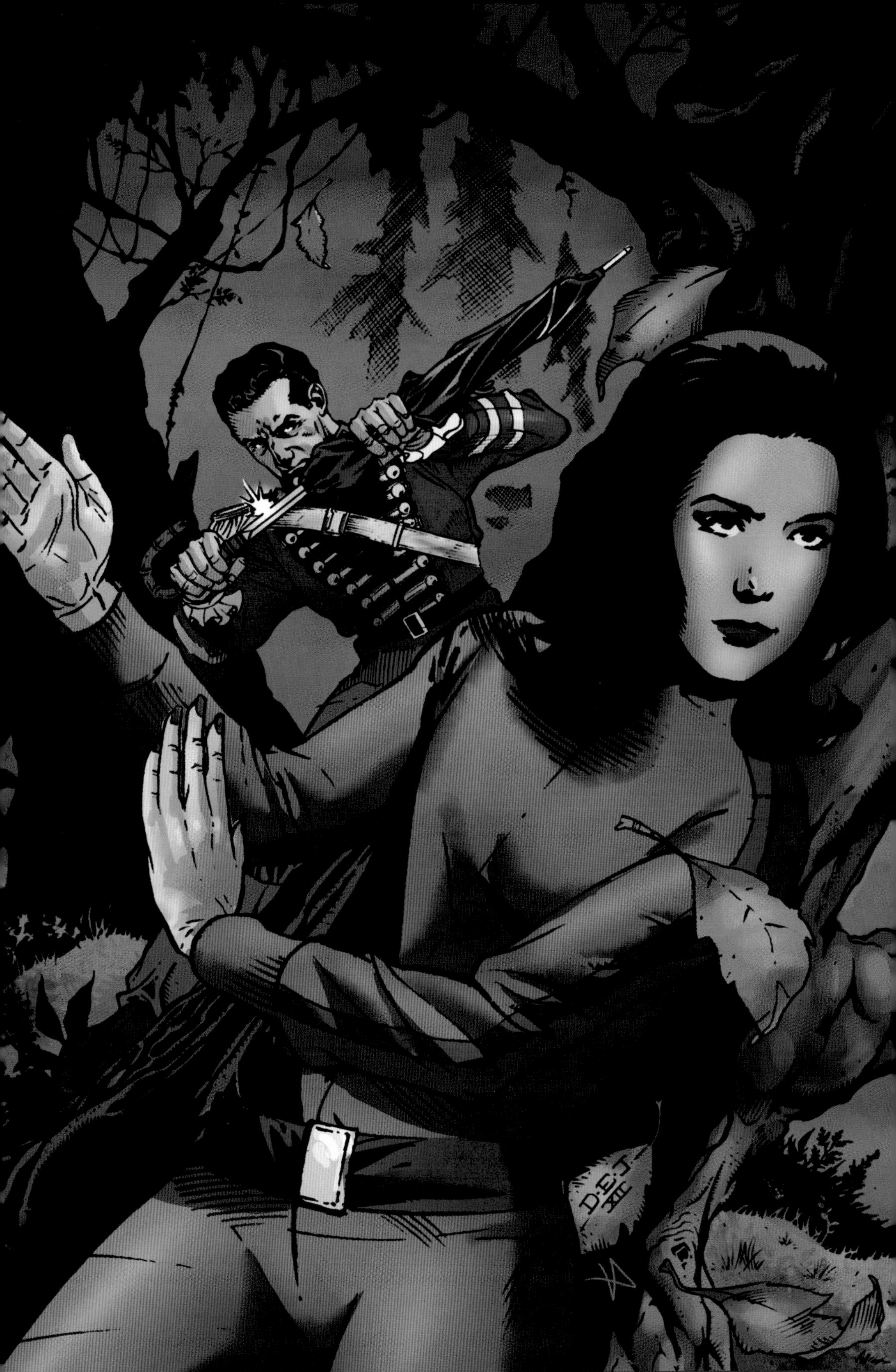

DREW JOHNSON
VLADIMIR POPOV

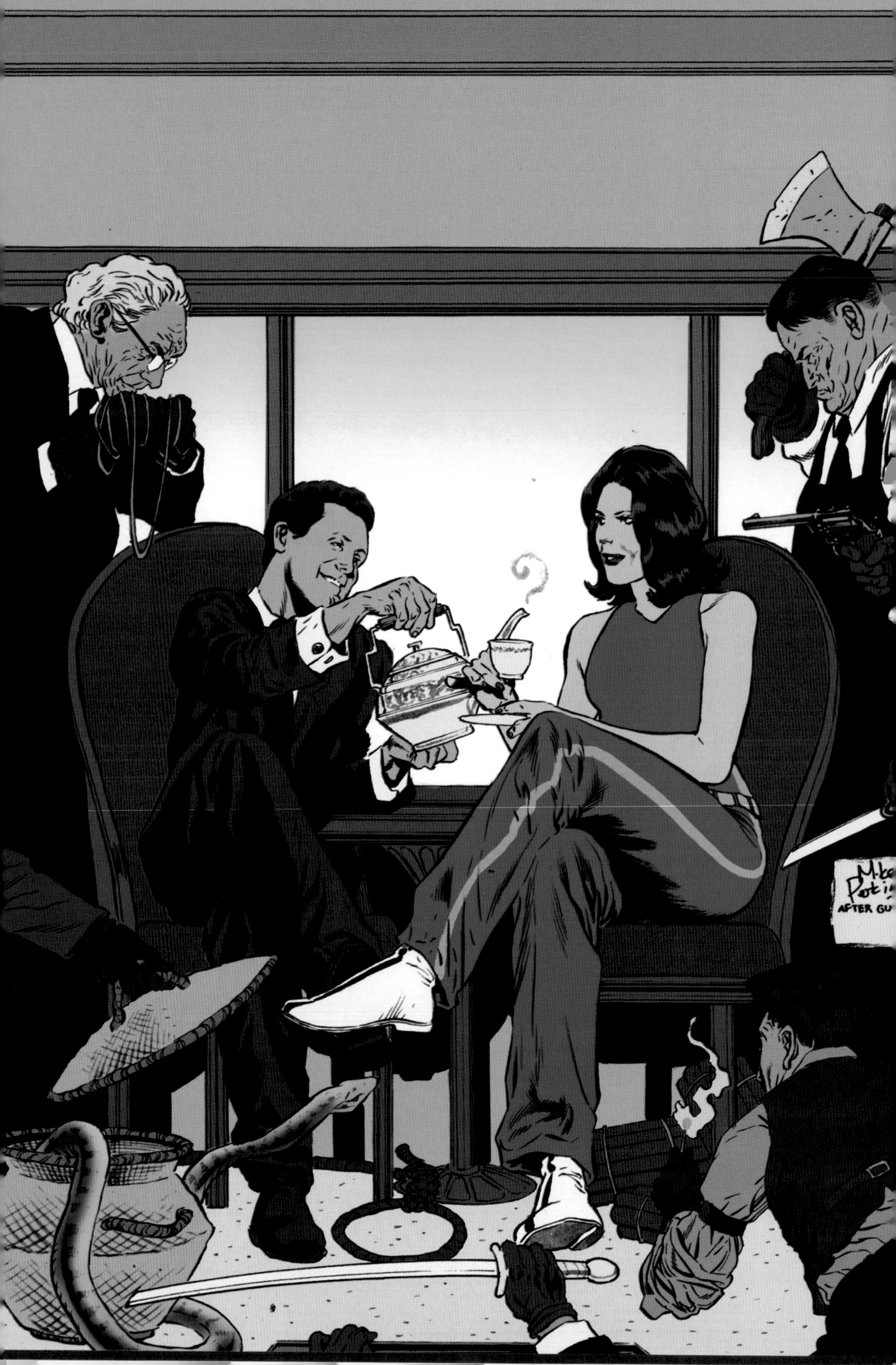

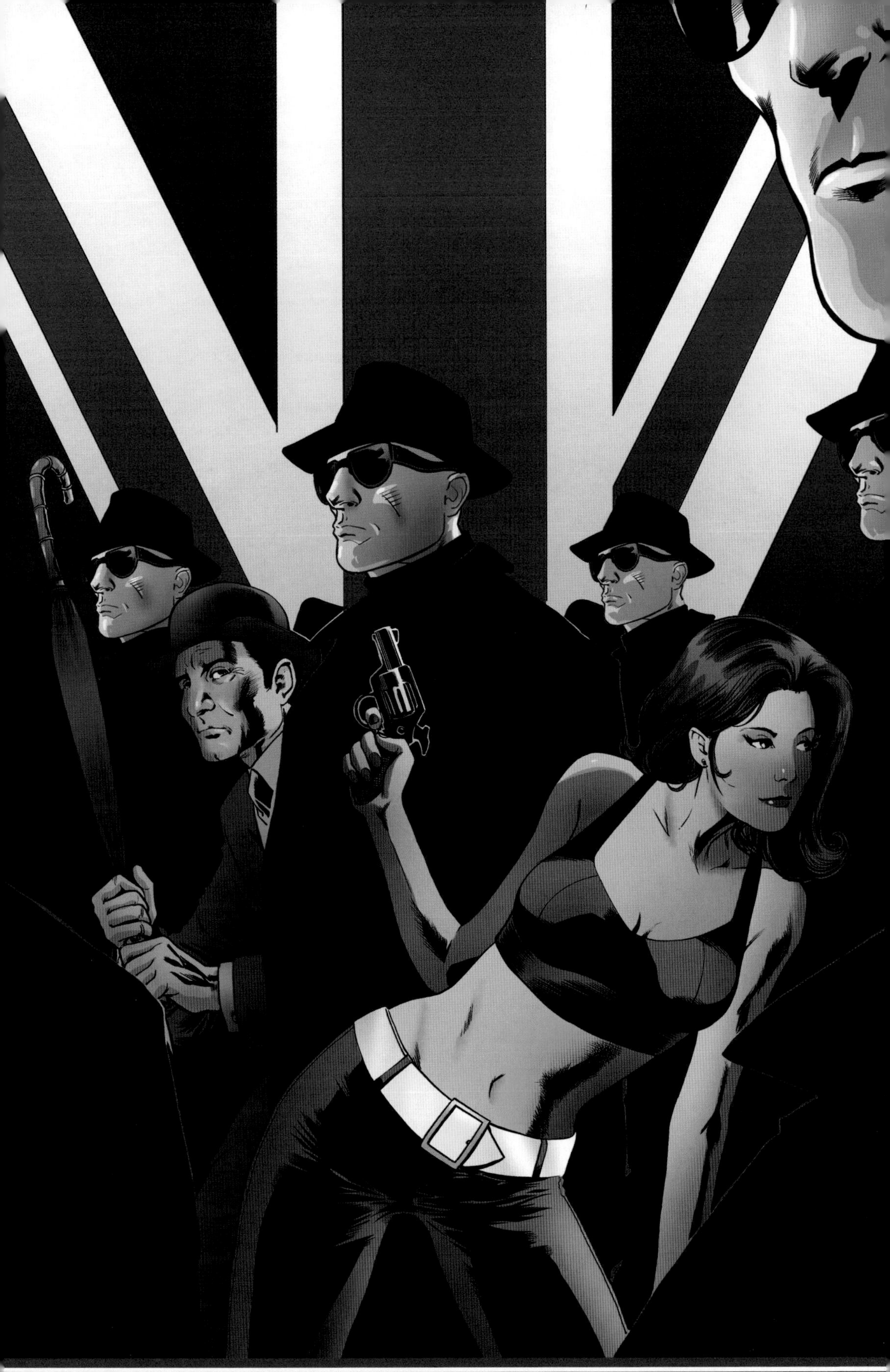

BARRY KITSON
VLADIMIR POPOV

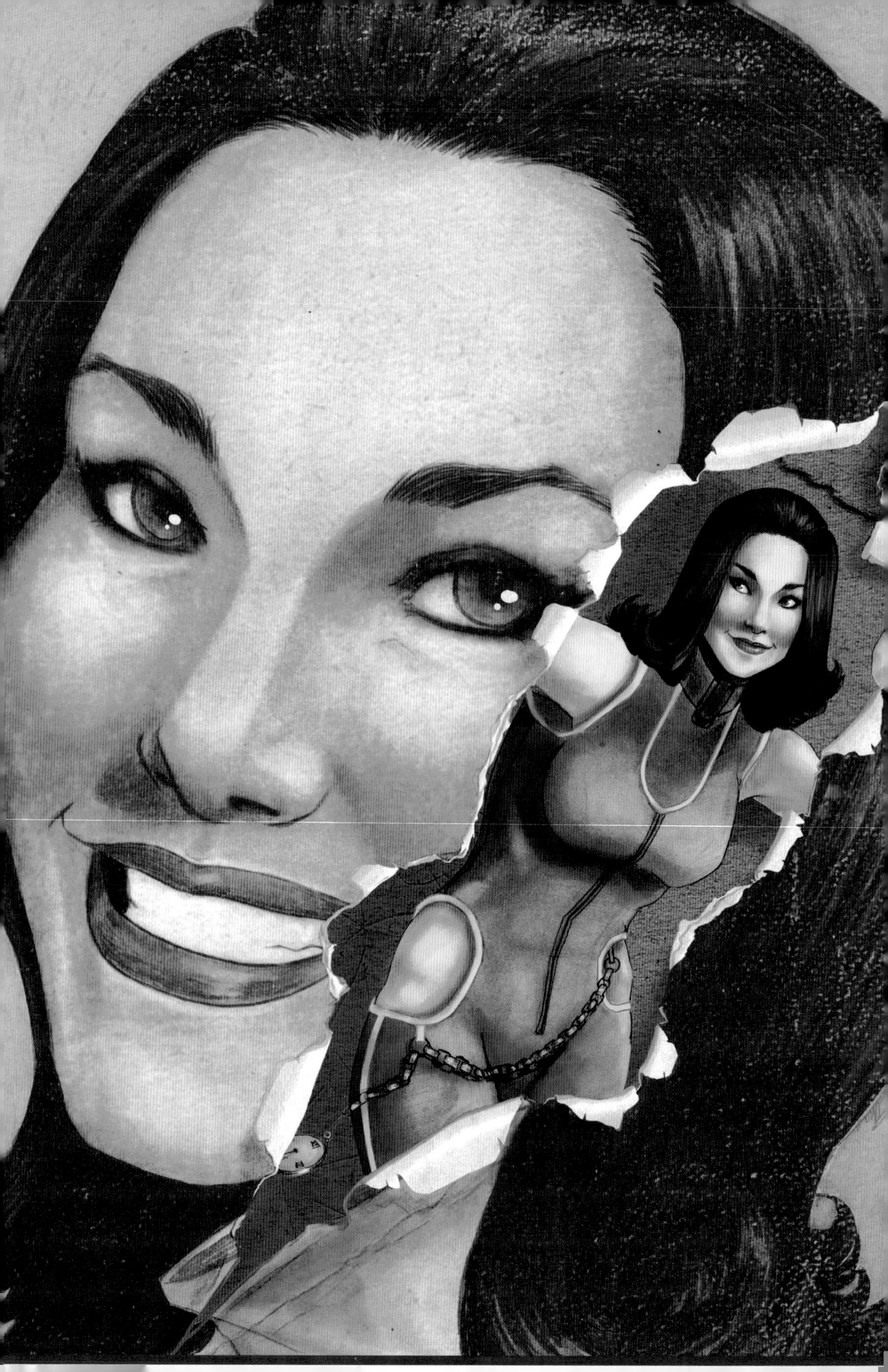

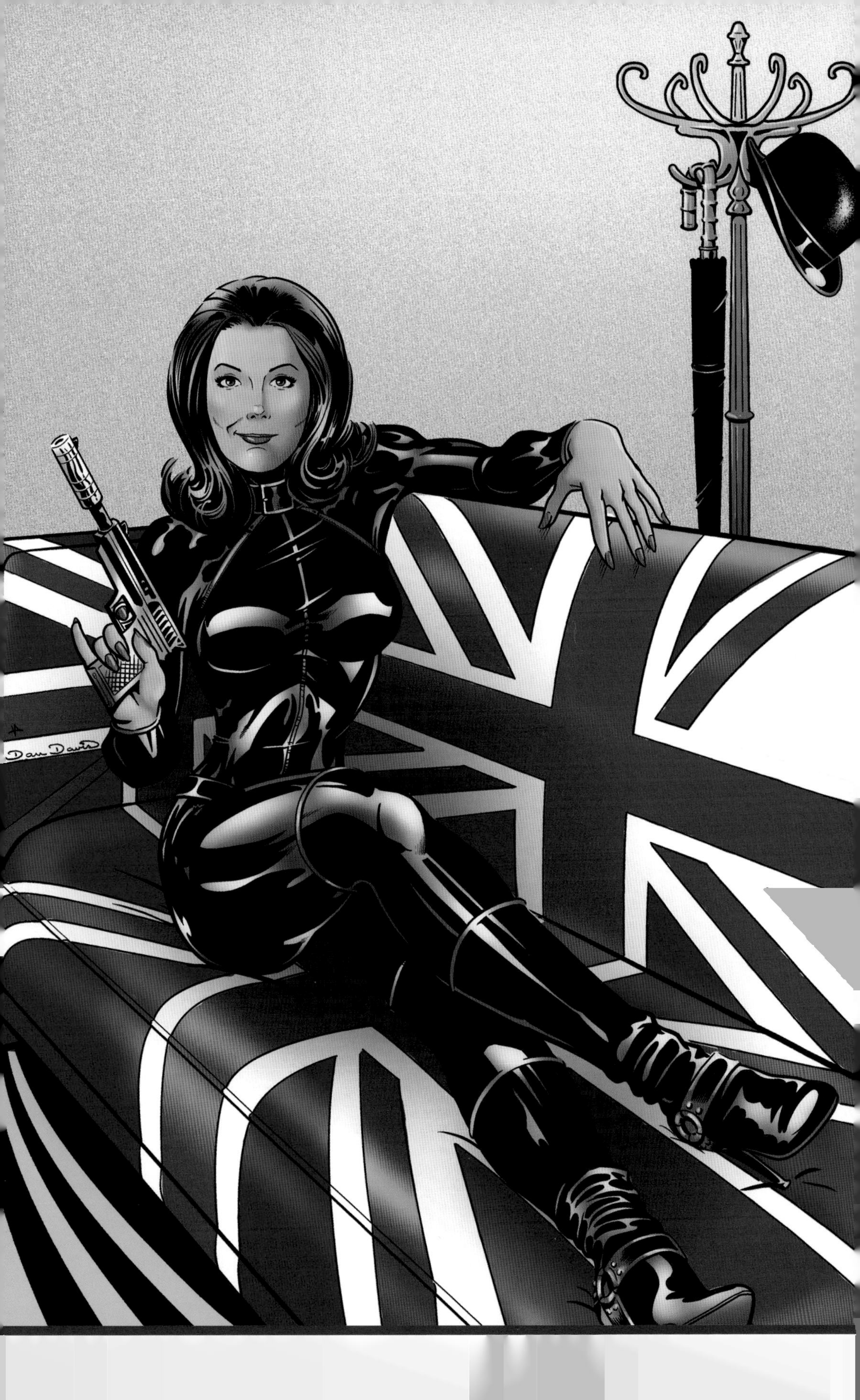
Dan Davis

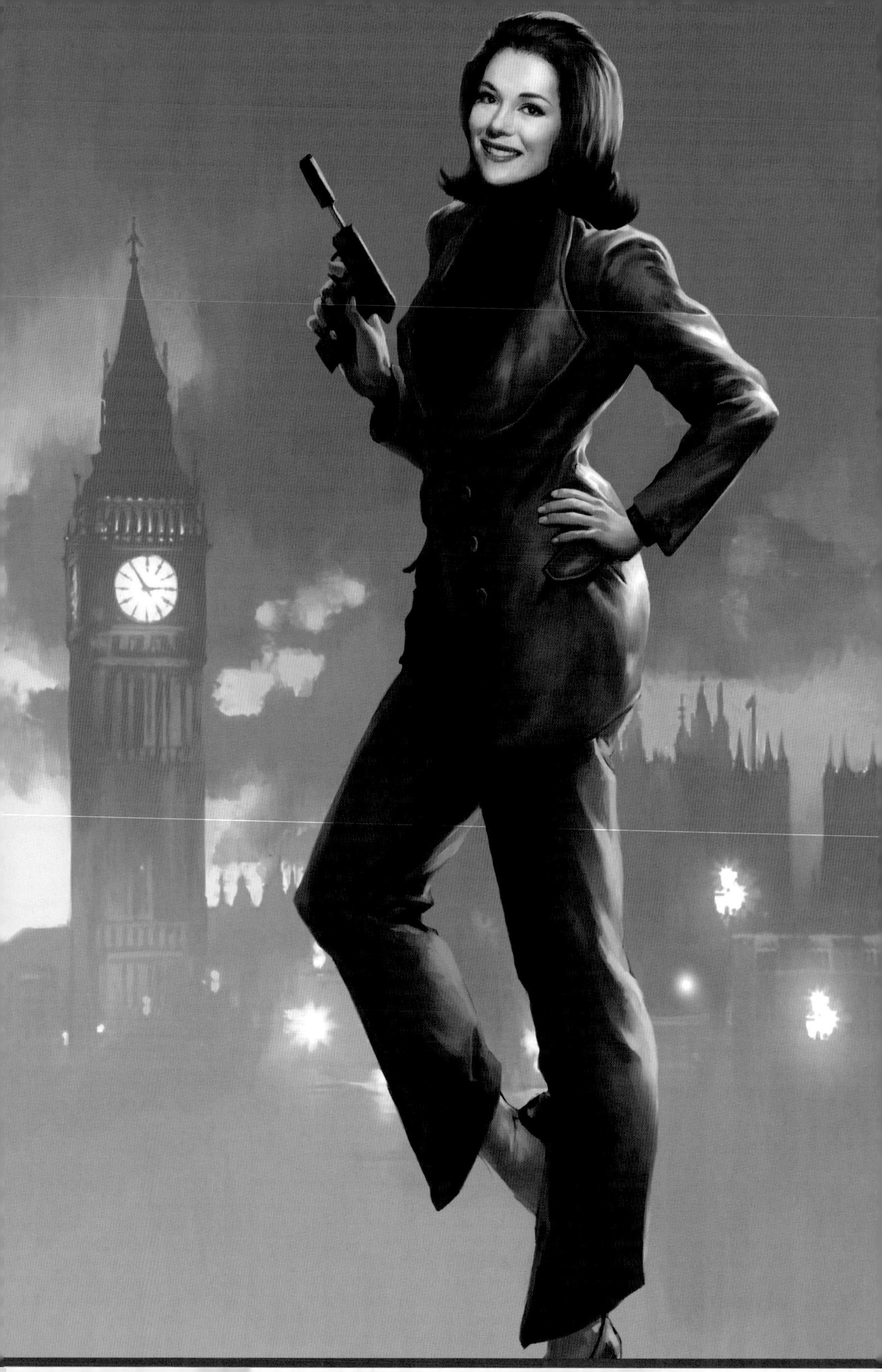

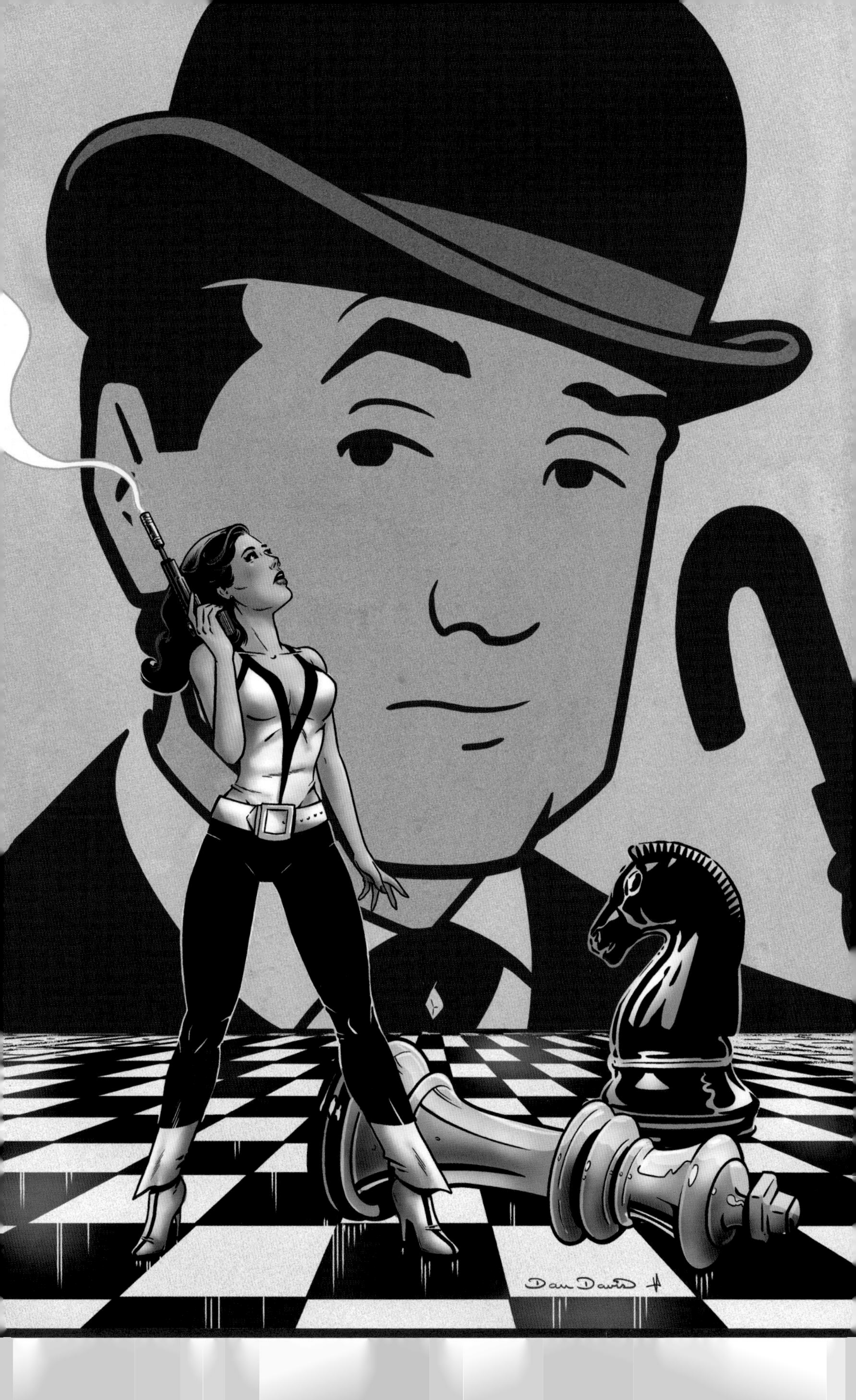
Dan Davis

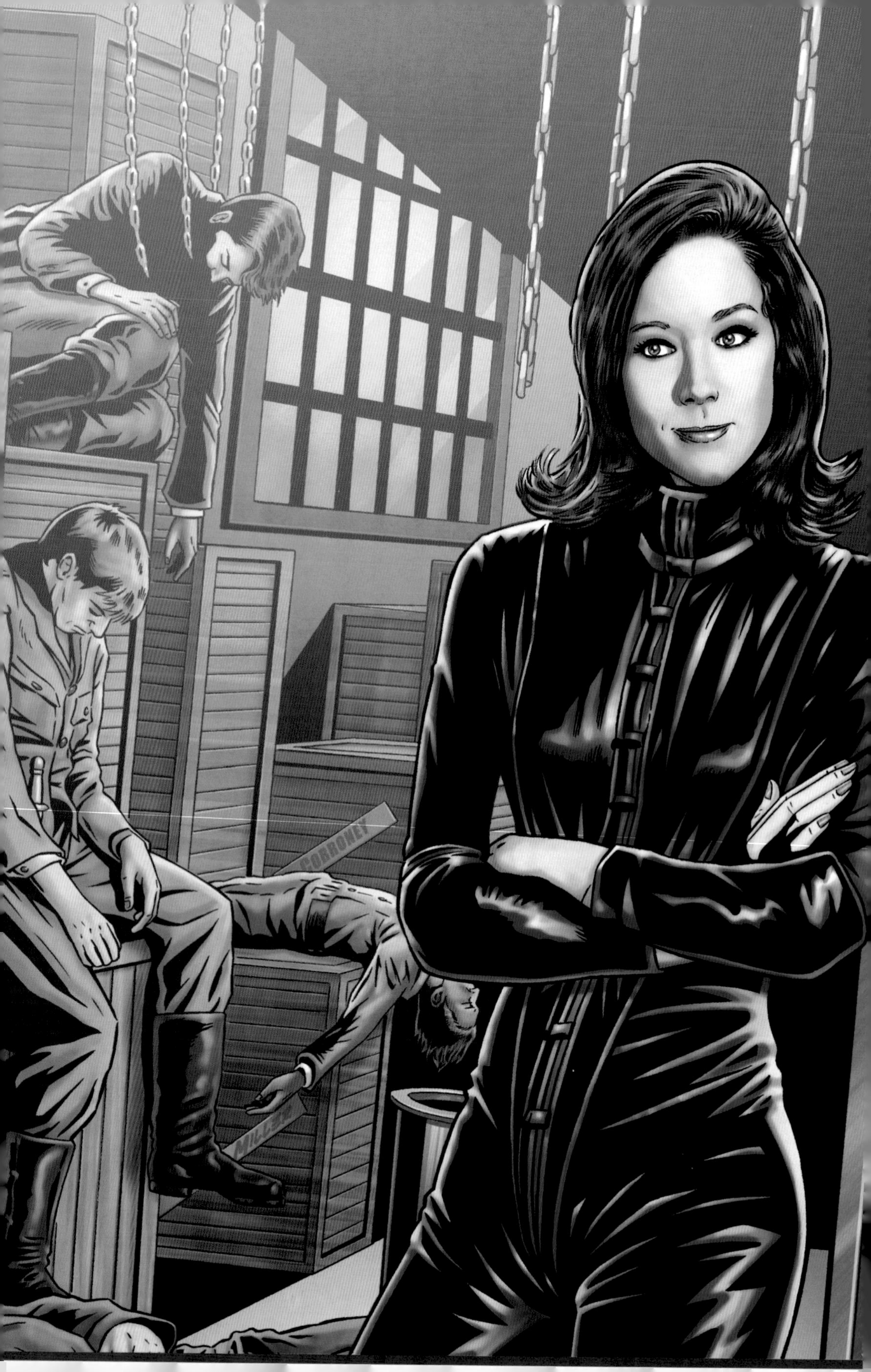
CORRONEY

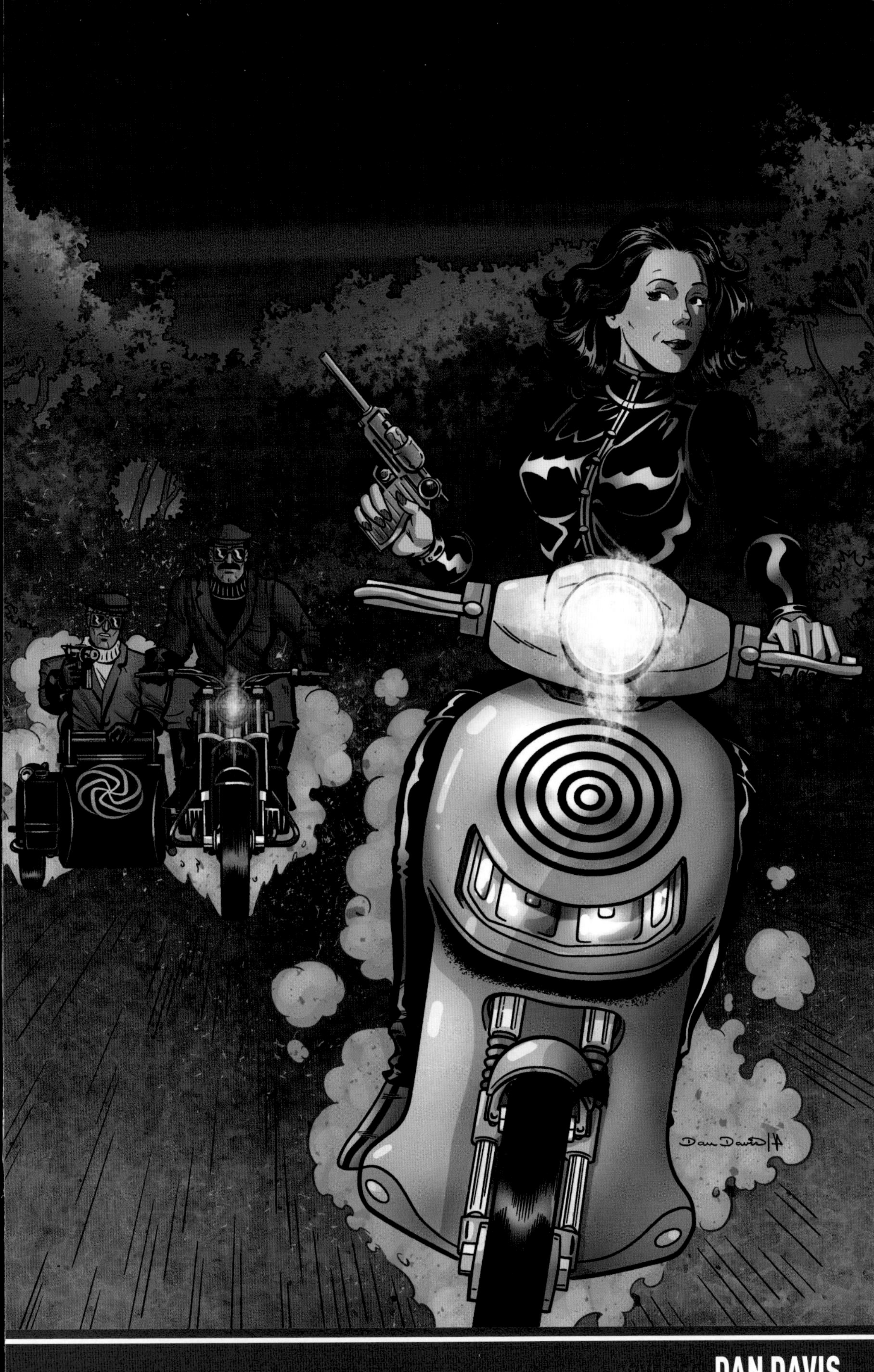
Dan Davis

DAN DAVIS
VLADIMIR POPOV

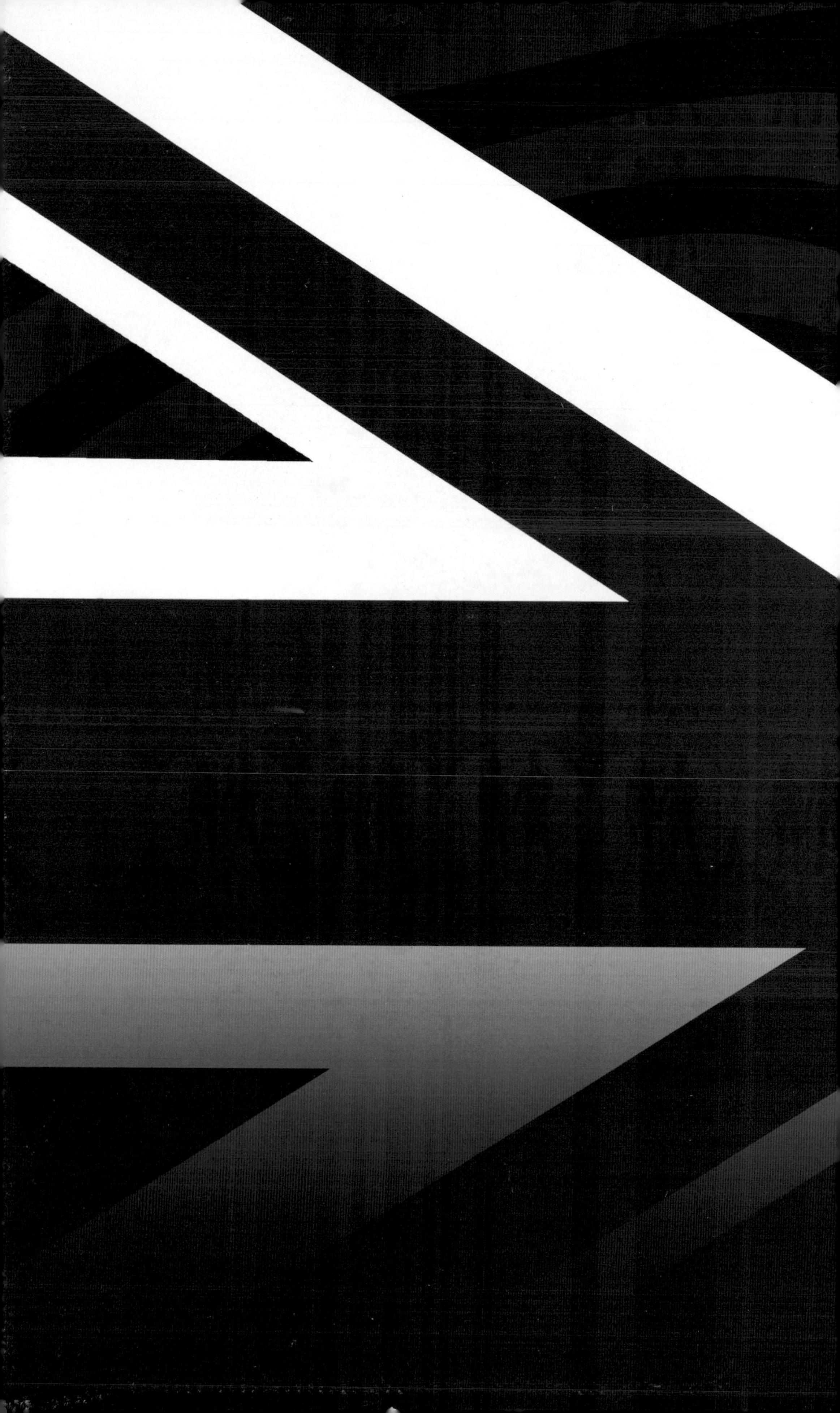